# Orwell's Roses

# Orwell's Roses

REBECCA SOLNIT

VIKING

VIKING

An imprint of Penguin Random House LLC
penguinrandomhouse.com

LIBRARY OF CONGRESS CATALOGING-IN-PUBLICATION DATA
Names: Solnit, Rebecca, author.
Title: Orwell's roses / Rebecca Solnit.
Description: New York : Viking, [2021] |
Includes bibliographical references and index.
Identifiers: LCCN 2021003710 (print) | LCCN 2021003711 (ebook) |
ISBN 9780593083369 (hardcover) | ISBN 9780593083383 (ebook)
Subjects: LCSH: Orwell, George, 1903–1950. | Authors, English—20th
century—Biography. | Orwell, George, 1903–1950—Homes and haunts. |
Orwell, George, 1903–1950—Knowledge. | Roses. |
Gardening. | Nature. | LCGFT: Biographies
Classification: LCC PR6029.R8 Z7895 2021 (print) |
LCC PR6029.R8 (ebook) | DDC 828/.91209—dc23
LC record available at https://lccn.loc.gov/2021003710
LC ebook record available at https://lccn.loc.gov/2021003711

Printed in the United States of America
3rd Printing

Set in Adobe Jenson Pro
Designed by Cassandra Garruzzo

# CONTENTS

## I
## The Prophet and the Hedgehog

## II
## Going Underground

## III
## Bread and Roses

## IV
## Stalin's Lemons

## V
## Retreats and Attacks

The very act of trying to look ahead to discern possibilities and offer warnings is in itself an act of hope.

OCTAVIA BUTLER

# I

## The Prophet
## and the
## Hedgehog

*D. Collings,* Muriel the Goat, *1939. (Portrait of Orwell at Wallington.)*

# ONE

# Day of the Dead

In the spring of 1936, a writer planted roses. I had known this for more than three decades and never thought enough about what that meant until a November day a few years ago, when I was under doctor's orders to recuperate at home in San Francisco and was also on a train from London to Cambridge to talk with another writer about a book I'd written. It was November 2, and where I'm from that's celebrated as Día de Los Muertos, the Day of the Dead. Back home, my neighbors had built altars to those who had died in the past year, decorated with candles, food, marigolds, photographs of and letters to those they'd lost, and in the evening people were going to promenade and fill the streets to pay their respects at the open-air altars and eat pan de muerto, bread of the dead, some of their faces painted to look like skulls adorned with flowers in that Mexican tradition that finds life in death and death in life. In a lot of Catholic places, it's a day to visit cemeteries, clean family graves, and adorn them with flowers. Like the older versions of Halloween, it's a time when the borders between life and death become porous.

But I was on a morning train rolling north from King's Cross in London, gazing out the window as London's density dissipated into lower and lower buildings spread farther and farther apart. And then the train was rolling through farmland, with grazing sheep and cows and wheat fields and clusters of bare trees, beautiful even under a wintry white sky. I had an errand or perhaps a quest to carry out. I was looking for some trees—perhaps a Cox's orange pippin apple tree and some other fruit trees—for Sam Green, who's a documentary filmmaker and one of my closest friends. He and I had been talking about trees, and more often emailing about them, for several years. We shared a love for them and the sense that someday he might be making a documentary about them, or we might join forces to make some kind of art about them.

Sam had found solace and joy in trees in the hard year after his younger brother died in 2009, and I think we both loved the sense of steadfast continuity a tree can represent. I had grown up in a rolling California landscape studded with several kinds of oak trees along with bays and buckeyes. Many individual trees that I knew as a child are still recognizable when I return, so little changed when I have changed so much. At the other end of the county was Muir Woods, the famous redwood forest of old-growth trees left uncut when the rest of the area was logged, trees a couple hundred feet tall with needles that condense moisture out of the air on foggy days and drip it onto the soil as a sort of summer rain that only falls under the canopy and not in the open air.

Slices of redwood trees a dozen or more feet across, with their annual rings used as history charts, were popular in my youth, and the arrival of Columbus in the Americas or the signing of the Magna Carta and sometimes the birth and death of Jesus would be marked on the huge disks in museums and parks. The oldest redwood in Muir Woods is 1,200 years old, so more than half its time on Earth had passed before the first Europeans showed up in what they would name California. A tree planted tomorrow that lived as long would be standing in the thirty-third century AD, and it would be short-lived compared to the bristlecones a few hundred miles east, which can live five thousand years. Trees are an invitation to think about time and to travel in it the way they do, by standing still and reaching out and down.

If war has an opposite, gardens might sometimes be it, and people have found a particular kind of peace in forests, meadows, parks, and gardens. The surrealist artist Man Ray fled Europe and Nazis in 1940 and spent the next decade in California. During the Second World War, he visited the sequoia groves in the Sierra Nevada and wrote of these trees that are broader than redwoods, but not quite as tall: "Their silence is more eloquent than the roaring torrents and Niagaras, than the reverberating thunder in [the] Grand Canyon, than the bursting of bombs; and is without menace. The gossiping leaves of the sequoias, one hundred yards above one's head, are too far away to be heard. I recalled a stroll in the Luxembourg Gardens during the first months of the outbreak of war, stopping under an old chestnut tree that had probably survived the French Revolution, a mere pygmy, wishing I could be transformed into a tree until peace came again."

THAT SUMMER BEFORE my trip to England, when Sam was in town, we had gone to admire the trees planted in San Francisco by Mary Ellen Pleasant, a Black woman born in slavery around 1812, who had become a heroine of the Underground Railroad and a civil rights activist, as well as a player in the elite money politics of San Francisco. She had died more than a hundred years before that day we stood under her eucalyptus trees, which felt as though they were the living witnesses of a past otherwise beyond our reach. They had outlived the wooden mansion in which some of the dramas of her life had played out. They were so broad they had buckled the sidewalk, and they reached up higher than most of the buildings around them. Their peeling gray and tan bark spiraled around their trunks, their sickle-shaped leaves lay scattered on the sidewalk, and the wind murmured in their crowns. The trees made the past seem within reach in a way nothing else could: here were living things that had been planted and tended by a living being who was gone, but the trees that had been alive in her lifetime were in ours and might be after we were gone. They changed the shape of time.

There's an Etruscan word, *saeculum*, that describes the span of time lived by the oldest person present, sometimes calculated to be about a hundred years. In a looser sense, the word means the expanse of time during which something is in living memory. Every event has its saeculum, and then its sunset when the last person who fought in the Spanish Civil War or the last person who saw the last passenger pigeon is gone. To us, trees seemed to offer another kind of saeculum, a longer time scale and deeper continuity, giving shelter from our ephemerality the way that a tree might offer literal shelter under its boughs.

In Moscow there are trees planted during the Czarist era that grew, shed their leaves in fall, stood steadfast through the winters, bloomed in springs through the Russian Revolution, shaded visitors in summers in the Stalinist era, through the purges, the show trials, the famines, the Cold War and glasnost and the collapse of the Soviet Union, dropped their leaves during the autumns of the rise of that admirer of Stalin, Vladimir Putin, and that will outlive Putin and Sam and me and everyone on that train with me that November morning. The trees were reminders of both our own ephemerality and their endurance long beyond ours, and in their uprightness they stood in the landscape like guardians and witnesses.

Also that summer, when we were hanging out at my home talking about trees, I had mentioned an essay by George Orwell I had loved for a long time, a brief, casual, lyrical piece he dashed off in the spring of 1946 for *Tribune*, the socialist weekly where he published about eighty pieces from 1943 to 1947. The essay that appeared on April 26, 1946, is titled "A Good Word for the Vicar of Bray," and it's a triumph of meandering that begins by describing a yew tree in a Berkshire churchyard said to have been planted by a vicar who was a famously fickle political player, switching sides repeatedly in the religious wars of the time. That fickleness let him survive and stay in place, like a tree, while many fell or fled.

Orwell writes of the vicar, "Yet, after this lapse of time, all that is left of him is a comic song and a beautiful tree, which has rested the eyes of generation after generation and must surely have outweighed any bad effects which he produced by his political quislingism." From there Orwell leapt to the last king of Burma, whose supposed misdeeds he mentioned, along with the trees that king planted in Mandalay, "tamarind trees which cast a pleasant shade until the Japanese incendiary bombs burned them down in 1942." Orwell had been a policeman in the British imperial service in Burma, so he would have seen those trees for himself in the 1920s, as well as the huge yew he described in the church cemetery in Bray, a small town west of London.*

---

* In 2019, Sam and I went to look for the tree in Bray and its outlying churchyards, to no avail, but we did have a very nice meeting on the banks of the Thames with the current vicar of Bray and we did see several immense yew trees.

He proposes that "the planting of a tree, especially one of the long-living hardwood trees, is a gift which you can make to posterity at almost no cost and with almost no trouble, and if the tree takes root it will far outlive the visible effect of any of your other actions, good or evil." And then he mentioned the inexpensive roses and fruit trees he had planted himself, ten years earlier, and how he had revisited them recently and in them beheld his own modest botanical contribution to posterity. "One of the fruit trees and one of the rose bushes died, but the rest are all flourishing. The sum total is five fruit trees, seven roses and two gooseberry bushes, all for twelve and sixpence.* These plants have not entailed much work, and have had nothing spent on them beyond the original amount. They never even received any manure, except what I occasionally collected in a bucket when one of the farm horses happened to have halted outside the gate."

I'd derived from that last line a picture of the author with a bucket and a gate beyond which horses passed, but I hadn't thought more about where and how he lived at the time and why he planted roses. Nevertheless, I had found the essay memorable and moving from the time I first encountered it. I thought it was a fugitive trace of an Orwell that remained embryonic, undeveloped, of who he might have been in less turbulent times, but I was wrong about that.

His life was shot through with wars. He was born on June 25, 1903, right after the Boer War, reached adolescence during the First World War (a patriotic poem, written when he was eleven, was his first published work), with the Russian Revolution and the Irish war of independence raging into the 1920s and the beginning of his adulthood, been among those who saw all through the 1930s the

---

* That is, twelve shillings and sixpence, a shilling being twelve pennies, for a total of 150 pence.

conflagrations of the Second World War being set up, who fought in the Spanish Civil War in 1937, had lived in London during the Blitz and been bombed out himself, and coined the term *cold war* in 1945 and saw that cold war and its nuclear arsenals grow more fearsome in the last years before his death on January 21, 1950. Those conflicts and menaces consumed a lot of his attention—but not all of it.

I had first read his essay on tree planting in a big, ugly, dog-eared paperback titled *The Orwell Reader*, which I bought cheap from a used bookstore when I was about twenty and wandered through for years, getting to know his style and tone as an essayist, his opinions about other writers, about politics, about language and writing, a book I had absorbed when I was young enough for it to be a foundational influence on my own meander toward becoming an essayist. I had come across his 1945 fable *Animal Farm* as a child, so that I first read it as a story about animals and mourned the faithful horse Boxer's death and not known that it was an allegory for the corruption of the Russian Revolution into Stalinism.

I'd read *Nineteen Eighty-Four* for the first time as a teenager, and then gotten to know *Homage to Catalonia*, his firsthand account of the Spanish Civil War, in my twenties. That latter book had been a major influence on my second book, *Savage Dreams*, for its example of honesty about the shortcomings of one's own side and loyalty to it anyway and of how to incorporate into a political narrative personal experience all the way down to doubts and discomforts—that is, how to make room for the small and subjective inside something big and historic. He had been one of my principal literary influences, but I had not gotten to know more about him than what he revealed in the books and whatever set of assumptions was ambient.

That essay of his I shared with Sam was in praise of the arboreal saeculum, and it was hopeful in that it looked to the future as something we could contribute to and, more than that, in that year after the first atom bombs had been detonated, as something we could have some degree of faith in: "Even an apple tree is liable to live for about 100 years, so that the Cox I planted in 1936 may still be bearing fruit well into the twenty-first century. An oak or a beech may live for hundreds of years and be a pleasure to thousands or tens of thousands of people before it is finally sawn up into timber. I am not suggesting that one can discharge all one's obligations towards society by means of a private re-afforestation scheme. Still, it might not be a bad idea, every time you commit an antisocial act, to make a note of it in your diary, and then, at the appropriate season, push an acorn into the ground." The essay took a tone common in his work, traveling nonchalantly from particulars to generalities, and from the minor to the major—in this case from one particular apple tree to universal questions of redemption and legacies.

That summer day when we fell to talking about trees, I told Sam about Orwell's garden, and he grew excited, and we went over to my computer to see if we could find out if the five fruit trees were still there. It took only a few minutes to dig up the address of the cottage Orwell had moved to in April 1936 and then a minute or two more to zoom in on the address on a mapping app, but the aerial views were full of indistinct blobs of green foliage that didn't tell us what we wanted to know.

Sam wrote a letter to the unknown inhabitants of the address we'd found, which was far more rural than the place I'd pictured all those years since I'd first read the essay. It was a very Sam letter that noted that "we are not kooks," offering the links to his website and mine to try to demonstrate that we were people who had a respectable history of taking interest in obscure facts and researching historical tangents. We hadn't heard back when I stepped off the train in Baldock in Hertfordshire, several stops before Cambridge, a little wobbly, a little anxious about knocking on that cottage door, but also more than a little exhilarated.

I'd had a hard year, and on top of being exhausted I'd gotten seriously ill and was supposed to be home convalescing. But in all that year's conflict about how much I should tour, I had signed a British contract that somewhere in its several pages of small print made me liable for a floor of ten thousand pounds in payments if I didn't show up, so I'd had to fly to London and talk about politics and ideas while fearful that I might faint on the street or disintegrate onstage. Since I was traveling so far, I agreed to go onward to Manchester so as not to spurn the north, and to Cambridge to have a public conversation with my old friend and fellow writer Rob Macfarlane.

I was about to find what I had not been looking for on this trip I would have canceled if I could. When I gave the address to the taxi driver, he knew exactly where to go. I wished that the journey out of the old market town and over the rolling Hertfordshire countryside had taken longer, because I was nervous about arrival and enchanted with the farmland we were passing through so rapidly. But it only took a few minutes to reach the village of Wallington or what I would see of it on that visit, a country lane lined with cottages, where the taxi driver saw a man outside and said, "Oh there's Graham now, I'll just introduce you."

I had thought it likely I would be rebuffed or reproached—and certainly anyone who lives in a famous writer's former home could come to feel besieged. I had expected that I might end up just snooping over fences for fruit trees, or asking a question or two at the door, but Graham Lamb—a slight older man with curling gray hair and, also, a Scottish accent—was cheerful and welcoming. He remembered Sam's letter, apologized for not replying—he was still gathering data to send us, he told me—and I was ushered into the back and introduced to Dawn Spanyol, his partner, who was working in the garden.

Dawn had come across the place when it was up for sale a few years earlier and told Graham about it and he rushed over to see it. They bought it immediately, after ascertaining that it was tiny and cramped and unsuitable for hosting their families at holidays and met absolutely none of their criteria about living near the sea or near pubs and shops. They joked that it had after all once been a shop and the house next door had been a pub, and he loved its literary lineage, she its garden. It was in a village full of people who expected to end up elsewhere, they added. The fruit trees were no more, cut down in the 1990s when the garden shed in the back had been expanded. But Nigel next door had been there much longer, and so we went over to say hello to Nigel and meander around his yard and peer back at Dawn and Graham's yard from it. The fruit trees were within his living memory, his saeculum, but there was nothing much he could say about them, except that they had been over there and nothing to see but some dank, ivy-choked, decaying stumps that might possibly have been last traces of some of those trees.

We stepped inside the cottage, and Graham showed me an aerial color photograph of the place as it had been some fifty years earlier. That too just showed green blobs for trees, and the main thing was that the fruit trees were now gone. The cottage interior had white-plastered walls, dark woodwork, and small rooms with low ceilings, more picturesque and pleasant than anything I would've associated with Orwell. Most of the accounts of the place make it sound grim, and in 1936 it did lack modern conveniences—including gas, electricity, and an indoor toilet, and the thatched roof was then a tin roof—but he liked being there immensely, so far as I can tell. Graham showed me the low door-way between the room off the kitchen Orwell used as an office and the room just beyond it that functioned as a shop in his time and as a sitting room in Dawn and Graham's; the tall writer must have had to stoop every time or bash his head on the lintel. A few slots were cut into the door so he could peer in from his work if a customer entered.

The trees in the garden were gone, but after we'd met Nigel and toured the stumps and viewed the photograph, they mentioned that the roses Orwell planted might still be there. The news startled me into alertness, and my mild disappointment about the fruit trees was overtaken by a wild rush of exhilarated interest. We went back out to the garden, where even on that November day two big unruly rose-bushes were in bloom, one with pale pink buds opening up a little and another with almost salmon flowers with a golden-yellow rim at the base of each petal. They were exuberantly alive, these allegedly octo-genarian roses, living things planted by the living hand (and shovel work) of someone gone for most of their lifetime. Graham told me that the roses were so prolific that the schoolmistress, Esther Brookes, who had purchased the cottage in 1948 after Orwell surrendered the lease, used buds from one of them as tickets for admission for the vil-lage fête. In 1983, she reported that the Albertine rose he planted was "the glory of the garden" and "still blooms."

His roses had been blooming in November 1939, when Orwell noted in his domestic diary, "Cut down the remaining phloxes, tied up some of the chrysanthemums which had been blown over. Diffi-cult to do much these afternoons now it is winter-time. The chry-sanths now in full flower, mostly dark reddy-brown, & a few ugly purple & white ones which I shan't keep. Roses still attempting to flower, otherwise no flowers in the garden now. Michaelmas daisies are over & I have cut some of them down." Nearly everyone who knew him is gone, but the roses are a sort of saeculum that includes Orwell. I was suddenly in his presence in a way I hadn't expected, and I was in the presence of a living remnant of the essay, and they rearranged my old assumptions.

The apparent directness of these two plants' connection to him and to that long-ago essay about roses and fruit trees and continuity and posterity filled me with joyous exaltation. So did the fact that this man most famous for his prescient scrutiny of totalitarianism and propaganda, for facing unpleasant facts, for a spare prose style and an unyielding political vision, had planted roses. That a socialist or a utilitarian or any pragmatist or practical person might plant fruit trees is not surprising: they have tangible economic value and produce the necessary good that is food even if they produce more than that. But to plant a rose—or in the case of this garden he resuscitated in 1936, seven roses early on and more later—can mean so many things.

I had not thought hard enough about those roses I had first read about more than a third of a century before. They were roses, and they were saboteurs of my own long acceptance of a conventional version of Orwell and invitations to dig deeper. They were questions about who he was and who we were and where pleasure and beauty and hours with no quantifiable practical result fit into the life of someone, perhaps of anyone, who also cared about justice and truth and human rights and how to change the world.

# Two

# Flower Power

There are many biographies of Orwell, and they've served me well for this book, which is not an addition to that shelf. It is instead a series of forays from one starting point, that gesture whereby one writer planted several roses. As such, it's also a book about roses, as a member of the plant kingdom and as a particular kind of flower around which a vast edifice of human responses has arisen, from poetry to commercial industry. They're a widespread wild plant, or many species of plant, and a widely domesticated one, with new varieties created every year, and when it comes to the latter, roses are also big business.

Roses mean everything, which skates close to meaning nothing. They've been used to make larger points, from the medieval philosopher Peter Abelard's use of roses as an example for an exploration of universals to modernist Gertrude Stein's "Rose is a rose is a rose." There's a line by the anthropologist Mary Douglas to the effect that just as everything symbolizes the body, so the body symbolizes everything else. The same could be said of roses in the western world. As images, they're so ubiquitous they're literally wallpaper and are routinely depicted on everything from lingerie to tombstones. Actual roses are used for courtships, weddings, funerals, birthdays, and a lot of other occasions, which is to say for joy, sorrow and loss, hope, victory, and pleasure. When the Black civil rights leader and congressman John Lewis died in the summer of 2020, his casket was taken by horse and wagon over the Alabama bridge where, as a protest marcher in 1965, he'd been beaten almost to death by state troopers. The whole route was scattered with red rose petals to symbolize the blood shed then.

Just as they crop up in ornament, so they pour forth from aphorisms, poetry, and popular songs. Flowers are often emblems of ephemerality and mortality, as in the vanitas paintings so common in seventeenth-century Europe, where elaborate bouquets were often paired with skulls, fruit, and other reminders that blooming and decaying, life and death, are inseparable. In songs roses often represent love and the beloved as the prize that cannot be grasped or kept. Among the popular songs of the last several decades are "La Vie en Rose," "Ramblin' Rose," "My Wild Irish Rose," "(I Never Promised You a) Rose Garden," "A Rose Is Still a Rose," "Days of Wine and Roses." In country singer George Jones's gorgeously lugubrious 1970 hit "A Good Year for the Roses," however, the rosebushes that go on blooming have proven to be more enduring than his marriage.

Thorns might be one of the things that distinguish roses and why they're sometimes anthropomorphized as capricious beauties or femmes fatales, like the conceited rose that's the beloved in Antoine de Saint-Exupéry's *The Little Prince*. In the Brothers Grimm version of "Sleeping Beauty," the princess is named Briar Rose (Dornröschen, or "rose with thorns" in German), unsuccessful suitors die after being trapped in the thornbushes around the tower in which she sleeps, and those thorns turn to flowers when the right suitor approaches. The blossom attracts, the thorns repel or exact a price for that attraction. "Truths and roses have thorns about them," says the old aphorism, and Marianne Moore's poem "Roses Only," which, like a surprising amount of poetry, is addressed directly to the rose, ends with the remark "Your thorns are the best part of you." Medieval theologians speculated that there were roses in the Garden of Eden, but the thorns came after the fall from grace.

Though flowers as the sexual organs of plants often have both male and female reproductive parts, they are routinely represented as feminine, and phenomena that have been feminized are often dismissed as ornamental and inconsequential. Perhaps when a flower is cut to adorn an altar or a table it becomes so, because it has been extracted from the plant's life cycle and will not produce fruit or seeds or a next generation. It may be the very uselessness of cut flowers, beyond the pleasure they give, that has made them a superlative gift, embodying the generosity and anti-utilitarianism of gift-giving. But flowers are powerful, and all human beings lead lives intertwined with them, whether we notice or not.

There's a cultural view in which flowers are dainty, trivial, dispensable—and a scientific one in which flowering plants were revolutionary in their appearance on the earth some two hundred million years or so ago, are dominant on land from the arctic to the tropics, and are crucial to our survival. "How Flowering Plants Conquered the World" is the way a recent scientific article put it. Flowers are the sexual parts of the plants called angiosperms and seeds the offspring of that sexual reproduction, and the revolution was at least as much about the seeds. *Angiosperm* means encased seed, and those cases— often a protective outer case, always a nutritional packet inside the seed to feed the embryonic plant, sometimes wings or burrs or other means of helping the seed travel—provided them with more robust, varied, and mobile methods of propagation than those of the earlier plants. They made their species capable of more varied techniques of survival and dispersal, and the seeds also made good food for other beings. The poet-paleontologist Loren Eiseley argued more than half a century ago that flowering plants were crucial props and prods to the evolution of mammals and birds, in an essay that made an impression on me when I was young.

"The agile brain of the warm-blooded birds and mammals demands a high oxygen consumption and food in concentrated forms, or the creatures cannot long sustain themselves," he wrote in a chapter of *The Immense Journey* called "How Flowers Changed the World." He continued, "It was the rise of the flowering plants that provided that energy and changed the nature of the living world. Their appearance parallels in a quite surprising manner the rise of the birds and mammals." Insects that coevolved with flowers received pollen and nectar in return for pollination services, as did the birds and bats that also pollinate as they feed at blossoms. The relationships were so important that species coevolved and some developed quasi-monogamous relationships, as with the Madagascar orchid with a neck so lengthy only one long-tongued sphinx moth can pollinate it, or the soapweed yucca that has for forty million years relied upon the *Tegeticula yuccasella* moth for its pollination as that moth relies on its seed as the sole food of its larvae. Seeds constitute a major food source for many other species, including ourselves, as grains, legumes, nuts, fruits, and those vegetables—squashes, tomatoes, peppers, and the rest—we forget are seed-bearing fruits. Seeds too developed mutually beneficial relationships—for example, the berries eaten by birds who sow the undigested seeds far from the parent plant. The complementary relationships between angiosperms and animals generated, Eiseley argues, a world more intricate and interconnected, and the concentrated foodstuffs sped mammalian evolution.

I write this with random bites and sips at my longtime usual breakfast, tea made of leaves from India, toast from wheat and rye with some other seeds mixed in, milk, butter, and yogurt from local cows whose pastures I know well, and honey from bees, a pastoral landscape on a platter. Most of what we eat is either angiosperm or, for nonvegans, from creatures who fed on angiosperms. There might be evolutionary reasons why we too find flowers so attractive, since our lives are so bound up with theirs, and we have domesticated and bred them to amplify and vary size, forms, colors, and scents. Our lives depend, if not exactly on flowers, then on flowering plants.

Roses are not a major human food anywhere on Earth, but their petals were used in medieval recipes, and their fruit still is for teas and other potions. During the Second World War, Britain's Ministry of Food (where Orwell's wife, Eileen O'Shaughnessy Blair, worked) launched rose hip–gathering campaigns to try to supply vitamin C to a nation cut off from imported foods, notably citrus. By 1942, two hundred tons, equivalent to 134 million hips, were reportedly gathered, mostly to be made into syrup, but the ministry also put out recipes for homemade rose hip marmalade, a product still common in Germany. Roses are also, of course, used for perfumes and scented oils.

They are part of a plant family, Rosaceae, of more than four thousand species, including apples, pears, quinces, apricots, plums, and peaches, as well as brambles and the thorny blackberries and raspberries whose flowers resemble wild roses' blooms. The flower of the wild rose, like those of the fruit trees, has five petals; roses bred from random mutations in China, Europe, and the Near East developed the

familiar many-petaled forms. In the third century BC the philosopher
Theophrastus wrote, "Most have five petals, but some have twelve or
twenty, and some a great many more than these; for there are some,
they say, which are even called hundred-petalled," and three centuries
later Pliny the Elder also spoke of hundred-petalled roses.

Over the last few centuries breeders have produced variations on
those forms so that there are now thousands of varieties of rose, rang-
ing from some of the old musks, damasks, and albas to the innumerable current versions of the hybrid tea rose, from miniature to hulking
cabbage roses, single blooms to clusters, bushes to climbers, stark
white to murky attempts at mauves and purples, and a vast array of
crimsons, pinks, reds, and yellows, and scents described as sweet,
spicy, citrus, fruity, myrrh-like, musky. Even as ornament, flowers
represent life itself, as fertility, mortality, transience, extravagance,
and as such they enter our art, rites, and language.

# THREE

# Lilacs and Nazis

O n April 2, 1936, a few months before his thirty-third birthday, Orwell had just arrived in Wallington, had just rented the cottage, and was preparing a garden and with it a life. That spring he was between two journeys that would awaken him politically and set him on the path to becoming a political journalist and essayist and eventually a writer of immense impact. He was also settling down for the first time, at an address he would keep longer than any other, and in which for the first time he would live the life he wanted, with a garden and a wife, in the countryside, making his living primarily as a writer.

Orwell's life was notably episodic, and a lot of the episodes are geographical. He was born in northern India, where his father remained for the first several years of his childhood, and raised by his mother in a series of pleasant English towns. His life with her and his two sisters was disrupted when he was, at age eight, sent away to live for five years at a preparatory school where, in return for reduced fees, he was hectored and shamed and groomed to win a scholarship to one of the elite public schools. The grief and bitterness were still strong when, at the end of his life, he wrote a memoir of the experience. At thirteen, he won a scholarship to the most elite of all, Eton, where he spent another four years, acquiring an accent that marked him as an outsider among the poor without making him an insider among the rich. There he was unable or unwilling to excel again, and without the family money for university or the accomplishments for a scholarship, he had to find work.

At nineteen, he went off to serve in Britain's imperial police force in Burma for five years, and there's a picture of him there, among his fellow officers, looking in his military-style uniform more strapping and neatly dressed than at any other point in his life. His job was to bully locals into submitting to an unwanted colonial authority, and he would write about it later in the novel *Burmese Days* and the essays "Shooting an Elephant" and "A Hanging." He officially left because of ill health in 1927, but refused to return. Thirteen years later he said of his Burmese job, "I gave it up partly because the climate had ruined my health, partly because I already had vague ideas of writing books, but mainly because I could not go on any longer serving an imperialism which I had come to regard as very largely a racket." That literary ambition and the low cost of living in France at the time might be why soon after he headed to Paris, but he had also decided to reverse the direction his parents had set for him and become downwardly mobile, not only poor himself but spending time by choice among the poor, as a kind of expiation of that colonial phase and an engagement with the classes he had been taught to shun.

His first book, *Down and Out in Paris and London*, is a picaresque account of his dive into the underworld of scrounging, hustling, and scraping by. Two essays also describe his time among the indigent. "How the Poor Die" recounts his two weeks in the squalid public ward of a Paris hospital when he had severe pneumonia, in March 1929. There his bodily needs were neglected and his illness treated with barbaric, outdated methods. At the end of 1929, he returned to England, living with his parents at first. The essay "Hop Picking" tells of his labors and social encounters among the harvesters—"East Enders, mostly costermongers, gypsies, and itinerant agricultural labourers with a sprinkling of tramps"—at a farm in Kent in 1931, as well as the dismal wages, rough living conditions, pleasures he found in the work itself, and subsidiary activity such as stealing apples. "They were the kind of people who . . . tack a 'fucking' on to every noun," he wrote in his diary of the experience, "yet I have never seen anything that exceeded their kindness." From 1932 to 1935 he worked as a schoolteacher in provincial schools and as a bookstore clerk in London, poorly paid jobs he loathed for their own sakes and for the time and energy they took from his writing.

His other places—the harsh prep school, Eton, Burma, Paris, then Spain during its civil war, London during those impoverished years and again during the Second World War, and the remote Scottish island on which he spent as much of his last years as he could—have attracted far more attention than Wallington. It's true that Burma, Paris, London, and Spain all became locations for his books and true that they accord better with the version of Orwell that I found again and again in the books about him I read after that encounter with the autumnal roses. These versions emphasized his political engagement, discordant relations with some of his peers, and exceptional insight into how propaganda and authoritarianism fed each other and how they threatened rights and freedoms, along with the miserable respiratory health that would kill him at forty-six. One is titled *Orwell: Wintry Conscience of a Generation*. The books painted a stern and gloomy portrait in shades of gray.

Perhaps his relentless scrutiny of the monstrosities and underlying dangers in the present and the future defines him, but it's also been used to characterize him as though he was what he saw, or that was all he looked at. I returned to his writing after the roses startled me, and there I found another Orwell whose other perspectives seem to counterbalance his cold eye on political monstrosity. One of the striking things was how much he recounted enjoyment, from many forms of the domestic comfort that might be called coziness to ribald postcards, the pleasures of nineteenth-century American children's books, British writers like Dickens, "good bad books," and a host of other things, and most of all animals, plants, flowers, natural landscapes, gardening, the countryside, pleasures that surface over and over again in his books all the way through *Nineteen Eighty-Four*'s lyrical evocation of the Golden Country and its light, trees, meadows, birdsong, and sense of freedom and release.

This unfamiliar Orwell brought to mind an essay by Noelle Oxenhandler about waiting and slowness and their value. In it she touches on the life of Jacques Lusseyran, who was blinded as a child and at seventeen became an organizer in the Resistance in Paris during the Second World War. "What impressed me as much as his heroic activity was the pause that preceded it," she writes, describing how he explored Paris under Nazi occupation, and how at the same time he learned to swing dance, because as he wrote in his own memoir, "Swing was really a dance to drive out demons." Oxenhandler and Lusseyran suggest that you might prepare for your central mission in life by doing other things that may seem entirely unrelated, and how necessary this may be.

Orwell seemed to have an instinct for this other work and a talent for giving it what it required. In the last phase of his life, he was both intent upon writing *Nineteen Eighty-Four* and devoting huge amounts of his time, energy, imagination, and resources to building up a garden verging on a farm, with livestock, crops, fruit trees, a tractor—and a lot of flowers—on the remote tip of a Scottish island. What is it that makes it possible to do the work that is of highest value to others and one's central purpose in life? It may appear—to others, sometimes even to oneself—trivial, irrelevant, indulgent, pointless, distracted, or any of those other pejoratives with which the quantifiable beats down the unquantifiable.

This unfamiliar Orwell also brings to mind a famous Buddhist parable about a person chased by a tiger who, in flight, stumbles over a cliff and grasps a small plant to prevent falling to her death. It's a strawberry plant that is gradually becoming uprooted and will soon give way, and it has one beautifully ripe strawberry dangling from it. What, asks the parable, is the right thing to do at that moment, and the answer is to savor the berry. It's a story suggesting that we are always mortal and might die sooner than we think: there are often tigers, there are sometimes strawberries. Orwell had his own personal tiger in the terrible health that must have meant he knew death was never far away.

Much of his life, he suffered from bouts of respiratory diseases. It began with bronchitis contracted as a toddler that seems to have caused bronchiectasis—a condition of damaged airways that made him more susceptible to subsequent pulmonary infection. He came down with pneumonia and bronchitis repeatedly, as a child and as an adult. He was often sick enough to require hospitalization and weeks to months of convalescence. In Spain in 1937 (or, other accounts suggest, in Burma a decade earlier) he seems to have contracted the tuberculosis that would lead to dangerous lung hemorrhages, shortness of breath, weakness, and exhaustion. He had several extended stays in hospitals and sanatoriums before his last decline institutionalized him for the year before his death of TB at forty-six in January 1950.

Sometimes the shadow of death frightens or depresses people, sometimes it makes them live more vividly and take life less for granted, and Orwell seems to be among the latter. He had an austere and martial disposition in many respects, didn't flee physical discomfort, and pushed himself through his bodily limitations until he was bedridden, then got back up, again and again, but he reached for the occasional strawberry. A friend said, "He was a rebel against his own biological condition and he was a rebel against social conditions; the two were very closely linked together."

None of this means he was an impeccable figure. He was not, he mourned after her death, as kind or faithful to his wife as he should have been. He held on to some of the prejudices of his class, his race and nationality, his gender, his heterosexuality, and his era. Those slights and sneers were particularly strong in his early published work and letters. Slashing away at others seemed to be a means of self-definition and self-enhancement that faded away as he grew more confident and more humane as a writer and a person.

The writing is sometimes brilliant, often useful, famously prophetic, and even occasionally beautiful, within a definition of beauty that doesn't have a lot to do with prettiness. Even there, of course, biases and blind spots are scattered. And though he wasn't exemplary in some respects, in others he was courageous and committed. He managed to both love Englishness and loathe the British Empire and imperialism and to say a lot about both, to be an advocate for underdogs and outsiders, and to defend human rights and freedoms in ways that still matter.

There is no Orwell book about Wallington—unless it's the austerely allegorical *Animal Farm*, set in a place named Willingdon, centered on a great barn on Manor Farm much like the actual Manor Farm barn still standing, tar black and imposing, around the corner from the cottage. But nearly every book of his contains evocations of rural English scenery and the pleasure taken in it that has much to do with this place and the places he wandered, fished, botanized, bird-watched, cultivated, and played in as a child, a youth, and a young man. His childhood seems to have been divided between the freedom and pleasure of life outdoors and the regimentation and misery of the schools he lived at from age eight to eighteen.

One day when he was eleven, he stood on his head in a meadow to attract the attention of the other three children nearby. The ploy was successful. Jacintha Buddicom, who was one of the three, wrote a memoir of her and her siblings' friendship with him during the school vacations when he returned to his own family in Shiplake, Oxfordshire. For the next several years, when he was at home, he spent much of his free time in their company, playing and exploring outdoors. They went on "not-too-long country walks," fished, went bird-watching, collected birds' eggs. She recalled that he was enthralled with books, reading, and telling ghost stories, with exploring the natural world, and that he intended to be not just a writer but a "Famous Author."

His 1939 novel *Coming Up for Air* has long passages that summon up some of the enchantment his surroundings had for him then. For example, "We used to go for long, trailing kind of walks—always, of course, picking and eating things all the way—down the lane past the allotments, across Roper's Meadows, and down to the Mill Farm, where there was a pool with newts and tiny carp in it (Joe and I used to go fishing there when we were a bit older), and back by the Upper Binfield Road so as to pass the sweet-shop that stood on the edge of the town."

He would become immensely famous for sentences such as this one in *Nineteen Eighty-Four*: "If you want a picture of the future, imagine a boot stamping on a human face—forever." He is much admired for sentences about the use and abuse of language such as this, from 1946: "Political language . . . is designed to make lies sound truthful and murder respectable, and to give an appearance of solidity to pure wind." He was good at scorn, as in this pair of sentences from 1944, when he launched a minor campaign against the lazy invocation of jackboots: "Ask a journalist what a jackboot is, and you will find that he does not know. Yet he goes on talking about jackboots."

But he also wrote sentences like these from the essay that had prompted me to visit the cottage: "In the good days when nothing in Woolworth's cost over sixpence, one of their best lines was their rose bushes. They were always very young plants, but they came into bloom in their second year, and I don't think I ever had one die on me." Or even this, in a letter from that April 1936 when he planted that garden: "The garden is still Augean (I have dug up twelve boots in two days) but I am getting things straight a little."

In his writing the hideous and the exquisite often coexist. When he went to Germany to report on the end of the Second World War, he came across a corpse near the footbridge that was one of the last unbombed bridges across the river through Stuttgart: "A dead German soldier was lying supine at the foot of the steps. His face was a waxy yellow. On his breast someone had laid a bunch of the lilac which was blooming everywhere." It makes a picture and strikes a balance, that yellow face and those lilacs, death and life, the vigor of the spring and the immense devastation of the war.

The lilacs don't negate the corpse or the war but they complicate it, as the specific often does the general. So does the unseen hand that had laid a bouquet on a soldier and the news that lilacs were blooming in Stuttgart, which in 1945 was shards and rubble from the thousands of tons of bombs dropped on it by British airplanes in the course of the war. The flowers say that this person a British reader would look upon as the enemy was someone's friend or beloved, that this corpse had a personal as well as a political history.

If you dig into Orwell's work, you find a lot of sentences about flowers and pleasures and the natural world. If you read enough of those sentences the gray portrait turns to color, and if you look for these passages, even his last masterpiece, *Nineteen Eighty-Four*, changes complexion. These sentences are less ringing, less prophetic than the political analysis, but they are not unrelated to it, and they have their own poetics, their own power, and their own politics. Nature itself is immensely political, in how we imagine, interact with, and impact it, though this was not much recognized in his era.

The German corpse has something to tell us, and it's about war and nationalism, and about an encounter with death. The flowers also have something to tell us in that sentence, perhaps that there's something beyond the war, just as there's cyclical time, the time of nature as seasons and processes imagined until recently as outside historical time. A human being lives in both, as a political actor, a citizen of this place or that, a seat for a mind with opinions and beliefs, but also as a biological entity, eating and sleeping and excreting and breeding, ephemeral like flowers. Emotions arise from bodily fears and desires, but also from ideas and commitments and culture.

In his 1946 essay "Why I Write," Orwell addressed this directly: "Anyone who cares to examine my work will see that even when it is downright propaganda it contains much that a full-time politician would consider irrelevant. I am not able, and do not want, completely to abandon the world view that I acquired in childhood. So long as I remain alive and well I shall continue to feel strongly about prose style, to love the surface of the earth, and to take a pleasure in solid objects and scraps of useless information. It is no use trying to suppress that side of myself. The job is to reconcile my ingrained likes and dislikes with the essentially public, non-individual activities that this age forces on all of us."

That middle sentence is remarkable, a credo driven by the verbs *feel*, *love*, and *take*. It's immensely specific about the objects of that love and pleasure. He devoted a lot of time to those phenomena and took a lot of pleasure in them, which his own writings reveal, but the books about him and the popular version of him mostly don't. He spent a lot of time with flowers and paid attention to them in pastoral and distinctly unpastoral settings. In 1944, while living in a London that had been bombed over and over for years, he asked readers if they knew the name of "the weed with a pink flower which grows so profusely on blitzed sites."

Around that time the poet Ruth Pitter came up from the country to visit him, and she recalled long afterward, "I had brought with me two things impossible to buy in London at that time—a good bunch of grapes from my mother's home in Essex, and a red rose—two rare treasures. I can see him now, holding up the grapes with a smile of admiration and delight on his face, and then cupping the rose in his wasted hands, breathing in the scent with a kind of reverent joy. That's the last vivid image I have of him."

He was not only a gardener but an avid naturalist and had been since childhood. As a poor man with few options for intimacy, he often relied upon parks and the rural outdoors as locations for sexual activity, a practice reflected in his novels *Keep the Aspidistra Flying* and *Nineteen Eighty-Four*, and that may have charged the natural world with another layer of allure. But that wasn't all he liked about the countryside. Richard Peters, whom Orwell tutored when Peters was a boy and he was a young man, said of the long walks they went on, "He commented on the actions of politicians in the same sort of way as he commented on the behaviour of stoats, or the habits of the heron. . . . His attitude to animals and birds was rather like his attitude to children. He was at home with them. He seemed to know everything about them and found them amusing and interesting."

A woman who used to go walking with him when he was young recalled, "He knew an awful lot about the countryside, and he would notice birds or animals and point them out to me. He'd say, 'Listen!' and he'd tell me what bird it was singing. By the time I saw them they were gone! And different trees—he knew the names of plants." The novelist Anthony Powell complained, "If you went with a country walk with Orwell . . . he would draw attention, almost with anxiety, to this shrub budding early for the time of year, that plant growing rarely in the south of England."

A young communist who went to visit him late in his life reported that Orwell "bored him to death with endless descriptions of the habits of birds," possibly to avoid discussing politics. This Orwell feels like a nephew of Thoreau (who botanized, kept diaries about the timing of bird migrations and first flowerings, grew produce for sale and for consumption by his circle, and, of course, advocated for radical political positions and actions in some of his most important essays). He is not someone I expected to encounter, but once you know what he looks like, you run into him often.

In 1935, he had published a poem that was not a very good poem— he was neither a talented poet nor a promising novelist, and it would take time for him (and others) to find out that he was a sublimely gifted essayist. It was a compelling portrait of his view of himself as someone who did what the age demanded of him.

*A happy vicar I might have been*
*Two hundred years ago*
*To preach upon eternal doom*
*And watch my walnuts grow.*

He mourns having missed this "pleasant haven," but then he got it anyway. Or rather his aunt got it for him, though in a letter to his friend Jack Common he said "a friend" got it for him, perhaps because at thirty-three "aunt" made him sound too juvenile. His mother's older sister, like the Wallington home, has often gotten short shrift in the accounts of Orwell's life, but she played a major role at a crucial time. (There's a whole history to be written about bohemian aunts and queer uncles, about those family members who swoop down to encourage misfit children in ways their parents won't or can't.) That aunt, Helene Limouzin, called Nellie, was a suffragist, a socialist (probably the first one he knew), a bohemian, an actress, and a contributor to left-wing publications.

Jacintha Buddicom recalled of her friend Eric Blair (who would assume the name George Orwell in 1933), "There was an Aunt Ivy

Limouzin and an Aunt Nellie, as I remember. One or two of these aunts and their friends were Militant Suffragettes. Mrs. Blair was in sympathy, but not so active. Some of this contingent, Eric said, went to prison and on hunger-strike as well more moderately chaining themselves to railings." When he was very young, Aunt Nellie introduced him to the first serious writer he met, E. Nesbit, who was known for her rambunctious novels for children, but who was also a cofounder of the democratic socialist group the Fabian Society.

When the nephew returned from Burma, the aunt helped him out as he fumbled his way into a new life. She herself was impecunious and adventurous, and while Orwell's parents were horrified by his decision to step off the ladder of upward mobility to pursue something as unreliable as writing, she was encouraging. At some point in the 1920s, she had gotten involved with a French anarchist, Eugène Adam, who had been a witness to the Russian Revolution in 1917. Nellie and Adam were living together in Paris during Orwell's time there at the end of the 1920s. Adam's firsthand knowledge of the Russian Revolution and rejection of what it had become may have influenced Orwell's own recognition of how terribly wrong the experiment had gone. Anarchists generally recognized this early, while too many communists continued to imagine it as the glorious realization of the dictatorship of the proletariat long after it was just another dictatorship.

The adult Orwell's first published piece was in a left-wing French magazine whose editor, the novelist Henri Barbusse, had been introduced to the young man by his aunt. On June 3, 1933, when he was a provincial schoolteacher, she sent him some money and asked him to renew her subscription to the left-wing magazine *Adelphi* and to keep the rest for himself. "It will pay the rent of your allotment, which I *hope* has brought you some profit; of course seeds must have cost something, perhaps some manure and also perhaps tools, although I hope you were able to borrow or steal those.... Here, while attending the Disarmament conferences, they are at the same time preparing for war pretty thoroughly." It's a long and affectionate letter, one in which she shows a kind interest in his jobs, his book, his garden, shares her own in politics, and accepts his choices and resultant poverty without question.

He was preoccupied with that allotment garden. Earlier that year, he wrote to a woman he was pursuing, "Forgive me for not writing for so long, but I have been as usual submerged with work & in the intervals trying to break the back of my garden. Today I nearly broke my own back, using the turfing iron & yesterday gave myself one on the shin with a pickaxe. Have you read *Ulysses* yet?" He added, likely in reference to some al fresco erotic activity, "It was so nice at Burnham Beeches & I should love to go there again when the trees are budding." And then in July he wrote to another woman he was pursuing about the allotment, where he was apparently raising vegetables he hoped to sell: "marrows & pumpkins, which are swelling almost visibly. We have had lashings of peas, beans just beginning, potatoes rather poor, owing to the drought I suppose. I have finished my novel, but there are wads of it that I simply hate."

Then he fell seriously ill with pneumonia, and after he was released from the hospital he had to move back in with his mother and father to convalesce for several months. It happened around the same time that he first began publishing under the name George Orwell, an endeavor to reinvent himself on his own terms and separate himself from his family. That project must have felt compromised by his return to the parental home in the coastal town of Southwold in Suffolk.

During his residence with his parents, he declared in a letter to one of his women correspondents, "This age makes me so sick that sometimes I am almost impelled to stop at a corner and start calling down curses from Heaven like Jeremiah or Ezra or somebody." Later he would excel at jeremiads and screeds about the age. But in the letter he did that interesting thing human beings do when they are talking informally: he made a seamless transition from Old Testament wrath to reportage of something that seems to have charmed him and piqued his curiosity. A little later in it, he writes, "The hedgehogs keep coming into the house, and last night we found in the bathroom a little tiny hedgehog no bigger than an orange. The only thing I could think was that it was a baby of one of the others, though it was fully formed—I mean, it had its prickles. Write again soon." It is often implied (or shouted) that if you enjoy hedgehogs you do not care about the evils of the age, but they routinely coexist in experience and imagination.

On September 23, 1934, Aunt Nellie wrote to her Welsh friend Myfanwy Westrope on her nephew's behalf. Westrope was a suffragist, a pacifist, a vegetarian, and a member of the Independent Labour Party, and she and her husband had a bookshop near Hampstead Heath in London. That husband had learned Esperanto while imprisoned as a conscientious objector during the First World War, and Esperanto had led him to Adam, and Adam to Limouzin. She connected her nephew to the Westropes and to an afternoon bookshop job that left mornings to write and came with a bedroom at their nearby home. At some point his aunt too moved to London; Ruth Pitter recalls, "Yes, I remember we went to supper with Aunt Nellie once. Ooh, what a supper it was. She was living with some ould Anarchist, I think. She was a coughdrop. She gave us some fearsome dish such as one would have in Paris if one was a native Parisian and dreadfully hard up."

During those years as a teacher and then a bookstore clerk, he published three not particularly successful novels one right after the other in 1934, 1935, and 1936, before he went on those journeys and found a political perspective to orient himself by. The books, which he was himself unsatisfied with, are all noteworthy for a view of the world that is less political analysis than personal resentment. Perhaps it originates in his formative years as a poor boy in schools for rich boys, this taking the side of the underdog and loathing of the powers that crush them. He said of his youthful self, "I was both a snob and a revolutionary. I was against all authority . . . I loosely described myself as a Socialist. But I had not much grasp of what Socialism meant, and no notion that the working class were human beings."

Each of his novels features an individual estranged from the people around her or him, and those adversaries compound into the system that is society, and society grinds each of his protagonists down. (*Nineteen Eighty-Four*'s plot and its physically and morally frail antihero bear a striking resemblance to the protagonist of *Keep the Aspidistra Flying*, though the earlier book features poverty and the pressures to conform of Orwell's own society and the later book, a totalitarian state that breaks down its lead character through torture and terror.) Each book also shifts into a more passionate and vivid prose when describing immediate experience, particularly of the natural world. They seem like ingredients that haven't stewed together long enough, these chunks of dubious plot, dismal lives, furious tirade, and lavish evocation. In *A Clergyman's Daughter*, the protagonist named in the title is a cringing servant to her selfish father, a diligent tender of the sick and elderly of the parish, and generally a thwarted soul who will be swept away by a series of not-very-credible events and then plopped back in her rustic misery at the end.

But after a visit to nurse a miserable old woman in her father's parish, she pauses on her bicycle ride home to bask where "the red cows were grazing, knee-deep in shining seas of grass. The scent of cows, like a distillation of vanilla and fresh hay, floated into Dorothy's nostrils. . . . Dorothy caught sight of a wild rose, flowerless of course, growing beyond the hedge, and climbed over the gate with the intention of discovering whether it were not sweetbriar. She knelt down among the tall weeds beneath the hedge. It was very hot down there, close to the ground. The humming of many unseen insects sounded in her ears, and the hot summery fume from the tangled swathes of vegetation flowed up and enveloped her." The lives he invented are miseries studded with epiphanies. Orwell did not believe in permanent happiness or the politics that tried to realize it, but he did believe devoutly in moments of delight, even rapture, and he wrote about them often, from these early books to *Nineteen Eighty-Four*.

He was being looked after by multiple older women, including Mabel Fierz, who had known his parents in Southwold. Fierz had introduced him to some of the men she knew in London, figures who would become his literary agent, his publishers, and some of his most lasting friends. When the Westropes asked him to move out of their home, Fierz introduced him to Rosalind Obermeyer, a student of psychology in her forties who had a spacious flat with an unoccupied bedroom in which he took up residence. There he cooked primitive dinners in what his letters describe as a Bachelor Griller—a sort of toaster oven—and served them to friends on a table he otherwise used for writing.

In the spring of 1935, Obermeyer and Orwell threw a joint

party at the place, and one of the guests who strolled in was Eileen O'Shaughnessy, a fellow student of Obermeyer's in University College London's master's of psychology program. Orwell was immediately and immensely taken with the self-possessed twenty-nine-year-old and pursued her eagerly that night and thereafter. O'Shaughnessy was from a more prosperous if less established family than his—her father was an Irish Catholic who had settled in northern England. An Oxford graduate, she had immense intelligence, an arch sense of humor, considerable wit, and, soon, reciprocated ardor for an unusually tall, unhealthy, unsuccessful novelist with a brush of dark hair springing upward from his head, sunken blue eyes, and strong and often cranky opinions. She loved him enough to leave behind her friends and her London life and join him in the rural village he chose to land in, and to devote herself to him instead of the career for which she was training. When he was planting the garden in Wallington, he was preparing for Eileen's arrival from London and their marriage.

"The garden is potentially good but has been left in the most frightful state I have ever seen," he wrote to his friend Jack Common on April 3, the day after he arrived. "I am afraid it will be a year before I can get it nice." There was a small area for planting in front of the cottage, where some of the roses went, a larger garden area behind it, and a field across the lane he managed to lay hands on for a more extensive vegetable garden, rented from the postmaster at nearby Sandon. Later on he'd graze goats on the village common and milk them twice daily (one of his letters to Common, a blue-collar writer who took over the place for a while in 1938, includes extremely detailed instructions on the correct way to milk his goats).

The cottage had been a village shop, and he bought a bacon slicer and some modest groceries and set up as a grocer to the small community. The tiny profit off the sale of a small assortment of goods, including sweets, aspirins, bacon, and eggs from the chickens they raised, helped with the minuscule rent while he was barely scraping by as a writer. He attended the Adelphi summer school that year, participating in its political discussions, but mostly he wrote and tended his garden, at least for those six months after his marriage. (Eileen apparently took on most of the housecleaning and cooking and some of the shopkeeping.)

At the end of 1936, Orwell reversed direction from rustic withdrawal and journeyed to Spain and to war. But his tendency, perhaps forged in those schools full of richer boys, to remain an outsider would keep him from being swept up during that war and ever after in what would later be called groupthink, a spinoff of the word *doublethink* he coined in his last novel. Also, he hated London and city life, and the cottage with the low rent paid for by the shop might have given him his only chance at writing full-time.

Eileen O'Shaughnessy became Eileen Blair on June 9, a Tuesday, with a small ceremony at the church that was a short walk from her new home up a shady lane, past the great tar-black Manor Farm barn and a small pond fed by a spring.* The little church has been built in bits and pieces since the twelfth century, and it is made of flint—or rather its exterior walls are pale cement holding together curiously

---

* Eileen's beloved brother Dr. Laurence Frederick O'Shaughnessy went by Eric in their family, and so while Eileen took Eric Blair's surname, she took to calling her husband George. While his use of the name George Orwell happened abruptly in print, it happened gradually in letters and in friendships, until he was George Orwell to many of those who knew him personally. So though there was a George Orwell there was never an Eileen Orwell. Her tombstone and his say Blair, and the son they adopted in 1944 is named Richard Blair. I regret having to refer to Eileen O'Shaughnessy Blair by her first name, but like too many married women it is the only one she really owned throughout her life. When Sonia Brownell married Orwell a few months before his death, she took Orwell as her surname, as if she were marrying the legend, rather than the man.

shaped chunks of dark flint, the local stone. The rows of stones look like hieroglyphics or ciphers on a page. The whitewashed interior is luminous and spare, with angels carved long ago into the wooden rafters and a floor paved with black eighteenth-century tombstones inscribed in flowing script.

Orwell once called himself a Tory anarchist, and though he had elements of the rebel and the revolutionary about him, he was a lover of tradition, stability, rusticity, and domestic routine. "He was traditional in a way which goes back to a very old tradition in English life, before industrialism, to the English village," proposed the poet Stephen Spender. "He believed essentially in small communities of neighbours who knew one another very well and therefore he had a great deal of sympathy with the anarchists. . . . Therefore you might say that the basic reason why he wasn't a Communist was because the Communists weren't Communists and George Orwell was one." Like William Morris, he believed that paradise was behind us, in the old ways of life, and in the organic world, rather than ahead of us in an urbanized and industrialized future.

The choice to get married in a church was perhaps part of this embrace of the old ways, though it might also have been about choosing a place that didn't require him to leave the village or the shop, which was open most days. The wedding lunch was at the pub next to his new home. Some of the biographies describe the next several months as among the happiest of his life. Eileen Blair had her own version, which she wrote in a letter to a friend in November of that year. "I lost my habit of punctual correspondence during the first few weeks of marriage because we quarrelled so continuously & really bitterly that I thought I'd save time & just write one letter to everyone when the murder or separation had been accomplished. Then Eric's aunt came to stay & was so dreadful (she stayed *two months*) that we stopped quarrelling & just repined. Then she went away & now all our troubles are over. . . . I forgot to mention that he had his 'bronchitis' for three weeks in July & that it rained every day for six weeks during the whole of which the kitchen was flooded & all food went mouldy in a few hours. It seems a long time ago now but then seemed very permanent." When she wrote, the newlyweds were in Southwold on the Suffolk coast, visiting Orwell's parents, but she added, "If I'd written this from Wallington it would have been about the real things of life—goats, hens, broccoli (eaten by a rabbit)."

The hens had a starring role in their lives. When Orwell returned to Wallington from the Spanish Civil War, where he enlisted at the end of 1936—and from a series of places where he thereafter convalesced from his war wound and another round of lung trouble—he recorded the daily egg production and the behavior of the individual birds and the minutiae of feeding and tending them. The Wallington diary begins with an exuberance of flowers on an April three years from when he first landed there. "We have now 26 hens, the youngest about 11 months. Yesterday 7 eggs (the hens have only recently started laying again.) Everything greatly neglected, full of weeds etc., ground very hard & dry, attributed to heavy falls of rain, then no rain at all for some weeks. . . . Flowers now in bloom in the garden: polyanthus, aubretia, scilla, grape hyacinth, oxalis, a few narcissi. Many daffodils in the field," he wrote. "These are very double & evidently not real wild daffodil but bulbs dropped there by accident. Bullaces & plums coming into blossom. Apple trees budding but no blossom yet. Pears in full blossom. Roses sprouting fairly strongly." On May 25, 1939, he reported that his hens had laid two hundred eggs in the previous two weeks.

These domestic accounts—which take up a lot of the nearly six-hundred-page compilation of his travel, war, and domestic diaries published in 2009—stand out in his work as records of something almost antithetical to the subjects of a political writer: places in which nothing was seriously wrong and no conflicts raged. The minor troubles—a jackdaw hanging around the chicken coops, potatoes rotted by frost, goats terrified by thunder, birds eating the strawberries, greenfly on the roses, and lots of slugs—worked against the gardener's agenda but not against any law of nature or morality. The majority of his entries are concerned with his own activity with his domesticated plants and animals, but he makes notes as well on the agricultural fields beyond and the wild things around him. Occasional speculations and small experiments are also recorded.

While a writer like Henry David Thoreau might sow beans and reap metaphors and aphorisms, Orwell's beans came up strictly as beans in these accounts. That is, he never uses these observations and records as a springboard for flights of imagination or overt literary groundwork. It's an impersonal private diary, not intended for publication but also not recording his emotional, creative, social, or bodily life, only his toil and intentions. Sometimes there are lists of things he intends to buy and do, visions of the future so simple and near at hand as to be realizable when so much else was not. It's not clear why he kept these detailed records, but he was so committed to them that when he left Wallington to attend his father's deathbed Eileen kept up the entries, and in the postwar time on the Isle of Jura, his sister Avril wrote some entries while he was away. Committed to them, but not as his particular voice and views, though they are present nonetheless.

In 1940, he offered this biographical sketch of himself in answer to an author questionnaire: "Outside my work the thing I care most about is gardening, especially vegetable gardening." The measure of how much it mattered to him is in the attention he paid to it, and the considerable labor he put into it, from his 1933 allotment garden to the last garden he exerted himself to bring to life as he was dying. And it's in something less measurable and more significant: the pleasure he took, and the meaning he found. He wanted a garden, and wanted to work in it, to produce his own food and more intangible things. He wanted flowers, fruit trees, vegetables, chickens, goats. He wanted to watch birds and skies and the seasons change. He clearly, as he said in that credo, loved the surface of the earth. He was curious about daffodils and hedgehogs and slugs; he spent a lot of time observing flora and fauna and weather.

Pursuits like that can bring you back to Earth from the ether and the abstractions. They could be imagined as the opposite of writing. Writing is a murky business: you are never entirely sure what you are doing or when it will be finished and whether you got it right and how it will be received months or years or decades after you finish. What it does, if it does anything, is a largely imperceptible business that takes place in the minds of people you will mostly never see and never hear from (unless they want to argue with you). As a writer, you withdraw and disconnect yourself from the world in order to connect to it in the far-reaching way that is other people elsewhere reading the words that came together in this contemplative state. What is vivid in the writing is not in how it hits the senses but what it does in the imagination; you can describe a battlefield, a birth, a muddy road, or a smell—Orwell would become famous for all the stenches mentioned in his books—but it is still black letters on a white page, with no real blood or mud or boiled cabbage.

A garden offers the opposite of the disembodied uncertainties of writing. It's vivid to all the senses, it's a space of bodily labor, of getting dirty in the best and most literal way, an opportunity to see immediate and unarguable effect. At the end of the day if you dug, how much you dug is as clear and definite as is the number of eggs collected from the chickens. The literary critic Kunio Shin notes of Winston Smith, the protagonist of *Nineteen Eighty-Four*, "In a world where '[n]ot merely the validity of experience, but the very existence of external reality, [is] tacitly denied' by the Party, Winston's attempt to hold on to the truth of truisms—'Stones are hard, water is wet, objects unsupported fall towards the earth's centre'—is itself a desperate gesture of political resistance." Elsewhere in the book, Orwell declares, "The Party told you to reject the evidence of your eyes and ears," which makes direct observations and firsthand encounters in the material and sensory world likewise acts of resistance or at least reinforcements of the self who can resist. To spend time frequently with these direct experiences is clarifying, a way of stepping out of the whirlpools of words and the confusion they can whip up. In an age of lies and illusions, the garden is one way to ground yourself in the realm of the processes of growth and the passage of time, the rules of physics, meteorology, hydrology, and biology, and the realms of the senses.

The American poet and devoted gardener Ross Gay told an interviewer, "There's probably been nothing else in my life that's trained me to go slow the way gardening has, that's compelled me to look very closely. Part of the delight of my garden is that you just get lost in it before you've even started to do anything. I walk out to my backyard garden at certain times of the year and I can't get 30 feet without stopping for 20 minutes because the goumis need trimming. And then I watch the wasps and notice that the lavender and the thyme right next to it need weeding. I love how my garden is very productive outside of the logic of productivity—it makes a lot of stuff that's edible and nourishing and all that, but it's also 'productive' in ways you wouldn't think necessarily to measure." Most of writing is thinking, not typing, and thinking is sometimes best done while doing something else that engages part of you. Walking or cooking or laboring on simple or repetitive tasks can also be a way to leave the work behind so you can come back to it fresh or find unexpected points of entry into it.

If you write for a living, the return (as impact, as income, as appreciation) can be a nebulous thing, but you reap what you sow in a garden—if the weather holds and the pests don't devour everything. Growing food plants can be a touchstone, a way to come back to your senses and your sense of self after wandering in words. Or it can be an encounter with a creative process full of unpredictabilities and interventions, by weather, other creatures, and unforeseen forces, that are very different than what happens on the page (or the computer screen), a collaboration with the nonhuman. A manuscript is rarely flattened by hail, though one of Orwell's was scattered by a German bomb. The kind of metaphoric, evocative, image-rich speech that *Nineteen Eighty-Four*'s Newspeak is trying to root out is grounded in the natural, rural, and agrarian world: the language of plowing ahead, having a hard row to hoe, reaping what you sow, making a beeline, going out on a limb, not seeing the forest for the trees, rooting out itself, and all the rest. Orwell in going rural was, among other things, returning to the source of metaphor, aphorism, and simile.

An incident he recalls that likely took place in Wallington shows how—to use another rustic metaphor—fruitful the rural was for him: "I saw a little boy, perhaps ten years old, driving a huge carthorse along a narrow path, whipping it whenever it tried to turn. It struck me that if only such animals became aware of their strength we should have no power over them, and that men exploit animals in much the same way as the rich exploit the proletariat." Thus was *Animal Farm* born. Though he wrote it in London, during the war, it benefited greatly from his familiarity with the dispositions of various farm animals.

Gardens are also places in which the inseparability of life and death is apparent in innumerable ways. In late October 1939, Orwell noted in his garden diary that, thanks to a sharp frost, "the dahlias blackened immediately, & I am afraid the marrows I had left to ripen are done for." That day, he was collecting dead leaves for mulch, working on his compost heap, noting that "the turves old H stacked earlier in the year have rotted down into beautiful fine loam, but I think I had first killed the grass on these," and saving a hen from freezing to death. The Zen practitioner and gardener Wendy Johnson writes, "Watching the things of the world come apart and recombine is core Zen work and the fundamental anchorage of every gardener's life." She notes that garden fertility comes out of "the discarded waste of our lives." Kylie Tseng, a young climate activist I know, inscribed on her well-built compost bin, "Death is never an ending in nature." And because a garden is always a place of becoming, to make and tend one is a gesture of hope, that these seeds planted will sprout and grow, this tree will bear fruit, that spring will come, and so, probably, will some kind of harvest. It's an activity deeply invested in the future.

Orwell's anarchist friend George Woodcock wrote, "The source of his self-regenerative power lay in his joy in the ordinary, common experiences of day-to-day existence and particularly of contact with nature. He fed from the earth, like Antaeus." The distinction between happiness, which is often imagined as a steady state, like endless sunshine, and joy, which flashes up like lightning, is important. Happiness seems to require having a well-ordered life avoiding difficulty or discord, while joy can and does show up anywhere, often unexpectedly. In their book *Joyful Militancy* carla bergman and Nick Montgomery draw the distinction thus: "Joy remakes people through combat with forces of subjection [i.e., subjugation]. Joy is a desubjectifying process, an unfixing, an intensification of life itself. It is a process of coming alive and coming apart. Whereas happiness is used as a numbing anesthetic that induces dependence, joy is the growth of people's capacity to do and feel new things, in ways that can break this dependence."

Orwell is renowned for what he wrote against—authoritarianism and totalitarianism, the corruption of language and politics by lies and propaganda (and sloppiness), the erosion of the privacy that underlies liberty. From those forces, it's possible to determine what he was for: equality and democracy, clarity of language and honesty of intentions, private life and all its pleasures and joys, the freedom and liberty that also depend to some extent on privacy from supervision and intrusion, and the pleasures of immediate experience. But they don't have to be detected via their opposite; he wrote about those things a lot, in a number of essays that amount to a significant part of his work, and in passages in other works that crop up everywhere and also add up. His grimmest writings have moments of beauty; his most lyrical essays nevertheless grapple with substantive issues.

II

## Going Underground

*Sasha, untitled image showing coal miners and coal wagon,*
*Tilmanstone Colliery, Kent, 1930.*

# ONE

# Smoke, Shale, Ice, Mud, Ashes

In the spring of 1936, a man planted roses. To write it that way makes the man the protagonist, but the roses were protagonists as well. You could, for example, say some domesticated roses—in the family Rosaceae in the genus *Rosa* that has succeeded in getting humans to hybridize and propagate it throughout much of the world—benefited from a man spending his sixpences and then toiling to plant and tend them. As Michael Pollan wrote in *The Botany of Desire*, we think of these plants as something we domesticated, but it could be argued that they domesticated us to tend and propagate them.

The roses flourished. They grew, drank water with their roots, and, fueled by sunlight in the process called photosynthesis, pulled carbon dioxide out of the atmosphere with their leaves and water up from the soil with their roots. They transmuted the carbon into carbohydrates to build themselves out of or consume for energy and broke the water down to release the oxygen back into the air. They flowered, carried out their symbiotic romance with pollinating insects, and brought forth the hips that are their seed-stuffed fruit. Plants are anything but passive. They made the world. The story of how this particular person and these particular plants came together has many beginnings and unfolds in many directions. One lineage begins a little earlier in that year, another in the history of the Industrial Revolution, and a third about 330 million years ago. Those last two time spans were part of what he had just come from investigating and what he would be writing about during most of the rest of 1936.

That spring, Orwell had come to Wallington from the north of England and from places utterly unlike Wallington's bucolic setting. He had been researching what would become his 1937 book, *The Road to Wigan Pier*, titled after an outlying area of Manchester then notable for its poverty (and a music-hall joke about the gritty place having a pleasure pier). It was a book his left-wing publisher, Victor Gollancz, had commissioned as a study of the depressed areas, and it was an invitation to once again delve into how the poor live, as he had in London, in Paris, and among the hop pickers of Kent. The result was a curious book that clearly annoyed Gollancz, who would have preferred to publish only the first half, which was superb reportage on the conditions and characters he encountered. The second half was a torrent of Orwell's still-forming opinions about politics and class, with plenty of autobiography and observations such as "the modern English literary world, at any rate the highbrow section of it, is a sort of poisonous jungle in which only weeds can flourish."

From London, he set off by foot, train, and bus to the north in midwinter and spent almost two months staying in boardinghouses, with friends of friends, with working-class contacts he made, in a youth hostel, and at one point with his older sister, Marjorie, and her family in a suburb of Leeds, talking to whoever would talk to him.

He reported on the conditions of the homes people lived in, on their incomes and expenses and views, and their scramble to find food, fuel, and housing. He was appalled at how they lived and moved by how much people trusted and opened up to an outsider with an alien accent. The region had been particularly devastated by the depression that arrived earlier in the 1930s, though life there had already been hard for generations: it was where the Industrial Revolution had begun and with it the industrial proletariat.

He scrutinized the place as well as the people in this mining and manufacturing country. Coal—as work, as dust, as fuel, as smog, as danger, as illness, as death, as the abundant stuff quite literally underneath everything—was everywhere. He approached it by degrees. First there was the landscape: "The monstrous scenery of slag-heaps, chimneys, piled scrap-iron, foul canals, paths of cindery mud crisscrossed by the prints of clogs." Soot blackened all the buildings, and even the snow was black; black smoke hung over the towns. Wigan seemed to be "a world from which vegetation had been banished; nothing existed except smoke, shale, ice, mud, ashes, and foul water." He described stagnant pools of water where mining pits had subsided, covered with ice "the color of raw umber." Elsewhere were slag heaps that had caught fire, and "in the darkness you can see long serpentine fires creeping all over them, not only red but very sinister blue flames (from sulphur) which always seem on the point of going out and then flicker up again."

Some of the most vivid scenes he describes are of men, women, and children scrambling in the bitter weather to find scraps of coal in the slag the mining companies dumped, sometimes hauling their gleanings away on homemade bicycles. He noted the listlessness of hunger and chronic undernourishment, defeat and despair, the way long-term unemployment left men stranded and families barely hanging on, the injuries and illnesses of those who worked in the mines, and the shadow of death hanging over this most dangerous of occupations. He observed the bodies of miners who came home blackened with the coal dust that would kill many of them. And he described the scarring of their faces: they often banged their heads on the low ceilings of the mines, and these workplace cuts were turned into blue tattoos by the coal dust embedded in them, so that "some of the older men have their foreheads veined with it like Roquefort cheese."

"Our civilization . . . *is* founded on coal, more completely than one realizes until one stops to think about it," he wrote afterward. "The machines that keep us alive, and the machines that make the machines, are all directly or indirectly dependent upon coal." And then he noted, "It is only very rarely, when I make a definite mental effort, that I connect this coal with that far-off labour in the mines." London had since the late sixteenth century been foul with the fumes of coal burning, and Orwell lived most of his life in houses heated by coal—sometimes a furnace but often by a coal fire in a room (and those fumes and particles surely contributed to the miserable condition of his lungs and worsened the tuberculosis that killed him).

He mentioned, in *The Road to Wigan Pier*, that he was writing the above passages in front of a coal fire from coal delivered by a wagon and workmen shooting it into the coalhole under the cottage's stairs, and how easy it was to not think past the workmen or the coalhole. It was clear that he assumed he was writing for other people like himself, left-leaning southerners for whom the details of the lives of the poor and the jobs and conditions of the mines and mills were not so familiar.

That invisibility or that obliviousness is one of the defining conditions of the modern world. Orwell was rectifying this obliviousness when he went up north to meet the working class out of work and down in the mines and to bear witness to that foundational commodity, coal, and the conditions of its extraction. To go down into the earth is to travel back in time, and to excavate it is to drag the past into the present, a process mining has done on a scale so colossal it's changed the earth all the way up to the upper atmosphere. You can tell this story as a labor story, but you can also tell it as an ecological story, and the two dovetail in the end, as a story of devastation.

# Two

# Carboniferous

The ecological story looks something like this: Most of the coal on Earth came into existence in the geological period that takes its name from coal, the Carboniferous, which lasted from about 359 to 299 million years ago. The planet was not much like the one we live on now: The continents were at another phase of their drift across the globe, and their modern forms had not emerged. Some places were still under shallow seas, others were mashed together: at the earlier end of the Carboniferous, Europe and North America were amalgamated into Laurasia, while other landmasses had agglomerated into the supercontinent Gondwana farther to the south. England and Scotland had not yet separated themselves from larger landmasses or crashed into each other.

In one of the lyrical, semi-opaque sentences I came across as I tried to understand the genesis of coal, I read, "After Laurentia had converged with Avalonia and Baltica, bringing the two halves of the UK together in the Caledonian Orogeny, Gondwana continued to drift north." It was an alien planet, long before flowering plants, long before mammals, very long before the conditions under which humans would evolve had emerged. There were no words on this planet, and no names: many worlds rose and fell away in succession on the same planet, a planet that changed again and again when it came to its geology, its geography, its biology, the contents of its atmosphere, and its climate, an Earth on which we did not belong and that we would not recognize.

By the Carboniferous, the once barren surface of the earth had gone green with growing things that had crept out of the oceans and evolved and built soils atop the stony expanses. The land near the equator was riotously alive with plants. The coal forests, as these equatorial abundances were known, were made up of giant club mosses, immense tree ferns, hundred-foot-tall horsetails, and primitive trees. The angiosperms, the flowering plants, would not appear for more than a hundred million years, but these plants did what plants do. They broke down water and released the oxygen and took in carbon dioxide and used it for energy and building materials.

The hectic, lavish plant life of the Carboniferous intensified these processes, with strange effects. One of them was oxygen levels far higher than in recent geological eras. We live on a planet whose atmosphere has long been about 21 percent oxygen, but in the Carboniferous it reached 35 percent. The richer air relaxed the limits on growth and flight. Animal evolution ran riot: there were dragonfly-like creatures with thirty-inch wingspans, millipedes eight feet long, huge mayflies and cockroaches, and an ancestor of newts like a gigantic crocodile, all crashing through the swampy forests. The high oxygen levels were the result of another peculiarity of the Carboniferous.

Usually when plants die, much of their carbon returns to the atmosphere by decay or other transformation, including burning, and it bonds with oxygen to form carbon dioxide, a greenhouse gas, a heat-trapping part of the atmosphere. But in the Carboniferous, vast amounts of carbon dioxide taken out of the air by plants did not return. The cycle was broken. As dead plant matter, the carbon went into the swamps and water-soaked earth and became peat. The peat over eons compressed, dried out, and became coal. In boggy places around the earth, the process of peat formation is still going on, and peat bogs, most notably in Ireland, hold huge amounts of carbon.

The black stuff that lay underground in darkness for hundreds of millions of years began with the photosynthesis of sunlight. As my friend Joe Lamb, who's a tree surgeon and poet with a degree in evolutionary biology, remarked to me, "One way of looking at trees is that they are captured light. Photosynthesis, after all, captures a photon, takes a little energy from it before re-emitting it at a lower wavelength, and uses that captured energy to turn air into sugars, and then sugars into the stuff that makes leaves, wood, and roots. Even the most solid of beings, the giant sequoias, are really light and air."

Some of the original organic matter kept its form in the coal beds, and the geologists documenting Britain's coalfields from the nineteenth century onward often included accounts of fossil plants in their reports. In 2009, scientists reported on a North American coal mine in which an ancient forest extending for miles could be seen from below: leaf litter, great trunks rising into branches, roots, stumps with a dangerous tendency to fall out of the mine roof. Which means that it was clear to at least some of the miners and engineers that they were excavating an ancient world to burn up in the present one.

Plants made the world, over and over, from when single-celled organisms in the seas first put significant quantities of oxygen into the atmosphere of the earth. In the age of the coal forests, plants pulled so much insulating carbon dioxide out of the atmosphere that the era ended in a climate crash—an ice age. Scientists believe that the carbon crash came close to producing "snowball Earth," a planet frozen over from pole to pole. In 2017, Potsdam Institute climate scientist Georg Feulner theorized that the cold itself slowed or stopped the cycle of vegetation growth that was drawing down carbon from the air and freezing the earth. He ended by noting that we are reversing that process. Think of the Carboniferous as a sixty-million-year inhale by plants, sucking carbon dioxide from the sky, and the last two hundred years as a monstrous human-engineered exhale, undoing what the plants did so long ago.

You could imagine coal miners shoveling the carbon out of the bowels of the earth directly into the upper atmosphere, but that would not be fair to them, who are not responsible for climate change, or recognize that it's in burning it, not excavating it, that we put back into the upper atmosphere the carbon that plants long ago buried. Miners supply it. Others burn it—and the oil and gas that are likewise the product of ancient plants, likewise sequestered carbon, likewise catastrophically changing the carbon dioxide levels of the earth. By dumping the residue of the distant past into the sky we are heating the globe and breaking the elegant orchestration of organic and inorganic systems, of the seasons and growing cycles, the weather and migrations and blooms and fruitings, of the currents of air and ocean. Perhaps if we were not burning so rapidly, in the span of a few hundred years, the result of tens of millions of years and more of carbon deposits into the earth, it would not be so devastating, but we have outpaced the capacity of plants to recapture the carbon.

"All that is solid melts into air," Marx and Engels famously wrote in *The Communist Manifesto*, and though they were talking about social and technological change, they could have been describing the return of buried carbon to the upper atmosphere. In 1931, a cheerily brutal book, *New Russia's Primer: The Story of the Five-Year Plan*, was published in English. An ode to the Soviet Union's industrialization, it circulated widely in the United States. In a section titled "We Will Force the Dead to Work," it declares, "The remains of the swamp grass, the ferns, the horsetails rotted under the layers of sand and clay, became black, and turned into coal. And to this cemetery we intend to go, drag the dead out of their tombs, and force them to work for us." That language frames it as a zombie movie, a horror story, the dead come back to haunt us, in this case with their carbon.

# THREE

# In Darkness

There's a short story by Ursula K. Le Guin called "The Ones Who Walk Away from Omelas." It's about a city-state that appears to be magnificent and admirable, enlightened and progressive, but that somehow depends upon the abuse of one child locked in a dim basement, isolated, undernourished, deprived. The misery of that child serves metaphysical purposes, but in England not long before Orwell's day there were many such children, and their misery served practical ones. An 1842 report titled *The Condition and Treatment of the Children Employed in the Mines and Collieries of the United Kingdom* details some of this.

It describes children sent down into mines to work so many hours they only saw daylight on Sundays, sent to drag out coal from passages so cramped they had to crawl for long distances. Some wore the hair off the crown of their heads from pushing carts in front of them. Others on all fours dragged coal carts by chains around their waists that passed between their legs to the carts, and the chains often wore holes in their clothes and sores into their skin. Orwell reported, "There are still living a few very old women" who had dragged coal thus, some well into their pregnancies, "but most of the time, of course, we should prefer to forget that they were doing it."

The women in that 1842 report described how they lived like animals, working until they went into labor or giving birth to children in the pits deep underground, and of how often the children died. The youngest workers, too small at five or six or seven for much physical labor, were employed as "trappers," as keepers of the trapdoors that regulated the ventilation of the mines. Sometimes a small child would get into position before dawn, remaining there alone for twelve hours, except for when miners passed, when the child was expected to open and then reclose a door. They were often left in pitch darkness, because a candle or lamp was not provided, sometimes beaten for being asleep or absentminded.

Sarah Gooder, who was an eight-year-old trapper, told the inspectors, "I have to trap without a light, and I'm scared. . . . I never go to sleep. Sometimes I sing when I've light, but not in the dark; I dare not sing then." Friedrich Engels also wrote about the condition of the miners in his 1845 *Condition of the Working Class in England*, noting that some of the children emerged back into the upper world so depleted they fell asleep on the way home or at home fell so fast asleep their parents could not feed them after work. He described how the children were often stunted and sometimes deformed by the work, and how everyone in the mines was prone to often-fatal lung diseases. When it's burned, coal produces many kinds of toxin, but the dust miners and others inhale is also deadly.

The mine tunnels often collapsed, the air in them often exploded from built-up gases, so mine workers could also anticipate being crushed or maimed or blown to pieces or badly burned or cut off from all possibility of escape by a collapse between themselves and the upper world. Or suffocating in bad air. The conditions deep underground were often so hot that women and children wore nothing but trousers, and men often worked entirely naked. The inspectors were scandalized by what they saw as immodesty, but what seems striking now is the terrible vulnerability of these people with little or nothing to protect them from the rough, foul underworld. In Le Guin's story, those who disapprove of the submerged brutality of Omelas walk away, and the possibility of revolt is not mentioned. In the coal mines, some who abhorred the conditions struck, organized, worked to expose and reform the working conditions, passed laws to keep women and children out of the underground realms.

This was the lurid misery on which Britain's puissance was built, its railroads, steamships, and warships, its iron foundries and textile mills, its great cities. It was, along with colonial labor exploitation and resource extraction, the deprivation underlying its newfound abundance. It is perhaps not so far from the contemporary world that depends on oil platforms in the Gulf of Mexico and the North Sea, foul bitumen strip mining and steam extraction in the tar sands of Alberta, oozing oil projects in indigenous homelands in the Niger Delta and the Amazon, and exploited labor forces around the world exposed to toxins, injury, and death.

Coal had been mined for centuries before this industrial supernova, but in the eighteenth and early nineteenth centuries new technologies had both made deep-pit mining possible and generated machines voracious for the coal that such mining produced, a feedback loop that went faster and further. Locomotives on iron tracks and steam engines were deployed for British mining—to move ore and coal, to pump out water so mining could go deeper. They then became more widespread technologies that made it possible to transcend the limits that had always bounded human life, the limits of how fast and far we could move ourselves and goods and then information, how much we could make, ultimately how much we could change the earth itself and then its air and seas. It was all fueled by fires, millions of them in fireplaces and stoves and below the boilers driving steam loco-motives, steam pumps, and steamships, tens of millions of fires all going at once, the industrial-scale ones so voracious that "stoker" be-came a job: the person who shoveled the coal into the furnace. The Brit-ish navy was so dependent on these feeders that it counted six ranks of stoker. All these coal fires put the buried carbon back in the sky.

Human beings remained slow and frail and vulnerable to the ele-ments compared to many other species but able to construct devices and systems, machines and tools that overcame the limits of the human body and of the animal bodies we had harnessed (though horsepower remains the measure of our machines long after the horses had left the roads and streets and most of the fields). It was a kind of mechanical self-transcendence, and also a way to make and become monsters. The machine power driven by burning coal and then oil produced economic and political power, and the concen-trated sources of energy allowed for unprecedented concentrations of power in the hands of the few, including, eventually, the major fossil fuel corporations and petro-nations.

In 1800, Britain mined and used 10 million metric tons of coal; by 1853, that had risen to 71 million tons, peaking at 292 million tons in 1913. By 1920, more than one in twenty British workers was in coal, and the country was still mining and using 232 million tons in 1936, when Orwell went to Wigan. In 2015, the last deep coal mine closed; by 2017, coal production had dropped to 3 million tons; and in 2019, the country went a fortnight without using coal to generate power for the first time since 1882. The country had replaced coal with oil and gas, which are also fossil carbon and also contribute to climate change when burned but are cleaner and more efficient overall. Wind was increasingly important in the energy mix, particularly in Scotland. *Carboniferous*, that term used to describe the age in which coal was produced, could apply equally well to our own age that has consumed it so voraciously. Coal is itself a dead thing, the remains of ancient forests, and the death of coal as a fuel and an industry is predicted to be complete in the United Kingdom by 2025. It will be the death of a kind of death.

Orwell went down into the mines three times. On February 23, he went down in a cage that dropped nine hundred feet into a mine whose low roof was one of the first things that surprised him. They got to where the miners were working in an area less than three feet high, some places where he thought they must lie on their bellies to excavate the coal in temperatures he estimated at 100 degrees Fahrenheit. "After a few hundred yards of walking doubled up and once or twice having to crawl, I began to feel the effects in a violent pain all down my thighs." On his way back he grew so tired he had to stop every fifty yards and his knees failed him repeatedly. On February 25, he showed up shivering and nearly collapsed on the doorstep of some kind left-wing acquaintances in Liverpool, who put him to bed and kept him there for a few days.

On March 19, he went down again into a mine where the workers had to crawl or run long distances doubled over and breathed in clouds of coal dust from the machinery and noted, "The place where these men, and those loading the broken coal onto the tubs, were working, was like hell." Two days later he went down once more, admiring the men's forms when they worked stripped to the waist and noting that with one bath a week they must live blackened from the waist down six days out of seven. Women and children were no longer in the mines, if you didn't count the boys who went down in their midteens, and there were better lights, but in some crucial respects the conditions he saw were much like those of 1842. He wrote in *The Road to Wigan Pier*, "When I am digging trenches in my garden, if I shift two tons of earth during the afternoon, I feel that I have earned my tea. . . . At a pinch I could be a tolerable road-sweeper or an inefficient gardener or even a tenth-rate farm hand. But by no conceivable amount of effort or training could I become a coal miner; the work would kill me in a few weeks."

When he started his garden in Wallington, he was between two journeys. The first was this expedition to the mining and manufacturing districts of England to research *The Road to Wigan Pier*; the second was to Spain in December 1936, to join the Loyalists in the Spanish Civil War and report on that war in essays and the book *Homage to Catalonia*. With those two books he had found himself politically. His friend Richard Rees ruefully remarked that he spent three years trying to convert Orwell to socialism, but the trip to the north did the job he could not. In "Why I Write," Orwell declared, "The Spanish war and other events in 1936–37 turned the scale and thereafter I knew where I stood. Every line of serious work that I have written since 1936 has been written, directly or indirectly, *against* totalitarianism and *for* democratic socialism, as I understand it." With three novels in quick succession behind him, and only two more ahead in the next thirteen years, in 1939 and 1949, he also shifted his focus to essayistic nonfiction.

It's possible to see both journeys as journeys to wars and both books as war correspondence. He wrote in *The Road to Wigan Pier* about class war as the brutality and inequality that produced that grim poverty and that terrible labor in the mines. The mines were a sort of one-sided battlefield with terrible casualties—both directly in the explosions and collapses that maimed and killed and indirectly in the terrible illnesses for the miners and those in the mining districts and in the fights over wages and working conditions.

That framework of war can be extended more broadly. Coal burning was (and is) a colossal disaster for human health, and the famous fogs of London into the mid-twentieth century were mixes of mists and fogs from the river with fumes from coal that were intensely toxic and sometimes fatal over the centuries they persisted. The best-known incident is the Great Smog of 1952, which shut down the city for four days with fumes so dense that vehicles and pedestrians couldn't navigate the streets and even theaters and other indoor spaces lost visibility. The content of that smog has been described as "1,000 tonnes of smoke particles, 2,000 tonnes of carbon dioxide, 140 tonnes of hydrochloric acid," as well as 370 tonnes of sulphur dioxide that turned into 800 tonnes of sulphuric acid.

It's a formula a little like some of the poison gases of the First World War, and like chemical warfare it produced casualties. Earlier estimates that four thousand people died from the 1952 smog incident have been upped to suggest that three times as many Londoners ultimately died from the event, and others were dying of the persistent air pollution all along. A 2019 study in the *European Heart Journal* estimated that 800,000 Europeans and 8.8 million worldwide die annually from air pollution, mostly from burning fossil fuels, and a 2021 study went further to charge fossil fuel emissions with one in five deaths worldwide in 2018, and one in three in eastern Asia that year. Like the domestic coal fires Orwell celebrated in his prose, the

London smog he inhaled during his sojourns there in the 1930s and 1940s must have contributed to the abysmal condition of his lungs and early death.

The extraction of fossil fuels has been so lucrative a business that it has prompted wars and shaped foreign policy around the world. It's also been so foul a project that it's destroyed immense expanses of land and contaminated water on all the continents on Earth except Antarctica. And it has changed our sky and then our seas and earth. It has been a war against the earth and the atmosphere. But looking back at 1936, what is most striking is how long ago it was in ecological terms.

Even a decade later, even amidst the terrible ruins of the Second World War that had killed more than eighty million and shattered cities from London to Dresden to Tokyo to Leningrad, you can pull back from contemplating human life and human structures to see that the nonhuman world was largely or at least comparatively thriving. The oceans had not acidified and heated up; the polar ice, Greenland ice sheet, and glaciers and the climate itself appeared to be stable; the weather was reasonably predictable; far more of the great temperate and tropical forests stood intact and were performing their carbon sequestration work; a host of species now endangered or extinct were flourishing; and whole classes of chemicals and plastics had yet to be deployed.

There had, of course, been many kinds of damage: the Tasmanian emu, the African bluebuck, the North Atlantic great auk, the mysterious starling of the South Pacific, and numerous other species in numerous other places had become extinct. The earth was far from pristine. Much of western Europe had been deforested long ago and many of its species hunted out; the Near East overgrazed before that;

mining had already broken the landscape and polluted the air and water around the world. In the nineteenth century, the North American prairie had been chopped up into real estate and bisected by wood-burning and then coal-burning railroads for which wars against the Native tribes of the plains had been fought in part by decimating the great bison herds there; the Great Plains had become the Dust Bowl earlier in the 1930s, as agriculture created massive soil erosion and wind picked it up. Engels describes the black rivers of the industrial north, and unregulated pollution of air and water, with few exceptions, was the norm into the postwar era. Even so, it was far more intact and sustainable than the world we inhabit today. It looks like Eden from 2021.

Though coal had been intensively used in Europe since the late eighteenth century and then in North America, though petroleum extraction had begun in the later nineteenth century, though gas lighting was as common as coal heating in the era of Orwell's youth, though the oil booms had begun in Texas and Saudi Arabia, though Britain's Rangoon Oil Company (later Burmah Oil Company) had been founded in 1871 and then its Anglo-Persian Oil Company had been founded in 1908 (and both would become part of British Petroleum, now known as BP), though Standard Oil had already grown so titanic in the United States that the government sought to break it up in 1911, much of the damage was yet to come.

Atmospheric carbon, which as I finish this book is at about 416 parts per million (it was 413 when I began it), began to rise in the early nineteenth century after long being at about 280 parts per million. In 1936, it was at only 310 parts per million, well within the limits to maintain the climate of this Holocene interglacial. Even in 1984, those levels were just below the 350 ppm settled upon by climate scientist James Hansen as the upper limit for a stable Earth. Orwell's final novel looked forward to 1984 as a year deep into political horror. We can look back across the huge divide that is our terrible knowledge and our worse actions to 1984 as the last good year, in terms of climate. And 1936: it was as different imaginatively as it was ecologically.

The people of 1936 had a confidence so deep it was like an unexcavated strata in their consciousness: that the world was big enough and resilient enough to absorb our harm, that the damage was always going to be local, that whatever we did to the parts would not undermine the whole, that there would always be more. Human beings behaved like a child who believes his mother is immortal no matter what, but the child had grown huge and powerful with powers beyond the human in his tools, machines, and chemical inventions, and he was striking blows that were damaging and changing the system itself. It was a war, and when we woke up to it, making peace with what the plants had done became the task. That sometimes took the form of reforestation, protecting existing forests, grasslands, topsoil, and otherwise joining the side of the plants, as well as drawing back from the project of throwing long-buried carbon into the sky.

A MAN PLANTED roses and fruit trees in a world in turmoil and strife. Perhaps what he was doing in his new Hertfordshire garden was making a place and a set of relationships as unlike what he had just seen, as unlike the deathliness that hung about those places, the uprootedness and alienation, the sheer ugliness in his eyes. It's not hard to see the garden as a reaction against where he had just been. What he saw up north made a profound impression on him, not just as subject matter for a book but as a harrowing encounter with suffering and exploitation that furthered his transformation into a political writer.

The gesture of planting the roses and launching the garden could mean a thousand things, but for now let it mean a collaboration with the world of and work of plants, the establishment and tending of a few more carbon-sequestering, oxygen-producing organisms, the desire to be agrarian, settled, to bet on a future in which the roses and trees would bloom for years and the latter would bear fruit in decades to come or even, as he wrote, a century hence. To garden is to make whole again what has been shattered: the relationships in which you are both producer and consumer, in which you reap the bounty of the earth directly, in which you understand fully how something came into being. It may not be significant in scale, but even if it's a windowsill geranium high above a city street, it can be significant in meaning.

He was thinking about the future and how to contribute to it when he advocated for the planting of trees as perhaps the most long-lasting gesture most human beings can make. No one was thinking about carbon sequestration in 1936, of course, but even without that consciousness, you could choose to be on the side of the plants, and in that proposal from "A Good Word for the Vicar of Bray," the man who planted those roses knew that this also meant being on the side of the future.

# III

# Bread and Roses

*Tina Modotti, Roses, Mexico, 1924.*

# ONE

# Roses and Revolution

In the year 1924, a woman photographed roses. Despite the few prints Tina Modotti made from her large-format negative, the image became one of the most celebrated in the history of photography. Sixty-seven years after its making, a contact print that had been inherited by the artist's last partner, an international operative for Stalin, went up for auction. The pop star Madonna reportedly bid on it, but the winning bid came from the fashion mogul Susie Tompkins Buell. Her purchase made the news because at $165,000 it was then the highest price ever paid for a photograph. Reproductions of the image can be found for sale in a huge variety of forms today.

Like the photograph, its creator had a startling trajectory: Tina Modotti was born into a poor socialist family in northeastern Italy in 1896, became a factory worker and the main support of her family at fourteen, and emigrated to San Francisco at sixteen. There she worked as a seamstress and found success as an amateur actress and then, in Los Angeles, in early motion pictures. In Southern California, she met the photographer Edward Weston, who became both her lover and her instructor in photography. In 1923, he left behind his wife to join her in Mexico City. In the wake of its recent revolution, Mexico was full of the dream and promise of further revolution in art and culture, and a vibrant artistic community had gathered in the capital. Modotti became for a few years Weston's partner in life and in a photography studio and began making work that resembled his sharp-focus abstracting modernism in some respects and diverged from it in others.

Her 1924 photograph *Roses, Mexico* is printed on paper saturated with palladium rather than the usual silver to produce an image in shades of golden brown rather than gray. The four pale blooms are seen head-on and their concentric rings of petals fill the frame. One bud is beginning to open. One wide-open rose that takes up far more room than the others is beginning to wilt. The two others are in stages in between. It is like a portrait of a child, an adult, and two youths, these four flowers in three stages of life. Modotti's biographer Patricia Albers says that she had laid them on their side to make the image, and it appears that gravity has gently pressed the arrangement of petals of the two intermediate flowers into something closer to an oval than a circle. These pale roses are both entirely recognizable and shown in an unfamiliar way, and they are individuals, at different stages of their lives, with forms that are distinct from one another. It is a sensuous, voluptuous image, all softness and yieldingness and mystery.

The beauty of roses may lie in part in their tenderness, in the petals as soft as the cheek of a child—a youthful complexion was once described as "blooming." The petals of this domesticated flower are fleshy without being thick or tough like a magnolia petal, delicate without being as frail as one of the wildflowers that wilts as soon as you pick it, and this quality that resembles human skin lasts as they lose their crispness and sag, as though gravity first arrived in middle age, before their smoothness erodes into tiny wrinkles that fracture the smooth surface as the flower begins to wither in earnest. The mortality of flowers is also part of their essential nature, and they've been used to represent the fleeting, evanescent nature of life again and again, with the implication that that which does not last is more precious for it.

*Fresh* is another word that indicates youth, newness, but also mortality or transience. Something that will never fade or die was never fresh. The writer and actor Peter Coyote once remarked that no one cries over artificial flowers, and there's a particular kind of disappointment when you begin to admire a bouquet or a blossom at a distance and find out closer up that it's fake. The disappointment arises in part from having been deceived, but also from encountering an object that is static, that will never die because it never lived, that didn't form itself out of the earth, and that has a texture coarser, dryer, less inviting to the touch than a mortal flower.

The beauty of flowers is not merely visual; it's metaphysical, and tactile, and with many of them olfactory: they can be smelled and touched and sometimes tasted. Some lead to fruit or seeds or other bounty humans value or even depend upon, so a flower is also a promise. You look at a flower at one stage and know that other stages came before and will come after. The beauty of roses may also lie in the way they are appealing at every phase from bud to dried and dead, and that their fading is slow and graceful. Camelias in full bloom have a form close to roses, but they go briskly from hard bud to wide-open flower to a brown sodden mess that drops from the stem to rot on the ground, and a lot of other flowers also decline this way. "Lilies that fester smell far worse than weeds," but roses rarely fester.

Wild roses are frail and uncomplicated compared to the domesticated rose. I've seen them from subarctic Canada and the Rocky

Mountains to coastal California and the hedgerows and byways of southern England, but the most remarkable were on the Tibetan plateau. At altitudes near twelve thousand feet, long after aridity, harsh conditions, and overgrazing had eliminated nearly every other plant, dense rosebushes flourished. Many were taller than I am, wider than they were high, sometimes in groves or long clusters alongside the glacial-melt rivers snaking across the dry lands. I traveled too late to see them in bloom. The rosebushes of Dolpo as I met them were domes of closely packed, small, bright-green leaves punctuated with crimson rose hips about the size of small grapes. They felt heroic and supremely tough, vivid in a landscape otherwise drained of color.

It was Buddhist country, but Buddhism developed in more humid regions, and its most celebrated flower is the lotus. "Like a pure lotus in muddy water" is one phrase that's common, and another is the Sanskrit mantra that translates as "Hail to the jewel in the lotus." Aztecs had their ceremonial marigolds, and Christianity made both lilies and roses sacred symbols. Roses were domesticated and bred to multiply their petals and create a larger, lusher, more intricate flower and a more intensely fragrant one. Once, in a public rose garden, looking at old-fashioned roses whose cupped petals curve in concentric rings, I caught myself thinking they were like mandalas, but of course it's the other way around. Mandalas—including Asian sacred paintings and Gothic churches' rose windows—are like multipetaled flowers.

Dante at the end of his *Divine Comedy* journeys through a series of concentric rings to a great rose that is the heart of Paradise itself. He addresses the Virgin Mary, who was often represented as a rose:

*Within your womb was lit once more the flame*
*Of that love through whose warmth this flower opened*
*To its full bloom in everlasting peace.*

I photographed those roses in the public garden, and when I looked at the resulting images, some of the close-ups of individual flowers with their tousled, tender petals looked like labia and vulvas. You never see everything with a rose; the bud is mostly closed, the petals folded together, but even a rose in full bloom has layers of petals overlapping one another and creating interiors, shadows, secrets. Around the same time that Modotti and, in California, Imogen Cunningham were photographing flowers close-up, Georgia O'Keeffe had begun making enormous paintings of single flowers seen head-on that are also often thought to resemble the genitalia of women.

Flowers are, of course, the sexual organs of plants, designed to reproduce the genes and also, for many species, to do so by attracting pollinators that can be insects, birds, or bats. And, arguably, humans, who have done so much to cultivate flowers and incorporate them into homes, offerings, and ceremonies. Though they're often seen as feminine in themselves and associated with women, they commonly have male parts as well. The photographer Robert Mapplethorpe masculinized flowers in a series of photographs with an emphasis on long stems, bold forms, lilies' out-thrust filaments, the phallic spadix at the center of calla lilies.

Nevertheless, in Henry Miller's 1934 novel *Tropic of Cancer*, which Orwell wrote about with exhilarated enthusiasm, there's a sex worker whose pudenda Miller calls her "rosebush." Dante's Paradise is a rose that opens through the warmth of the Virgin Mary's womb.

Another medieval poem begun about three quarters of a century earlier, the *Roman de La Rose* (*Romance of the Rose*), is likewise both secular and spiritual. The rose is the beloved, the beloved is a destination, and the human lover a little like a bee pursues and celebrates this both erotic and spiritual rose at the center of a walled garden.

In Mexico, roses have a particular significance as the flower that cascaded forth from Juan Diego Cuauhtlatoatzin's coarse-woven cloak on December 12, 1531, only a decade after the Spanish conquest of the Aztec Empire. The legend relates that a radiant young woman had appeared to this indigenous man near what is now Mexico City, identified herself as the Virgin Mary, and commanded that a shrine be built to her. When the Spanish bishop of Mexico demanded proof, the Virgin caused the hilltop named Tepeyac to bloom with out-of-season flowers—a variety of flowers in some accounts, nonnative roses in the most common version—for Juan Diego to fill his cloak with in his quest to be believed.

He returned to the bishop, the roses tumbled forth, and the inside of his cloak was revealed to bear her image, as if the roses themselves had drawn her or become her. A cloak with its image of a dark woman wrapped in a blue robe scattered with stars and standing atop a crescent moon still hangs in the Basílica de Nuestra Señora de Guadalupe at the foot of Tepeyac, still so revered that to keep the huge crowds flowing, moving walkways transport people past it. The largest Catholic pilgrimage in the world is to that shrine complex on the Virgin of Guadalupe's feast day, December 12, and year-round the shrine is piled high with offerings of roses.

She is sometimes regarded as an Aztec goddess reappearing in Christian guise, and she spoke Juan Diego's language to him, Nahuatl. In D. A. Brading's history of the origins and evolution of the image and its worship, he notes that "when Mary commanded Juan Diego to gather flowers, she rooted the Christian gospel deep within the soil of Aztec culture, since for the Indians, flowers were both the equivalents of spiritual songs and by extension, symbols of divine life." She became Mexico's patron saint, and in 1810, when Father Miguel Hidalgo raised the cry for liberation from Spain, he did so in her name, and "Long live the Virgin of Guadalupe" became the indigenous and mestizo rallying cry, her image—the one from the miraculous cloak—the insurgent banner. When Modotti titled her photograph *Roses, Mexico*, she was following the modernist style of neutrally descriptive naming, but the conjunction of those particular flowers and that particular place had its own resonance.

In 1924, a woman who was an ardent supporter of revolutionaries photographed roses. It was a moment in time when avant-garde theories of art and radical political ideas seemed like they could share a bed, a dream, a path, when you could be for art, for beauty, and for revolution. Modotti learned from Weston, who was a leading proponent of a new style in photography emanating from the West Coast, a form of modernism that emphasized unconventional perspectives, simple, dramatic forms, sharp focus, and tight compositions. Objects were abstracted, as though meaning came from form alone, and Weston famously depicted the curve of a porcelain toilet base and bell peppers much the way he depicted nude women, including Modotti, whom he photographed many times. He was her teacher, her lover, her creative companion, and she wrote long, heartfelt letters to him for years after they parted ways, until she moved to Moscow in 1931.

In 1924, both were enchanted with Mexico in the aftermath of its revolution, and they fell in with its artists and organizers, including Diego Rivera and the other political muralists rendering on epic scale the narratives and aspirations of the moment. Modotti earned part of her living for the next several years by documenting the murals and their creation and by making studio portraits. Noted for her beauty, she was painted by Rivera at least twice. By the 1930s, Weston would largely disengage from left politics and Modotti would largely withdraw from making art, giving her large-format camera to the young Manuel Álvarez Bravo as she was deported from Mexico and headed into the last years of her life, as a supporter of the Soviet Union during some of its most brutal years.

# Two

# We Fight for Roses Too

In the year 1910, Helen Todd, a campaigner for women's voting rights, went on an automobile tour of southern Illinois, trying to recruit rural people to the cause. Women's suffrage was being won state by state in the United States before the Nineteenth Amendment to the Constitution established it as a right nationally in 1920. She wrote about the tour in *The American Magazine*, describing how she framed the issues of the day—food safety, child labor, workplace safety—as women's issues. On the last night, she stayed with a farm family. Her bedridden host, who was in her nineties, told her that her daughter Lucy had stayed home and let the "hired girl," Maggie, go to the rally, because someone needed to tend her and because Lucy already believed in women's suffrage, but Maggie needed to hear more.

In the morning, Todd, Maggie, and Lucy had breakfast together in the farmhouse kitchen, at a table with a bouquet of lady-slippers and a back door opening onto a yard full of hollyhocks. Maggie said, "If you want to know what I liked the best of all in the whole meetin' it was that about the women votin' so's everybody would have bread and flowers too." Lucy was so taken with this idea, Todd reports, that she asked Todd to send her mother a pillow stamped with the slogan. "Bread for All, and Roses Too" said the pillow Todd delivered.

In her magazine report, she reflected on the phrase that was to become a refrain for the suffrage movement, the labor movement, and then for radicals of the 1970s and after, declaring that women's votes would "go toward helping forward the time when life's Bread, which is home, shelter and security, and the Roses of life, music, education, nature and books, shall be the heritage of every child that is born in the country, in the government of which she has a voice. There will be no prisons, no scaffolds, no children in factories, no girls driven on the street to earn their bread, in the day when there shall be 'Bread for all, and Roses too.'"

The phrase that seems to have condensed out of the conversation between two farmwomen and a political organizer in response to a suffragist speech went on to have an extraordinary life. Later in 1911, the poet James Oppenheim published the poem "Bread and Roses" in the same *American Magazine* Todd published in (and he was often subsequently credited with originating the phrase). It reads in part:

*As we come marching, marching, in the beauty of the day,*
*A million darkened kitchens, a thousand mill-lofts gray*
*Are touched with all the radiance that a sudden sun discloses,*
*For the people hear us singing, "Bread and Roses, Bread and Roses."*

*[…]*

*As we come marching, marching, unnumbered women dead*
*Go crying through our singing their ancient song of Bread;*
*Small art and love and beauty their drudging spirits knew—*
*Yes, it is Bread we fight for—but we fight for Roses, too.*

Bread fed the body, roses fed something subtler: not just hearts, but imaginations, psyches, senses, identities. It was a pretty slogan but a fierce argument that more than survival and bodily well-being were needed and were being demanded as a right. It was equally an argument against the idea that everything that human beings need can be reduced to quantifiable, tangible goods and conditions. Roses in these declarations stood for the way that human beings are complex, desires are irreducible, that what sustains us is often subtle and elusive.

An earlier American labor song about the struggle for the eight-hour workday argued for roughly the same thing:

> *We mean to make things over,*
> *We're tired of toil for naught*
> *With but bare enough to live upon*
> *And ne'er an hour for thought.*
> *We want to feel the sunshine*
> *And we want to smell the flow'rs*

Thought, sunshine, flowers: they wanted intangible as well as tangible goods, pleasures as well as necessities, and the time to pursue them, the time to have an inner life and freedom to roam the outer world.

Bolsheviks had chanted, "Peace! Land! Bread!" in 1917, or in other versions "Bread, Land, Peace and All Power to the Soviets!" Bread was the staple of most of Europe's poor—the French Revolution had been prompted in part by hunger brought on by catastrophic weather and a poor wheat harvest. It often served as a synecdoche for food in general, and for the meeting of basic human needs—and a lot of poor people actually lived on little more than bread. People would have been familiar with the Lord's Prayer from the Book of Matthew that implores, "Give us this day our daily bread," and with the biblical phrase "not by bread alone." The Bible's prescribed supplement to bread was the word of God, with perhaps the implication that all you needed on this earth was that bread because your joy and solace lay elsewhere. The roses in "bread and roses" can be heard as an explicit rejection of religion as the other half of human need, a proposal for its replacement by the joys and comforts of this world rather than the next.

By mid-1912, the legendary New York labor organizer Rose Schneiderman had picked up the phrase and would use it many times (and she too would be credited with originating it). She declared in a speech in Cleveland, Ohio, that "what the woman who labors wants is the right to live, not simply exist—the right to life as the rich woman has the right to life, and the sun and music and art. You have nothing that the humblest worker has not a right to have also. The worker must have bread, but she must have roses, too. Help, you women of privilege, give her the ballot to fight with."

It became a common phrase in early twentieth-century labor circles, though it was only applied long afterward to the 1912 Lawrence, Massachusetts, factory workers' strike now remembered and celebrated as the Bread and Roses Strike, because a claim was made that a sign carried by a striker bore the phrase and inspired the poem. The poem had been published before the strike began, but after Helen Todd wrote of her conversation with the women on the farm in the same magazine, and Todd had used versions of the concept in her speeches.

The poem was set to music not long after its creation. In the 1930s, seniors at Mount Holyoke College in Massachusetts incorporated the song into their graduation rites. In the 1970s, singer-organizer

Mimi Fariña wrote new music for the poem, and Judy Collins and then Fariña herself and her sister Joan Baez recorded it. Fariña also started the Bread & Roses project to bring music to prisons, hospitals, and other institutions. She died in 2001, but the organization continues to bring music to the institutionalized as of this writing. In the twenty-first century, Pan y Rosas is a feminist-socialist organization launched in Argentina, now operating in Bolivia, Chile, Brazil, and several other Latin American countries, as well as France and Germany. There's no evidence that Tina Modotti was familiar with the phrase, though it was in wide circulation during her time in the United States.

## THREE

# In Praise Of

I f roses represent pleasure, leisure, self-determination, interior life, and the unquantifiable, the struggle for them is sometimes not only against owners and bosses seeking to crush their workers but against other factions of the left who disparage the necessity of these things. The left has never been short on people arguing that it is callous and immoral to enjoy oneself while others suffer, and somewhere others will always be suffering. It's a puritanical position, implying that what one has to offer them is one's own austerity or joylessness, rather than some practical contribution toward their liberation.

Underlying all this is a utilitarian ideology in which pleasures and beauties are counterrevolutionary, bourgeois, decadent, indulgent, and the desire for them should be weeded out and scorned. Would-be revolutionaries often argue that only the quantifiable matters, and that human beings should be rational creatures content with what should matter and fit into how things should be, rather than what does matter and how things are. The roses in "bread and roses" constituted an argument not only for something more, but for something more nuanced and elusive—as Rose Schneiderman put it, "The right to live, not simply exist." It was an argument that what makes our lives worth living is to some degree incalculable and unpredictable, and varies from person to person. In that sense, roses also mean subjectivity, liberty, and self-determination.

Orwell often weighed in as a defender of roses, sometimes literally. In *Tribune* in January 1944 he wrote, "A correspondent reproaches me with being 'negative' and 'always attacking things.' The fact is that we live in a time when causes for rejoicing are not numerous. But I like praising things, when there is anything to praise, and I would like here to write a few lines—they have to be retrospective, unfortunately—in praise of the Woolworth's Rose." And then he celebrated the ones he'd planted in 1936. He was writing as the Second World War was raging around him. A few months later, as the Royal Air Force stepped up its bombing campaigns over Germany, he noted, "Last time I mentioned flowers in this column an indignant lady wrote in to say that flowers are bourgeois."*

Sometimes he celebrated what was meant by the roses in "bread and roses": the intangible, ordinary pleasures, the joy available in the here and now. In his spring 1946 essay "Some Thoughts on the Common Toad," he wrote in praise of the creatures as they come, gaunt and famished, out of hibernation, a harbinger of spring, and of the beauty of their golden eyes, of spring, of pleasure itself. He published the piece in *Tribune*, and *Tribune* was a socialist magazine, so he wrote defensively. It was, being Orwell's, about toads and

---

* In the column, he explained that Woolworth's roses were inexpensive and often surprising. "One that I bought for a Dorothy Perkins turned out to be a beautiful little white rose with a yellow heart, one of the finest ramblers I have ever seen. A polyantha rose labelled yellow turned out to be deep red. Another, bought for an Abertine, was like an Abertine, but more double, and gave astonishing masses of blossom. . . . Last summer I passed the cottage where I used to live before the war. The little white rose, no bigger than a boy's catapult when I put it in, had grown into a huge vigorous bush, the Abertine or near-Abertine was smothering half the fence in a cloud of pink blossom. I had planted both of those in 1936." Presumably he meant Albertine.

spring but also about principles and values and arguing with an orthodoxy.

He took on directly the standard complaints of the left: "Is it wicked to take a pleasure in Spring and other seasonal changes? To put it more precisely, is it politically reprehensible, while we are all groaning, or at any rate ought to be groaning, under the shackles of the capitalist system, to point out that life is frequently more worth living because of a blackbird's song, a yellow elm tree in October, or some other natural phenomenon which does not cost money and does not have what the editors of left-wing newspapers call a class angle? There is no doubt that many people think so. I know by experience that a favourable reference to 'Nature' in one of my articles is liable to bring me abusive letters, and though the key-word in these letters is usually 'sentimental,' two ideas seem to be mixed up in them."

He identified one of them as the idea that pleasure makes us passive, acquiescent, self-absorbed, perhaps the belief that made the reader declare "flowers are bourgeois." A decade earlier, the idea that all art should further the communist cause in obvious and immediate ways took hold inside and outside the Soviet Union (as did the Nazi idea that all art should further or at least not conflict with their racist and reactionary agenda; in 1939, they reportedly burned five thousand modernist works that had been part of the *Degenerate Art* exhibition the year before). The British art historian and Soviet spy Anthony Blunt wrote, that April of 1936 when Orwell was planting his garden at Wallington, "A new art is beginning to arise, the product of the proletariat, which is again performing its true function, that of propaganda." A few years later, Blunt wrote, "If an art is not contributing to the common good, it is bad art" (which suggests confidence that the common good could be defined clearly and narrowly).

In a 2005 essay by Lawrence Weschler titled "Vermeer in Bosnia," I found a more open-ended idea of what art might do for politics that stuck with me. Weschler, who has devoted his long writing life to reports about human rights around the globe and essays about art, asked a judge in The Hague how he could stand to listen to the stories of atrocities day after day in the International Criminal Tribunal for the former Yugoslavia of the mid-1990s. The judge, reports Weschler, brightened as he answered: "As often as possible I make my way over to the Mauritshuis museum, in the center of town, so as to spend a little time with the Vermeers."

For a long time after I read the essay, I imagined the museum had many Vermeers, but it has three: the early *Diana and Her Nymphs*, the famous portrait *Girl with a Pearl Earring*, and the nearly as famous *View of Delft* with clouds far larger than anything else in the painting, up there in the delicately blue sky above tiny figures and dense buildings and a canal. The clouds are so light and evanescent; the buildings so solid and steadfast; the blue water reflects them both. In the foreground of all that spaciousness, two women converse. The Vermeer paintings have nothing, of course, to say directly about war or justice or the law or how you fix your society; they tell no news and propagandize no cause. In *Diana and Her Nymphs*, a kneeling woman washes another's feet while two others look on, and one turns her back, a plebeian moment among divinities. Weschler notes that Vermeer worked in a turbulent, war-plagued time, and that "the pressure of all that violence (remembered, imagined, foreseen) is what those paintings are all about" but that they are about it by being its opposite, about the peace we crave in times of war, the stillness in uproar, about the persistence of the everyday and its beauty.

The argument that all art must exhort us overlooks the needs and desires of those who are already engaged, and what fuels them, and what the larger work of building a society concerned with justice and compassion might be. What I found memorable in Weschler's essay was the idea that it's not necessarily the representation of injustice or suffering that might encourage someone to engage or help someone like the judge sustain that engagement. Art that is not about the politics of this very moment may reinforce a sense of self and society, of values and commitments, or even a capacity to pay attention, that equip a person to meet the crises of the day.

Politics is the pragmatic expression of beliefs and commitments shaped by culture. Works of art can and do help construct the self that engages in politics, and the mere exhortation to engage or tirades about what's wrong do not necessarily produce the empathic imagination, the insights, principles, orientations, collective memories that engagement requires. Of course other works of art, and lots of them in our time, help construct disengagement, by telling us that we are private individuals unimpacted by and unobliged to larger forces, or present those forces as fixed and unchangeable, or just erase all traces of their existence. The Vermeers could be read either way, and the judge's response suggests that some of it is in the eye of the beholder.

Nevertheless, Weschler's essay suggests that the least political art may give us something that lets us plunge into politics, that human beings need reinforcement and refuge, that pleasure does not necessarily seduce us from the tasks at hand but can fortify us. The pleasure that is beauty, the beauty that is meaning, order, calm. Orwell found this refuge in natural and domestic spaces, and he repaired to them often and emerged from them often to go to war on lies, delusions, cruelties, and follies—and to go to war as a soldier in Spain. In his essay on T. S. Eliot he famously noted that "all art is to some extent propaganda," insofar as propaganda is advocacy, and every artist's choices are a kind of advocacy for what matters, what deserves attention, but he was opposed to propaganda in the sense that Blunt called for it: as art and artists subservient to a party's or state's agenda. Elsewhere he wrote, "There is no such thing as genuinely non-political literature."

A Vermeer painting makes the case for stillness or looking at canals or the color blue or the value of the domestic lives of the Dutch bourgeoisie or just for paying close attention. Close attention itself can be a kind of sustenance. In "Why I Write," Orwell declared that he did so "because there is some lie that I want to expose, some fact to which I want to draw attention, and my initial concern is to get a hearing. But I could not do the work of writing a book, or even a long magazine article, if it were not also an aesthetic experience." Even when the agenda is bread, what spills over is roses.

These artworks and the pleasure that arises from them are like the watershed lands on which nothing commodifiable grows, but from which waters gather to fill the streams and rivers that feed the crops and people, or where wildlife lives that is part of the agrarian system— the insects that pollinate the crops, the coyotes who keep the gophers down. They are the wildlands of the psyche, the unexploited portion, preserving the diversity, the complexity, the systems of renewal, the larger whole as the worked land does not. Orwell defended both the literal green spaces of the countryside and the garden in which he spent so much time and the metaphysics of free thought and unpoliced creation. And he did battle with his opponents on these issues.

In that essay on toads and spring and pleasure, he identified the other standard objection to the enjoyment of spring or nature or the rural: "This is the age of machines and that to dislike the machine, or even to want to limit its domination, is backward-looking, reactionary and slightly ridiculous." Some years ago, I visited the Detroit Institute of Arts, where in the early 1930s Diego Rivera painted one of his grand murals celebrating industrial labor and production at the behest of Henry Ford's son, and I wondered why an avowed communist was working for one of the world's most successful capitalists— and would go on to work for the Rockefellers in New York (who had Rivera's mural destroyed when the artist refused to paint over an image of Lenin in it).

Gazing upon the walls filled with images of auto assembly lines and workers dwarfed by machinery, I realized that capitalists and communists of the era shared a devotion to mechanization and to industrialization as phenomena that would allow human beings to transcend the limits of nature. While they disagreed about the ideal structure of society, they agreed about humanity's destiny in crucial respects. That belief in science and technology as means to dominate the natural world and the misplaced confidence that those in charge would deploy those forces wisely were crucial to modernism. Avant-garde artists, communists, technicians, and capitalists of the era shared a vision that looked forward to a shining future. Looking back it seems like hubris and dangerous delusion.

The collapse of modernism and that hubris had many causes, including the rise in audibility of nonwhite and nonwestern voices, but environmental science and politics were key ingredients too. Environmentalists look at where human activity harms the natural world and seek to reverse or prevent that harm. They recognize what is reckless, shortsighted, and destructive about our species and suggest caution is due in all our actions and respect for the nonhuman world is essential to human survival. Orwell was never an enthusiast for the factory, the machine, or the city, and in important ways he was not a modernist. He believed socialism could build a better society by changing social relations and the distribution of wealth and power but was skeptical about industrialization and urbanization. He loathed centralized authority and believed that the natural world was something to which we should turn our faces, not our backs.

Those questions about pleasure, happiness, and paradise come up again and again in his work. A few years before the pro-toad essay, he wrote about the necessity to "dissociate Socialism from Utopianism. Nearly all neo-pessimist apologetics consist in putting up a man of straw and knocking him down again. The man of straw is called Human Perfectibility. Socialists are accused of believing that society can be—and indeed, after the establishment of Socialism, will be—completely perfect; also that progress is inevitable." He disagrees with the conservative critique, arguing, "Socialists don't claim to be able to make the world perfect: they claim to be able to make it better."

Nevertheless, many socialists and communists did believe an ironclad utopia was achievable, anything that brought it closer was justified, and that technology was crucial to achieving it. Elsewhere Orwell mounted arguments against perfectionists too. In that context, perfectibility was a dangerous thing, and so was utopia when it meant imposing ideals determined by people convinced they could use that destruction of rights called violence and that destruction of facts called lies to produce and protect it. The novelist Milan Kundera wrote not long after he escaped communist Czechoslovakia in 1975, "Once the dream of paradise starts to turn into reality, however, here and there people begin to crop up who stand in its way, and so the rulers of paradise must build a little gulag on the side of Eden. In the course of time this gulag grows ever bigger and more perfect, while the adjoining paradise gets ever smaller and poorer." Versions of Kundera's argument have often been used as an argument against left-wing idealism, but it could just as well be an argument against gulags—against ends that are supposed to justify means, against the idea that humanity can be reinvented through brute force, and against rulers with outsize power.

Orwell took on the subject again in a 1943 *Tribune* essay he published under the pseudonym John Freeman, perhaps to avoid blowback, titled "Can Socialists Be Happy?" He argued that "all 'favourable' Utopias seem to be alike in postulating perfection while being unable to suggest happiness," and he took a swipe at various utopian novels, ending with the sheer joylessness of the ideal society at the end of *Gulliver's Travels*. That society is populated by cerebral horses who "live uneventful, subdued, 'reasonable' lives, free not only from quarrels, disorder or insecurity of any kind, but also from 'passion,' including physical love." It is an elaborate proof, in other words, that the perfect is the enemy of the good or at least the joyous and the free.

In *Nineteen Eighty-Four*, he would write, "The sexual act, successfully performed, was rebellion. Desire was thoughtcrime." The totalitarian society in that novel attempts to dominate and wither away private and personal life, so independence of thought, the pursuit of privacy, desire, passion, and pleasure are dangerous acts of resistance. And desire is subjective, personal, unpredictable, corruptible, but not entirely controllable, either by individuals or their societies. Desire and its fulfillment are not happiness, when happiness means a steady-state emotion, a placated heart and mind; they are closer to joy, which erupts and subsides unpredictably and can appear amid danger and difficulty. Permanence—the idea of stabilizing something, which is usually predicated on controlling a lot of other things—is part of what he objects to.

He also objects to the gutting of privacy. A society seeking to reinvent human nature wants to reach down into every psyche and rearrange it. Bread can be managed by authoritarian regimes, but roses are something individuals must be free to find for themselves, discovered and cultivated rather than prescribed. "We know only that the imagination, like certain wild animals, will not breed in captivity," Orwell declares at the end of "The Prevention of Literature," and the roses in "bread and roses" mean a kind of freedom that flourishes with privacy and independence.

His version of socialism doesn't involve captivity. He writes, "The real objective of Socialism is not happiness. . . . The real objective of Socialism is human brotherhood . . . a world in which human beings love one another instead of swindling and murdering one another. And they want that world as a first step." Love is hard to engineer, if easy to corrupt and undermine. And then came one last dismissal of utopia: "They wanted to produce a perfect society by an endless continuation of something that had only been valuable because it was temporary." That is, they wanted to fix and control something that was of its essence fluid and uncontrollable, like desire, like joy. They wanted to make roses into bread, or win the bread and throw away the roses.

# Buttered Toast

In pursuit of socialism and brotherhood, he went to Spain at the end of 1936 to join the civil war that had begun in July of that year, not quite sure if he would work as a journalist or a soldier in defense of the Spanish Republic. Spain had elected a left-leaning government that February, and a cabal of right-wing forces led by General Francisco Franco and backed by fascist Italy and Germany sought to overthrow it. The Loyalists, as the anti-Franco side was called, consisted of people with a variety of political positions—including communists, Marxists, trade unionists, and anarchists—some of whom wanted to defend the status quo of the republic as it was before the conflict, some of whom wanted a full-fledged revolution. Revolution was underway in many Spanish places, as an expropriation of property, an attack on the Catholic Church, and an ardent joy and sense of equality and possibility.

Orwell's description of this joy and freedom in Barcelona when he first arrived is incandescent. It was an extraordinary moment for the idealistic and left leaning. The anarchist George Woodcock writes, "And 1936 particularly was a year when many people were filled with a secular faith that would not have seemed possible even at the end of 1935, and which was to be no longer possible after the middle of 1937.

Remembering that season when the millennium did not seem an impossible dream."

Orwell was still so poor that to cover his travel costs, he asked his bank for a loan and pawned the family silver (Eileen, when asked where it was by his visiting sister and mother, said they'd sent it out to have the family crest engraved upon it, and a few months later set out for Spain herself, where she did administrative work for the cause in Barcelona while he was at the front). Before he left, he went looking for introductions. Harry Pollitt, general secretary of the British Communist Party, considered him too idiosyncratic and unreliable to give him a recommendation, apparently after Orwell refused to pledge to join the International Brigades before he had a chance to vet it. (A few months later, Pollitt wrote a scathing review of *The Road to Wigan Pier,* calling Orwell "a disillusioned little middle-class boy" and "a late imperialist policeman.")

Instead he set out with a pair of size-twelve boots, aware that it would be hard to find footwear that fit him there, papers from the Independent Labour Party, and an introduction to ILP member John McNair in Barcelona. En route he stopped off in Paris and visited Henry Miller, who told him he was an idiot for joining up and gave him a warm corduroy coat. When he got to Spain, McNair took him to the Lenin Barracks of the POUM, the Partido Obrero de Unificación Marxista (the Workers' Party of Marxist Unification). Had Orwell known the lay of the land better, he might have joined the anarchists instead, but he became a soldier in the POUM, led by Andrés Nin, who had briefly been Trotsky's secretary and long afterward corresponded with the brilliant architect of the Russian Revolution about politics and strategy. (Trotsky had been driven into exile and demonized by Stalin; Orwell's portraits of the dissident pig

Snowball in *Animal Farm* and Goldstein in *Nineteen Eighty-Four* bear pointed resemblance to Trotsky.) Most of the foreigners who came to support the Loyalist cause—thirty-five to forty thousand—joined the International Brigades set up by the communists. The Americans tended to be working-class men; a significant portion of the Britons were middle-class, many of them literary figures, from the poet Stephen Spender to the lesbian novelist Sylvia Townsend Warner to Virginia Woolf's nephew Julian Bell, who died there.

By early 1937, Orwell was at the front. His youth shooting rats and rabbits in the countryside and his years in the imperial police force in Burma had made him competent with a rifle and familiar with military discipline, and he was appalled at the lack of training and equipment for the soldiers around him and moved by the generosity of spirit of the Spanish people he met. Though he described the smell of war as rotting food and excrement, he found some pleasure and beauty in the places he was stationed: "The winter barley was a foot high, crimson buds were forming on the cherry trees (the line here ran through deserted orchards and vegetable gardens), and if you searched the ditches you could find violets and a kind of wild hyacinth like a poor specimen of a bluebell. Immediately behind the line there ran a wonderful, green, bubbling stream."

He passed days and weeks in squalor and stagnation, got lice, helped seize a fascist machine-gun nest from which, it turned out, the machine gun had been removed, watched the spring come in. "On a bullet-chipped tree in front of our parapet thick clusters of cherries were forming. . . . Wild roses with pink blooms the size of saucers struggled over the shell-holes round Torre Fabian. Behind the line you met peasants wearing wild roses over their ears." He spent 115 days on the line before his first break, and he wrote in *Homage to Catalonia* that though he did not do much for the Spanish Republic, the Spanish Republic did a lot for him. If in the north of England he had found a sense of solidarity with the poor, in Spain he found a set of ideals and possibilities.

"One realized afterwards that one had been in contact with something strange and valuable. One had been in a community where hope was more normal than apathy or cynicism, where the word 'comrade' stood for comradeship and not, as in most countries, for humbug. One had breathed the air of equality." This is another kind of joy that matters in his work, the joy in ideals affirmed and realized, in solidarity, in spirit, in possibility, in meaning. The absence of all those things is the everyday condition of life in *Nineteen Eighty-Four*.

*Homage to Catalonia* is a vivid first-person book in which, unlike *The Road to Wigan Pier*, he's a full participant as well as an observer, and a far more mature observer than in the earlier book. (Some biographers credit Eileen for his significant growth as a writer around this time.) It has long explanations of the political situation but also a lot of description of what it meant to be a soldier in that war, what the bodily experience was, what the countryside looked like, how it felt to be so filthy, ill-fed, and cold. He also conveys the emotional impact of everything from the ebullience of drinking in the revolutionary spirit to the shock of being shot. The coexistence of these things is striking. The particulars are always challenging the general, the tangible countering the ideological.

He wrote about the slogans he heard the two sides shout back and forth across the trenches. The fascists would shout "Viva España! Viva Franco!" or when the population of foreign antifascists was sufficiently high, "Go home, you English!" And the Loyalist anarchists would shout out slogans, in Orwell's words, "full of revolutionary sentiments, which explained to the Fascist soldiers that they were merely the hirelings of international capitalism, that they were fighting against their own class, etc., etc., and urged them to come over to our side." He commented, "Everyone agreed that the trickle of Fascist deserters was partly caused by it."

Orwell calls the principal shouter on his side "an artist at the job. Sometimes, instead of shouting revolutionary slogans he simply told the Fascists how much better we were fed than they were. His account of the Government rations was apt to be a little imaginative. 'Buttered toast!'—you could hear his voice echoing across the lonely valley—'We're just sitting down to buttered toast over here! Lovely slices of buttered toast!' I do not doubt that, like the rest of us, he had not seen butter for weeks or months past, but in the icy night the news of buttered toast probably set many a Fascist mouth watering. It even made mine water, though I knew he was lying."

A couple of decades ago, I fastened onto that last shout, partly because it was so festively unserious, but partly because it signified something more. It struck me as playful, humorous, expressing some of the freedom of the Loyalist soldiers to embroider and improvise, to leave the official ideology behind, to issue an invitation instead of a threat. It also contained a serious recognition of the reality of cold and hunger and the complexity of human beings who were bodies as well as minds. You might be fighting for your ideals but you might want toast as well as justice. And that craving might be something you had in common with those you disagreed with about more ideological issues. Sometimes even lovely slices of buttered toast are about more than bread alone.

Like Hannah Arendt, Orwell distrusted rigid ideologies, seeing them as shields or perhaps cudgels against the complexity and contradictions life might present you with. Stephen Spender, who became a friend of Orwell's, wrote about that in his retrospective repudiation of his brief time as a Party member: "With the Communist intellectuals I was always confronted by the fact that they had made a calculation when they became Communists which had changed the whole of reality for them into the crudest black and white. . . . The Revolution was the beginning and the end, the sum of all sums. Someday, somewhere, everything would add up to the happy total." In that context the cries about toast were a minor attack on absolutes and abstractions.

Orwell writes repeatedly about being surprised by the immediate and particular and how they undermine categorical thinking. In his 1931 essay "A Hanging," he describes seeing a Burmese prisoner being marched to his death step aside to avoid a puddle. That little gesture struck him powerfully. "It is curious, but till that moment I had never realised what it means to destroy a healthy, conscious man. When I saw the prisoner step aside to avoid the puddle, I saw the mystery, the unspeakable wrongness, of cutting a life short when it is in full tide."

Something similar happened when he was in Spain. While he was was at the front, a man appeared on the fascist side "half-dressed and . . . holding up his trousers with both hands as he ran. I refrained from shooting at him. . . . I did not shoot partly because of that detail about the trousers. I had come here to shoot at 'Fascists'; but a man who is holding up his trousers isn't a 'Fascist,' he is visibly a fellow creature, similar to yourself, and you don't feel like shooting at him." He distrusted absolutes and abstractions and theories that attempted to browbeat the actualities. (In 1938, he and Eileen named their dog

Marx "to remind us that we have never read Marx," Eileen wrote to a friend, adding "now we have read a little and taken so strong a personal dislike to the man that we can't look the dog in the face.") When Woodcock compared Orwell to Antaeus, who draws his strength from the earth, he might also have meant that he drew his intellectual strength from the specific and tangible and from firsthand experience. It set him at odds with an era in which ideologies led many astray, not least as doctrines defending authority and delegitimizing dissent and independence.

# FIVE

# The Last Rose of Yesterday

Orwell went back to Barcelona on leave and was reunited with Eileen, who supported the war and his participation in it enough to join it herself. She had been working at POUM headquarters. On May 1, 1937, she wrote her brother that he was "almost bare-foot, a little lousy, dark brown, and looking really very well." It was on this leave that he fully realized that he was in a three-sided war. There was an overt war against Franco in which all other sides were supposed to be united. But in reality, the Soviet-backed communists were fighting for power against the anarchists and dissident socialists, and they were fighting to prevent revolution, or rather to murder the one underway. As Adam Hochschild puts it in his book about the conflict, "If the Soviet dictator appeared to support the far-reaching social revolution emerging in Catalonia and other parts of the Republic, it would horrify Britain and France, the allies he would need in case of war with Germany." The republic was dependent on Soviet arms—no other country would supply it—and so Stalin dictated to Spain: no revolution.

To be a communist had often come to mean being a supporter of the Soviet Union after its founding in 1922, and to support the Soviet Union came to mean supporting Joseph Stalin when he seized control of the nation, and so by degrees people who had begun with noble ideals of freedom and equality and revolution came around to supporting one of the most brutal dictatorships the world has ever seen (in part because it was seen as a bulwark against another, Hitler's Germany, and while at the time they were routinely portrayed as opposites, afterward their resemblances would become more widely recognized). This support often meant swallowing or spreading lies and denying facts. Much of the left of the first half of the twentieth century was akin to someone who has fallen in love, and whose beloved has become increasingly monstrous and controlling. A stunning number of the leading artists and intellectuals of that era chose to stay with the monster—though unlike in an abusive relationship, the victim was for the most part not these ardent lovers but the powerless people of the USSR and its satellites. (Past and present support for authoritarians and denial of their crimes among those who are supposed to be the left has long made me wonder what, if anything, the term *left* means, since at other times it means those who support the human rights, freedoms, and egalitarianism that are antithetical to this.)

When he saw the triangular war more clearly, Orwell at first wanted to join the International Brigades fighting around Madrid, convinced that their piece of the war was more important than the POUM's action in Aragon, and that fighting fascism was more important than anything. He also found that Barcelona's revolutionary atmosphere that had so amazed and delighted him had dispelled, and the POUM was under ferocious attack by the communists. Some of it was literal—there was gunfire between anarchists, communists, and the POUM over who would control Barcelona's telephone exchange—and some of it was propaganda that the POUM was secretly allied with Franco. He was fighting in a war he was just beginning to understand.

Despite the conflict between the factions, Orwell went back to his corner of the war with the POUM, and very early on the morning of May 20, he stuck his head above the parapet of his side's trench and was shot through the neck by a fascist's bullet. Had the bullet punctured rather than passed a hairsbreadth away from his carotid artery, he would have bled out on the spot. It damaged his vocal cords, temporarily reducing his voice to a whisper, and left him seriously injured. He described the physical and psychological experience in detail: "My first thought, conventionally enough, was for my wife. My second was a violent resentment at having to leave this world which, when all is said and done, suits me so well. I had time to feel this very vividly."

The POUM's leader, Andrés Nin, was assassinated that June. Alberto Besouchet, a young Brazilian volunteer who had arrived with a letter of recommendation to Nin, was by some accounts part of the street fighting around Barcelona that month, while Orwell was convalescing. Like Nin, Besouchet would die in Spain in uncertain circumstances, and it's generally assumed the Stalinists killed him that month or later in the war. Modotti is said to have helped condemn him by transmitting a letter from the Communist Party of Brazil to the Communist Party of Spain identifying him as a Trotskyist, according to her biographer.

She had in those years gradually abandoned roses to devote herself to bread. In 1927, Modotti joined the Communist Party of Mexico and soon after began working for International Red Aid, a project of the Communist International. "Being a model Communist, she believed, meant letting her old preoccupation with personal and sexual self-expression fall by the wayside," wrote Albers, noting that she quit her work as an artist's model and had "abandoned themes of flowers and architecture to focus on the soulful and heroic qualities of the Mexican masses." These transitional works were moving portraits, sometimes of individuals, often young and haggard figures akin to who she must have been during her phase as a child laborer, sometimes of groups, many times of mothers with children.

She did make more still-life photographs in this phase. One shows a bandolier full of bullets crossed by the neck of a guitar and an ear of corn between them, another the corn and bandolier with a sickle, a third the sickle with a hammer atop a Mexican sombrero, a fourth the hammer and sickle laid out alone, exactly as in the Soviet emblem. In the photograph, the tools cast shadows, the light plays along their handles, picking out the grain of the hammer handle and gleams on the sickle's blade. She translates a symbol back into the actual tools, bringing us from the abstract to the particular, and this specificity so intrinsic to photography is antithetical to dogma and its generalizations. But she also allows established meanings to dominate the work, rather than finding her own or questioning the orthodoxies.

In 1928, Diego Rivera put her in one of his murals holding a bandolier like the one in her photographs of the year before, amidst a crowd of armed men, a red flag with a hammer and sickle flying above them all. Rivera was a Trotskyist and a friend of Trotsky during the latter's Mexican exile. When she herself returned to Mexico, Modotti would repudiate him as part of her Stalinism, and then Rivera and his wife Frida Kahlo would eventually embrace Stalinism too. Rivera had already been purged from Mexico's Communist Party in 1929, and in a letter to Weston at the time, Modotti condemned him as a traitor. The same year, the man who seems to have been her greatest love, the dashing Cuban revolutionary Julio Antonio Mella, was assassinated as they walked arm in arm one evening in Mexico City. She was blamed, attacked in the press, and deported.

After this devastating episode, a light seems to have gone out of her, and a new life began. Vittorio Vidali, an operative for a subdivision of the NKVD—the Soviet secret police—in charge of assassinations, terror, sabotage, and abductions, was, apparently unbeknownst to her, on the ship that took her into exile from Mexico. One theory is that Vidali was fleeing Mexico, where he had arrived from the USSR two years earlier, because he was Mella's assassin. Somewhere in the long journey across the Atlantic, the two Italian radicals became close, and perhaps it was then they became lovers. They were sometimes together, sometimes apart thereafter, but he loomed over her the rest of her life and was often called her husband, though I found no report that they ever married. She spent years with him in Moscow and in postings in Europe, a diligent worker in the fields of international communism, translating foreign press articles, writing propaganda, serving on counterintelligence and counterespionage missions, obeying the strict rules of communism become totalitarianism, surviving in an increasingly paranoid and punitive society in Russia and in the increasingly ruthless communist organizations outside it.

Was it the very joy or sense of agency she took in beauty, in art, in her own creative vision that convinced her she must relinquish it to be a revolutionary? So many people had a similar trajectory to hers, submitting to a doctrinaire communism that compelled strict obedience and provided stern oversight. And that prewar slippage was far from the only time that leftists who were supposed to be for human rights and equality ended up backing authoritarians who violated those rights extravagantly. She too went to Spain in 1936, earlier than Orwell, before the war erupted, and she stayed for the duration of the conflict. There, she called herself Maria, and her biographer notes that the name evokes humble women, servants, and the Virgin Mary. "Like Mary, Tina became a paragon of devotion, gentleness, asceticism, and grief. She sought the most abject and dangerous tasks."

At one point she was running a hospital while wearing a nun's habit. That costume, donned as a disguise, recalls Emma Goldman's famous bread-and-roses reaction to a man telling her "it did not behoove an agitator to dance." She replied, "I did not believe that a Cause which stood for a beautiful ideal, for anarchism, for release and freedom from conventions and prejudice, should demand the denial of life and joy. I insisted that our Cause could not expect me to become a nun and that the movement should not be turned into a cloister. If it meant that, I did not want it. 'I want freedom, the right to self-expression, everybody's right to beautiful, radiant things.'"

It's hard to know what Modotti wanted at that point, but Modotti as Maria swept floors, emptied bedpans, tended children mowed down and mutilated by machine guns fired from fascist planes, continued her work for Red Aid. Perhaps she believed there would be beautiful, radiant things in the end. There are allegations that Modotti served as Vidali's assistant in counterespionage. According to the Mexican writer Octavio Paz, Modotti warned Paz's wife that the café in Valencia they frequented was "a rendezvous of Trotskyite and anarchist elements, of traitors to the revolution and enemies of the people, and another series of phrases along these lines."

Vidali under the pseudonym Carlos Contreras was in his glory, fighting in the Spanish Republic's Fifth Regiment, roaming the country, interrogating quantities of prisoners, organizing execution squads and executing others himself. He had become a communist in Italy many years before, in part to fight fascism; in Spain he was not fighting fascism but dissent from the Soviet position and communist orthodoxy, so the people he was executing were primarily anarchists, Trotskyists, and the like. His immediate superior called him "almost a monster." He was not fighting for Spain. Spain was the battlefield

on which he was fighting for Russia. He is reported to have participated in the interrogation, torture, and assassination of Nin, the
leader of the POUM, that June of 1937.

Orwell's association with the POUM made him a target, and his
time in Spain ended in his being a hunted man in Barcelona, posing
as an affluent tourist by day, hiding in ruins by night, desperate to
escape the country. The warrant out for his and Eileen's arrests would
probably have led to their deaths. All his journals from his time in
Spain were confiscated when Eileen's hotel room was searched, and
they may still exist somewhere in an old Soviet archive in Russia.
They finally managed to get onto a train to France and safety on June
23, two days before his thirty-fourth birthday.

After Orwell went back to Wallington, he was ill at ease with the
pastoral placidity he at other times cherished. "Down here it was still
the England I had known in my childhood: the railway-cuttings
smothered in wild flowers, the deep meadows where the great shining
horses browse and meditate, the slow-moving streams bordered by
willows, the green bosoms of the elms, the larkspurs in the cottage
gardens," he wrote at the end of his book about Spain. "I sometimes
fear that we shall never wake till we are jerked out of it by the roar of
bombs." And he like many others knew the bombs were coming with
the world war to which the Spanish conflict was an opening act.

Nevertheless he settled back into life at Wallington, tended his
garden and hens, wrote polemics about the war in Spain and worked
on his book about it. *Homage to Catalonia* appeared in a small edition
of fifteen hundred copies in April 1938, only about half of which sold
in his lifetime. Some of the reviews were good, but he feared his socialist publisher was trying to prevent its circulation, and the communists
were predictably hostile. But he had little capacity to pay attention to

the fate of his book, because the month before his own had been called into question when he began to cough up blood in quantity. He was transferred by ambulance to a sanatorium in Kent, and the presence of tuberculosis in his lungs was first confirmed there. He lost a year to illness—first almost six months in the sanatorium (where he was forbidden to use his typewriter but allowed to go fishing), then another six in Morocco with Eileen, in the hope that the warm dry air would help—and then restarted his Wallington life once again in April 1939. His first domestic diaries begin in Wallington just before they went to Morocco and resume there upon their return with the observation on April 10, 1939, that he'd just spent a week in bed, wild daffodils were out, roses were sprouting, and "larks singing hard."

Modotti stayed on until the war was fully lost to Franco and she too had to flee for her life into France. She spent the last years of her life with Vidali, hovering in the shadows in Mexico, living under pseudonyms. Vidali is sometimes said to have masterminded the assassination of Trotsky in Mexico in August 1940. Modotti herself died in a taxi on her way home from an evening with friends in January 1942, not yet forty-six. In response, Pablo Neruda wrote a poem, "Tina Modotti Is Dead." The poem addressed to her directly is full of roses, "the last rose of yesterday," but also "the new rose," and of regret and a rush to reassure her that she has not disappeared altogether. Her silence is burning, Neruda says, but the poem concludes, "fire does not die."

Many years before, in his mural for a provincial agricultural college, Rivera had painted her as a powerful figure whose strong, bare torso rises out of a tree trunk, as if she were growing directly from the earth. Neruda describes her as planted like a seed in the earth, as full of roots, as a flower, a heroine, a soldier marching across snow, but she was nevertheless gone. Fire doesn't die, but she had.

Among those who thought that Vidali had, in the parlance of the time, liquidated her, was the Russian writer Victor Serge, who was then living in Mexico, and the Mexican *La Prensa* newspaper. Serge, who was friendly with Orwell, wrote in his journal that "she's been in disagreement with the GPU [the Soviet secret police and intelligence agency], which she had long worked for, and that she feared for her life." Perhaps Vidali was "the assassin, the jackal, the Judas" from which Neruda vowed, in his poem, to take her far away. Or perhaps not. Neruda too was enthused about Stalin, later wrote an ode to him, and didn't acknowledge the atrocities of the regime until 1956, and Modotti did have a history of heart trouble.

Upon her death, Vidali came into possession of all her photographs and negatives. Like many of her prints, the photograph of roses sold for so much money has on its verso, like a cattle brand, a captive's tattoo, his stamp from that time when the communists were the enemies of revolution, and when he was in the middle of it all. It says "Comandancia General 5o Regimento Milicias Populares" around the periphery and in the center: "Comisario Politico." Political Commissar, General Command of the Fifth Regiment.

*Verso of Tina Modotti, Roses, Mexico, 1924, showing Vittorio Vidali's stamp.*

IV

Stalin's Lemons

*Yakov Guminer, 2 + 2, plus workers' enthusiasm = 5, 1931.*

# ONE

# The Flint Path

In the year 1946, a dictator planted lemons, or rather ordered them planted. Ten years before, Orwell planted his roses in the garden around his cottage. One of them is said to be an Albertine, a variety of rose bred by French grower Albert Barbier in 1921, or a near Albertine. It is not absolutely certain that the two rosebushes growing there now are those he planted, but the cottage was most definitely where he and Eileen O'Shaughnessy Blair lived on and off for years, starting in that spring of 1936. The rent is reported to have been seven shillings and sixpence (ninety pence) a week, a modest sum even then. The structure, which had probably housed tillers of the fields for most of its existence, was sometimes said to be from the eighteenth century, or the seventeenth, or when someone was exuberant about its antiquity, the sixteenth. (Esther Brookes, the schoolmistress who bought the cottage in 1948, calls it medieval but cites no evidence for a date.)

It was made out of stone, and brick, and trees, and plaster. Old beams, not trimmed into straight lines but curving and irregular as they came from the trees, are visible in the upstairs walls. A huge fireplace dominates the little front room that had served as the village shop. It includes an alcove in which bread was baked, and the chimney reaches up through the larger bedroom, where it was built up into a sort of heat-retaining brick ziggurat that Dawn and Graham's grandchildren took for a climbing structure. Up in the attic, Graham told me, the beams still have the branches from centuries before on them. All around spread wheat fields, and though the wheat is planted and harvested annually, the farming is more ancient than the houses, the church, the trees, in fields that have been tilled for a thousand years.

I came back to England in late summer, not quite two years after I had first encountered Graham and Dawn, the cottage, the roses, and the questions that arose then. I parked myself in Cambridge, so I could do research, which meant a little talking to people, a lot of reading, some time in Cambridge University's archives, and some looking around. One Thursday while I was there, I wrote a climate change editorial for *The Guardian* over breakfast and then put a raincoat and a water bottle in my knapsack and took a bus to the Cambridge train station. There I bought a sandwich, a chocolate bar, and a round-trip ticket for the short journey to Baldock. The outside of the Baldock station looked familiar from two years before, but I had hopped into a cab then, and the rest had been a blur of a few minutes.

Now, on a pleasant late-summer day, I would walk a little over three miles from station to cottage. I had no paper map of the area, no printer, and the map apps on my phone didn't work abroad, so before I left I had sketched a rough draft of the route and its turns as portrayed on Google Maps. It turned out to be useless, once I'd made my two or three turns on the streets in Baldock. I was going to wing it, and I looked forward to this small plunge into the mild unknown.

My mapped route ran out at the end of a footpath passing garden back fences on one side and a wheat field on the other. The footpath deposited me at the edge of an expressway along which cars zipped, so I hailed an older woman dressed in bright blue who came strolling along. She was the right person to ask, an old-timer who told me in a fluting voice where the path was and how it had once been the main road to Wallington, and then she gave me some details about the overpass that crosses the A505 road and kept an eye on me as I darted across the expressway and started out.

There was no one else on the route on that Thursday of scattered white clouds and sunshine, and so I fell into a happy introspective trance, taking in the details of the path, the fields, the sky. England often feels boxed in and small-scale to me, but the wheat fields were enormous, and the furrows curved to follow the contours of the land, and the land was a series of billows and swells, like the surface of the sea far from shore, a sort of ocean of earth I drifted along. In some of the fields, the wheat had been harvested and only dusty golden stubble remained, in some it stood ripe, each dry stalk bent over into a hook or a question mark by the weight of the ear of grain at its end, and in some places the stalks throughout whole regions of the fields had lain down in swathes. Some of the fields rose up on those billows to the horizon, gold all the way to the blue sky.

Other fields were bare and freshly plowed, and the pale chalky furrows were sown with flints. I had become captivated by this type of stone so unfamiliar to me when I had first come across it on Cambridgeshire walks with Rob Macfarlane in earlier years—with the black, blue, and white of them, with the way they curved like something organic, with the curious shapes, smooth surfaces, and razor-sharp edges. The flints in the fields between Baldock and Wallington were more beautiful than those I had seen before. Covetousness and curiosity seized hold of me, and I began stepping off the path to the edge of the fields, picking them up, discarding some, picking up some more, enraptured by the forms and the sense of so vast a quantity of them all around me.

Even after centuries of agriculture, they were thick on the ground. There were dozens every square meter, from chips and shards to big irregular lumps weighing several pounds. The latter resembled, at first glance, at least to my eye, small animals and large internal organs. They constituted a dictionary of flint possibilities and I was picking up a vocabulary of form from it. One was the shape of a large drumstick, glossy black on the inside, rough white on the outside. Others were shaped like cocks and balls, and some split-open lumps resembled small busts of human figures, at least to me, and I collected a little family group of anthropomorphic lumps with celestial blue or black faces.

The flints usually have a rough cement-textured whitish exterior that, like the outer layer of the brain's cerebellum, is called a cortex, and on the inside they are smooth as glazed ceramic or glass. The interiors are white or black or any shade of an exquisite stormy blue gray, from pale to midnight, or a mix of these colors. They curve, and their shape is sometimes described as a nodule, but their sharpest edges are sharper than scalpels. Flint, like obsidian, was a stone of choice in the Stone Age. Around the nearby town of Hitchin, which in Orwell's time had the Woolworth's where he appears to have bought most of his sixpence roses, hundreds of Stone Age flint tools have been found.

Flints were formed when this landscape was the bottom of the ocean; they began as the sediment that filled the burrows in that ocean floor or that moved into the space left as sea creatures decayed: they often have biomorphic forms because they are in fact often casts of what life left behind. The chalk itself that gave the soil its pallor was the remnant shells of innumerable tiny sea creatures, and so if the landscape billowed and swelled like the deep sea perhaps it was because it had once been exactly that. So I swam leisurely across an ocean of flint and wheat, not quite certain I was on the right path until I hit a narrow hedge-flanked road across which huge white letters spelled out the word S L O W. It curved down to enter Wallington.

There were hedgerows alongside some portions of the path and the roads it ran along, and there were scraggly, tough dog roses—the wild roses of England—in them, long past blooming, sprays of rose hips where the blooms had been, turning orange, not yet ripe like the wheat. It was quite literally a landscape of bread and roses, and also of blackberries, chalk, flint, and ancient paths that were still public rights of way across all this agricultural space. I strolled the short walk from the cottage Orwell and Eileen had inhabited, past the looming darkness of the Manor Farm barn to the churchyard full of old tombstones whose inscriptions were fading away under lichen and moss and ivy, and into the church, and then ate my sandwich seated on a wall outside and reversed course.

THINKING ABOUT ORWELL'S roses and where they led was a meandering process and perhaps a rhizomatic one, to deploy a word that describes plants such as strawberries that send out roots or runners to spread in many directions. The word was adopted by the philosophers Gilles Deleuze and Félix Guattari to describe a decentralized or nonhierarchical model of knowledge. "Any point of a rhizome can be connected to anything other, and must be," they declared. "This is very different from the tree or root, which plots a point, fixes an order." The branching of trees and of roots is often used as a model of lineage: of the evolution of species or languages, as a family tree, as any chronological, branching transmission, which is why they say later, "The rhizome is an anti-genealogy."

They wrote all that before the distinction between trees and rhizomes got a little blurrier with, for example, recognition of the 106-acre quaking aspen forest in Utah whose forty thousand or so trees share a common root system, are essentially clones of one another, and constitute a single organism larger than any other on Earth and about eighty thousand years old. Or with the underground mycorrhizal networks sometimes called the wood wide web that connect trees to one another in forests, circulating nutrients and information that make some forests a communicating community of not-so-individual trees.

Thoreau once noted that all animals are beasts of burden, "made to carry some portion of our thoughts." Plants too provide us with metaphors and meanings and images, with stems, offshoots, grafts, roots and branches, information trees, seeds of ideas, fruits of our labor, cross-pollinations, ripeness and greenness, and with the symbolic richness of the things we do to our domesticated plants: weeding and pruning, sowing and reaping, and so much more.

A FEW DAYS earlier, on another exploratory stroll, I had run into roses in Cambridge's botanical gardens, where the bushes featured almost no flowers—they had all gone to hips, some very beautiful— except for a wild prairie rose with bright pink petals. A sign said, "This planting demonstrates the complex ancestry of the modern rose, as unravelled by the geneticist Charles Hurst through a 25 year hybridization programme undertaken here in the earliest twentieth century." Genetics is a pursuit of exactly the kind of trees of lineage to which Deleuze and Guattari were seeking an alternative but also a crucial model for understanding how inheritance and evolution work. And so I went to the Cambridge University Library and got them to pull out the boxes of Hurst's papers and spent a day with them, unpacking folder after folder and with it the story of a man's life and work. He had cropped up in some of the literature about roses I'd read, but a more complex story was in the boxes.

Charles Chamberlain Hurst, a man with pointed moustaches and inherited money, was the right-hand man of William Bateson, the scientist who played a crucial role in establishing the modern field of genetics (including coining the word *genetics*). From 1900 on, when Gregor Mendel's experimental data was recovered and used as a foundation for further research, Hurst, Bateson, and several women scientists at Cambridge University did foundational work on heredity and evolution. In addition to deepening understanding of life itself and its processes of inheritance and evolution, discoveries in the field of genetics had immense practical application. Hurst's colleagues ran the spectrum from members of amateur flower-growing societies to the world's leading geneticists. Not a few souls were both—for example, Rose Haig Thomas, a wealthy rose connoisseur, a research sponsor and founder of the Mendel Society, and the author of both scientific papers and an illustrated children's book attempting to make aphids and other plant pests exciting to young readers.

Hurst put his financial resources, his time, and the hundred-acre nursery he inherited to work, first investigating orchids and then spending decades studying roses, with results that interested both rose breeders and research scientists. He also bred long- and short-haired rabbits to discover that the gene for long hair was recessive, and scoured the stud books—the records of British racehorse breeding going back many generations—to document how color was inherited in horses. He demonstrated that blue eyes were recessive in human beings and was tenacious in the face of opposition, of which there was a considerable supply—he got nicknamed "Bateson's bulldog" as a result. Although Bateson had moved on to become head of the John Innes Institute in Norfolk in 1910, Hurst settled in Cambridge after the First World War. His new wife, Rona Hurst, served as his lab assistant, doing microscopic work on rose chromosomes.

The Hursts looked at roses as a mystery to be deciphered and a family to be charted. In 1928, he wrote, "Since the War I have devoted myself entirely to a study of the genetics of the Rose. A comprehensive collection of the known species, sub-species and hybrids has been got together in the Cambridge Botanic Garden from various sources, including wild species collected by my wife and myself in England and in five Cantons of Switzerland, and plants raised from seeds sent to me by correspondents and travellers in North America, Mexico, Turkestan, Siberia, China and Japan."

Hurst's nursery, established in 1773 by his great-great-grandfather in Leicestershire in the English Midlands, had more than twenty acres devoted to roses alone—in 1922, a commercial catalogue he put out listed a thousand varieties for sale, including "the fifty best fragrant roses," fifty "standard and weeping roses," and the "twenty best roses for buttonholes." The names ramble all over the possibilities: Irish Fireflame, Adonis, Lady Reading, Snow Queen, Red Letter Day, Golden Ophelia, Lolita Armour, Mermaid, Los Angeles, and a whole host named after particular people, including several simultaneously commemorating and erasing married women with names such as Mrs. Arthur Johnson.

Wandering through books and archives can be a lot like wandering through landscapes. I'd run into Hurst in the university rose garden, and in an academic essay on Orwell's late years on the Isle of Jura, I'd come across a mention of his interest in the genetics controversies in Stalin's Soviet Union. It was a rabbit hole worth going down, since those controversies were for Orwell an occasion to contemplate larger questions about truth and fact, lies and manipulation, and their consequences. That is, they were an inspiration of sorts, particularly for *Nineteen Eighty-Four*.

THE TERM *INSPIRATION* is often thought to be about positive and desirable things, and there's a sentimental image of the muse as a pretty lady who's the object of the writer's ardor. For a political writer the inspirations or at least the prods to write are often whatever is most repellent and alarming, and opposition is a stimulant. Stalin was surely Orwell's principal muse, if not as a personality then as the figure at the center of a terrifying authoritarianism wreathed in lies.

# Two

# Empire of Lies

In August 1944, Orwell was riveted by a talk about what the Soviet Union was doing to scientists and science given by biologist John R. Baker at a PEN symposium in London on freedom of expression. Baker was, by his account, virtually the only one who spoke up about the violent repression of that freedom in the Soviet Union. In "The Prevention of Literature," published eighteen months later, Orwell wrote that one of the four main speakers "devoted most of his speech to a defense of the Russian purges." Some of the other speeches he called "eulogies of Soviet Russia," yet others defended the liberty to discuss sexuality, "but political liberty was not mentioned" except in this context of the politicization of science.

"His primary liberty," Baker said of scientists, "is freedom of inquiry. Without that he is as you would be if a dictator could control even your imaginations. When scientific autonomy is lost," said Baker, "a fantastic situation develops; for even with the best will in the world, the political bosses cannot distinguish between the genuine investigator on the one hand and the bluffer and self-advertiser on the other." And scientific autonomy had been lost. Baker declared that Trofim Lysenko, the director of the Institute of Genetics at the

Soviet Academy of Agricultural Science, "provides a vivid illustration of the degradation of science under a totalitarian regime."*

The story of the rise of Trofim Lysenko, the bogus scientist and brilliant political strategist, is also that of the fall of the magnificent agronomist Nikolai Vavilov, a story about the triumph of a liar over a truth teller and the immense cost of those lies. Vavilov was, as the contemporary ethnobotanist Gary Paul Nabhan writes, "the only man on earth who had collected seeds of food crops on all five continents, the explorer who had organized 115 research expeditions through some sixty-four countries to find novel ways that humanity could feed itself," and the scientist who published more than a hundred research papers.

His quest was first of all to understand agricultural biodiversity, the great resource against plant diseases and the resource for generating new strains of plants. Underlying all his exploration and research was a desire to improve food production, first of all for Russia and Russians, and behind that a humane desire to feed the hungry. His most celebrated achievement was establishing the world's largest seed bank in Leningrad, as Saint Petersburg was called from shortly after Vladimir Lenin's death in 1924 until the end of the Soviet era. The vast collection, part of the All-Union Institute of Plant Industry Vavilov directed from 1921 to 1940, offered the possibility of food security through biodiversity—species and strains that might be disease or pest resistant, grow in various conditions, increase yield or

---

* One might note that decades of fossil-fuel-sponsored climate denial and resultant inaction provide a vivid illustration of the degradation of science under capitalism. The long pretense by the mainstream media and by US and sometimes British government officials that there were two sides to the science, or no basis for the science, was a betrayal of facts and lives and the future. They often repeated frameworks and talking points originated by fossil-fuel corporations, whether they knew it or not.

nutrition, and the like (and it is celebrated in part because its devoted caretakers starved to death rather than devour its tons of seeds and other plant matter during the 872-day Siege of Leningrad).

Vavilov's career throve until he clashed with Lysenko. The latter man first came to public attention in October 1929, when his experiments with growing winter wheat were hailed as a messianic cure for the grain crises of the young nation. The conclusions Lysenko and the Soviet press drew from his slipshod work were unsound as science but useful for his self-advancement. From this starting point, he launched a successful two-headed campaign, to go to war against genetic science and to insinuate himself into Stalin's good graces. Lysenko understood how to flatter and denounce, and Stalin had already been inclined to oppose Darwinism's picture of random mutation and natural selection as drivers of evolution.

Like Lysenko, Stalin instead supported Lamarckism, the idea that acquired characteristics are inherited (the usual example is giraffe necks, with Jean-Baptiste Lamarck and his followers proposing that a giraffe who stretched her neck to reach for fodder might pass on longer necks to her children). Lamarck, who was born in 1744, can be forgiven for being a Lamarckian, but the twentieth-century figures have little excuse except ideological expediency in response to their misunderstanding of Darwinian evolution. As far back as 1906, Stalin had written in praise of "neo-Lamarckism, to which neo-Darwinism is yielding place."

A few years later a socialist wrote, "Socialism is a theory which presupposes natural equality for people, and strives to bring about social equality. . . . Darwinism, on the contrary, is the scientific proof of inequality." Karl Marx seems to have admired Darwin and saw an echo of his own idea of social evolution in the idea of the evolution of species. But Darwinism as filtered through Thomas Henry Huxley's Hobbesian interpretation emphasized conflict and competition, and Darwin himself did portray evolution as a struggle between members of a species competing for scarce resources. That was warped into a confirmation that free-market capitalism and personal selfishness were natural, inevitable, and even good by those who liked them.

Those who didn't seemed to see no way to reject the superimposed social values without rejecting the scientific theory. A beautiful third way is present in the anarchist philosopher Peter Kropotkin's conclusions from his time in Siberia, where survival was not an individualistic competition for resources, which were abundant, but a cooperative enterprise of coping with harsh conditions. He called that intra-species cooperation mutual aid, charted its roles in animal and human life, and emphasized that evolution and cooperation were often intertwined, not opposed, but his 1902 book, *Mutual Aid*, did not sway the arguments of the time. Contemporary evolutionary science has come closer to Kropotkin's version. The natural world is looking more and more collaborative and interdependent and less and less competitively individualistic.

But in Orwell's day, evolution was Darwinism and Darwinism too often social Darwinism. The Soviets did horrific things against both the facts of biological science and those who espoused and advanced them. The western scientists had their own sins. Many who presumed that Darwin's ideas of evolution confirmed the social status quo—the superiority of the rich to the poor, the aristocratic to the plebeian, the white to the nonwhite—became eugenicists, advocates of the notion of inferior and superior human groups and sometimes of ways of cultivating the latter and eradicating the former through punitive social controls or outright genocide. Hurst was a eugenicist, Baker, whose talk drew Orwell's attention to Soviet pseudoscience, was a eugenicist, and Darwin's own son was, for some years, the president of Britain's Eugenics Educational Society.

The Nazi regime took eugenicist ideas to an extreme, fortifying Stalin's justifications for opposing all genetic science. Thomas Henry Huxley's grandson Julian Huxley, vice president of the British Eugenics Society from 1937 to 1944, was at least right about other motives for Stalin and Lysenko's hostility: "Mendelian heredity," he wrote in 1949, in *Soviet Genetics and World Science*, one of the last books Orwell read, "with its self-copying genes and its random undirected mutations, seems to offer too much resistance to man's desire to change nature, and to elude the control he would like to impose. Lamarckism, on the other hand, holds out a promise of speedy control."

There was a broad and deep belief in the first two thirds of the twentieth century that everyone and everything could be reinvented, that the old ways could be swept away, the past forgotten, the future controlled, human nature reshaped, and it often was yoked to the idea that an elite—sometimes an elite of scientists, sometimes of politicians—could be trusted with these immense transformations. Eugenics was in its own way, like Lamarckism, an idea that human beings could be pressed into perfection, a monstrous means justified by dubiously utopian ends. Many then seemed to believe that human nature, as psychology as well as biology, was malleable enough that the way humans lived and thought and loved and worked could be reinvented.

Lysenko would convince Stalin that wheat, like men, was malleable, and that he could breed wheat that would inherit acquired characteristics. He was crafting a pseudoscience that aligned well with

Marxist ideology and Soviet aspirations. He was badly wrong about the underlying facts, but the corruption and ideological blinders all around him held off the consequences. Vavilov was also at work on producing hardier and more productive strains of wheat, but his sound methods required several years, while Lysenko promised impossibly quick results.

In 1928, the Soviet Union was at the start of its first five-year plan to pursue an accelerated program of industrialization that drew many people to the cities and increased bread shortages. Bad weather and Stalin's rural policies made the shortages far worse. Better-off and less-cooperative peasants were denounced as "kulaks," and at the outset of 1929, Stalin launched a swift and brutal "dekulakization" rampage to destroy members of this fluid category. Immense numbers of peasants, particularly in Ukraine, were executed, imprisoned, or shipped off to Siberia and other remote places.

The government seized the remaining peasants' grain, by force, by torture, at gunpoint. Even after the population was starving, Stalin was convinced they were holding out, and the brutality continued. Those who tried to leave the regions stripped of sustenance were prevented; those who tried to steal food were shot. The surviving peasantry was forced onto collective farms where conditions were often chaotic, brutal, and otherwise inconducive to productivity. Ideologues who knew nothing of agriculture were sent to run the farms. The conditions for a catastrophe piled up in the early 1930s.

In the resultant "terror famine" sometimes called the Holodomor, about five million human beings starved to death, mostly in Ukraine. Famished peasants came to the towns to beg for scraps, came to the train stations in hopes of escaping, or died en route. Their skeletal bodies were strewn along the roads. Deranged by hunger, some turned to cannibalism, even devouring their own children. The Soviet regime found the starved millions incompatible with its image of communism's success and so concealed their fate, with the help of most of the western journalists in Russia, who faced censorship and expulsion for telling the truth, but who were in most cases all too willing to comply.

Public figures—notably the playwright George Bernard Shaw, who had been flattered extensively by the regime—denied the existence of the famine, as did *The New York Times*'s Walter Duranty, who used his prestige to discredit other journalists who tried to report the facts. They hadn't been tortured; the process of making them go along with a lie had been more delicate. At the time, only a few journalists, including Orwell's friend Malcolm Muggeridge, told the truth about the famine and its causes. Gareth Jones, who in 1933 did so more boldly than anyone else, was in 1935 the victim of a still-unsolved murder.

Muggeridge wrote that showmanship was "the most characteristic product" of the Soviet Union, conjuring up illusions to conceal ugly realities rather than ameliorate them. Party members assured him that bread was plentiful and the agricultural future promising. When he went to see for himself, he found "cattle and horses dead; fields, neglected: meagre harvest despite moderately good climatic conditions; all the grain that was produced taken by the Government; now no bread at all, no bread anywhere, nothing much else either; despair and bewilderment." He reported of a despondent peasant and his malnourished children on a collective farm, "His pay was seventy-five kopeks a day. At open market prices seventy-five kopeks would buy half a slice of bread."

The American journalist Eugene Lyons repented afterward that he'd gone along with the lies, in a 1937 book called *Assignment in Utopia*. Orwell observed in his review of the book, "Like many others who have gone to Russia full of hope he was gradually disillusioned, and unlike some others he finally decided to tell the truth about it. It is an unfortunate fact that any hostile criticism of the present Russian régime is liable to be taken as propaganda *against Socialism*; all Socialists are aware of this, and it does not make for honest discussion." It may be Lyons's book that called Orwell's attention to what would become a famous part of the torture in *Nineteen Eighty-Four* that breaks down Winston Smith until he agrees that two plus two equals five. It was a real formula, a proposition to carry out the Soviet five-year plan in four years. Lyons wrote, "The formula $2 + 2 = 5$ instantly riveted my attention. It seemed to me at once both bold and preposterous—the daring and the paradox and the tragic absurdity of the Soviet scene, its mystical simplicity, its defiance of logic.... $2 + 2 = 5$: in electric lights on Moscow housefronts, in foot-high letters on billboards." Perhaps it was indoctrination in overriding one's intelligence, and certainly lies were the one crop with a bumper yield year after year.

Those who were insistent about science or history or inconvenient facts of any kind were silenced, exiled, or executed. This came to a head in the pivotal year of 1936. The first show trial began that August in Moscow. Sixteen former Soviet leaders were executed after confessions extracted by torture. It was another form of showmanship, a circus of terror. Such confessions became an established theatrical genre of self-accusation of terrible and often preposterous or impossible crimes and of self-abasement before the authorities. Truth and language and the historical record were themselves abased and tortured to produce these results. Stalin was intent not just on liquidating his potential rivals, especially Trotskyists, so that he could rule unchecked but on destroying them and their credibility in ways that terrified everyone else into silence and deference. As Orwell would convey more powerfully than almost anyone before or since, one of the powers tyrants hold is to destroy and distort the truth and force others to submit to what they know is untrue.

Inside the Soviet Union, the lies squeezed out of former leaders in their trials and the executions shredded the history of the young Soviet Union. The era of airbrushed photographs began—sometimes the same photograph would be doctored repeatedly as successive figures were erased, first from life and then from pictures and history. NKVD head Genrikh Yagoda, who had been in charge of the forced collectivization (as well as Stalin's poison laboratory), fell out of favor for reporting the negative public reaction to the show trials. He was demoted, then denounced, then tried in the third show trial in 1938, and executed. His replacement underwent a similar fate and was executed in early 1940.

"Execution was the favored solution to every problem, including those caused by previous executions," writes Adam Hochschild. "When the national census showed that his reign of terror was shrinking the country's population, Stalin ordered the members of the census board shot. The new officials, not surprisingly, came up with higher figures. Between about 1929, when Stalin had vanquished his rivals and concentrated power in his hands, and his death in 1953, most historians now estimate that he had been directly responsible for the deaths of somewhere around 20 million people."

The same year that the show trials began, the geneticists attempted to debate the Lysenkoists in a public conference. It was a proxy war for empiricism and the freedom to pursue knowledge. The consequence of this dissent for a dozen of Vavilov's colleagues was arrest and execution. Vavilov had been denounced by Lysenko, but he was unbowed. In March 1939, he stood up at a meeting of scientists at Leningrad's All-Union Institute of Plant Industry and declared, "We will go into the pyre, we shall burn, but we shall not retreat from our convictions." In November of that year, Stalin sent for him and told him at a midnight meeting, "You are the Vavilov who fiddles with flowers, leaves, grafts and other botanical nonsense instead of helping agriculture, as is done by Academician Lysenko."

In 1940, after a face-to-face argument with Lysenko, Vavilov went to Ukraine to collect seeds from cultivated and wild plants. While he was on a mountainside looking for specimens, officials pulled up in a black car and took him away. He was, over the next eleven months, interrogated four hundred times, mostly at night, accused of having been a spy, a traitor, saboteur, and principal cause of the famine. Almost ten hours into one of these interrogations he confessed falsely to being a member of a right-wing organization. His death sentence overturned by appeal, he was sent to a prison camp. There, on a diet of raw flour and frozen cabbage, the man who had done so much to address hunger starved to death, dying on January 26, 1943.

It was another scientist, C. D. Darlington, who in 1945 cowrote Vavilov's belated obituary for the journal *Nature*, as a denunciation of the Soviet regime, and it was to Darlington that Orwell wrote in 1947 to learn more about Lysenkoism. Darlington had trouble finding outlets for his critical pieces about Soviet science, because the USSR had been a British ally in the war and few wanted to address the nation's crimes. Orwell himself had had trouble publishing first *Homage to Catalonia* and then *Animal Farm*, because anti-Soviet positions were unpopular even after the British-Soviet alliance and the war had ended. While he was working on *Nineteen Eighty-Four*, he wrote to the left-wing publisher Victor Gollancz, who had published several of his earlier books, begging to be let out of the contract that gave Gollancz the right to future books for fear of future conflict and suppression.

Lysenko's career continued to rise, and the anti-geneticist became head of the Institute of Genetics. In 1948, he presided over a conference at which genetic science was denounced and his own pseudo-science became an official doctrine dangerous to criticize inside the country. Thousands who had previously dissented were removed from their positions as teachers and researchers. Three distinguished scientists committed suicide to avoid further persecution. Vavilov's physicist brother went along with the charade but wrote in his diary, "Everything is so sad and shameful."

In December 1949, about five weeks before his death, Orwell pasted into his journal the headline:

## "WHEAT CAN BECOME RYE"—LYSENKO

The article cited Lysenko's preposterous statement that "in mountainous areas possessing unfavourable wintry conditions winter wheat can turn into rye" and that this confirmed Stalin's views and his own theories. Orwell stood apart from his peers in his capacity to critique the sector of the left that had drifted toward authoritarianism and dishonesty without joining other leftists who became conservatives tolerating other forms of brutality and deception. Doing so meant charting his own path across the uneven ground of midcentury politics, and it made him after his death a totemic figure claimed by people across the political spectrum.

# THREE

# Forcing Lemons

At the 1945 Yalta Conference in Ukraine, where Stalin, Churchill, and Roosevelt negotiated the postwar order, Churchill or his daughter expressed a wish for lemons—to use in the drinks in one version, on caviar in another—and woke to find that during the long February night a lemon tree loaded with fruit had magically appeared at the palace in which they were lodged. In the postwar years, Stalin became preoccupied with pushing lemon trees beyond their natural limits. He was apparently convinced that the fundamental nature of citrus trees, like people, like wheat, could be remade through sheer force and tried to get them to grow outdoors at his dacha in Ukraine's Crimea region and at his Kuntsevo dacha on the outskirts of Moscow. Vyacheslav Molotov, a powerful official in the regime and one of the few Bolsheviks to survive all the purges, recalled long after Stalin was gone, "He arranged to have a lemon shrub planted at his dacha. I never saw him digging around it. Everyone oohed and aahed at it. Frankly, I oohed and aahed less than others. I wondered why the hell does he need that lemon shrub? A lemon shrub in Moscow!" Another high-level official told of being taken for a walk in this garden by Stalin, who fed him lemon slice after lemon slice, forcing praise out of him all the while.

He had extensive gardens at his several dachas and was much involved in giving orders to the gardeners in them. They provided the dictator and his family with abundant food. Stalin's daughter, Svetlana, reminisced, "He was unable merely to contemplate nature; he had to work it and be forever transforming it." In Moscow he had greenhouses the lemon trees overwintered in, but he told his gardeners, "Let them get used to the cold." It's conceivable that selective breeding over generations might have resulted in hardier lemon trees, but he seemed to be trying to toughen up individual specimens like a drill sergeant training recruits. His large-scale lemon planting in the Crimea region of Ukraine froze. Lemon trees did better in the mild conditions of his native Georgia, and he planted some—or rather decreed they be planted; he issued daily orders to his gardeners—at his Abkhazian dacha there. Even there, only one survived the bitter winter of 1947–1948. Perhaps he or someone else had them replanted, because a travel article reports that the dacha is presently surrounded by lemon trees.

*Alice in Wonderland* contains a scene in which panicky servants paint white roses red because red roses were what had been ordered for the garden, and if the Queen found out that there had been a mistake, "we should all have our heads cut off." How did Stalin take in the failure of the lemon trees to adapt to cold? Did he deny what happened and, as with the census takers, find someone to punish? Did gardeners provide the illusion of success by planting new lemon trees and pretending they were the old ones? Behind that is the question of how much he lied to himself while he forced everyone around him to lie about everything. Did he lose sight of the falsity as he commanded the nation to obey his dictates? What did it mean to be the enforcer of lies, to prop up illusions and conceal brutal realities, to demand obedience to a version of reality that was a result of your orders and suppressions rather than the data?

But this power couldn't make wheat obey bogus science or lemon trees survive harsh winters. Lamarckism in its time was a mistake; in their time, it was a lie. Lysenko's promises about wheat were lies. The denial of a great famine that led to millions of deaths in the early 1930s was a lie. The crimes that people were tortured into admitting to in the show trials were largely lies. People lied to stay alive, died of telling the truth, or lied and died anyway. Others lost track of what was true. History was rewritten regularly as the instigators of the Russian Revolution were executed by their fellow revolutionaries. Executioners were executed, interrogators were sent to gulags where they joined those they had interrogated. Books were banned, facts were banned, poets were banned, ideas were banned. It was an empire of lies. The lies—the assault on language—were the necessary foundation for all the other assaults.

Orwell wrote in 1944, "The really frightening thing about totalitarianism is not that it commits 'atrocities' but that it attacks the concept of objective truth; it claims to control the past as well as the future," a framework that would morph into Big Brother's "Who controls the past controls the future: who controls the present controls the past." The attack on truth and language makes the atrocities possible. If you can erase what has happened, silence the witnesses, convince people of the merit of supporting a lie, if you can terrorize people into silence, obedience, lies, if you can make the task of determining what is true so impossible or dangerous they stop trying, you can perpetuate your crimes. The first victim of war is truth, goes the old saying, and a perpetual war against truth undergirds all authoritarianisms from the domestic to the global. After all, authoritarianism is itself, like eugenics, a kind of elitism premised on the idea that power should be distributed unequally.

Russia's current authoritarian leader, Vladimir Putin, has been rehabilitating Stalin's reputation. Lysenko's seems to be coasting along on this revisionism and on some distortions of the significance of epigenetics. But it's Vavilov whose work lives on through seeds, the ones he found, collected, cultivated, the ones his followers protected in the seed bank during the Siege of Leningrad. Nabhan writes, "Roughly a quarter century after his death, four hundred new crop varieties selected from the seeds he collected were indeed feeding such a large percentage of Soviet citizens that the frequency of famines . . . declined precipitously."

Stalin's lemons failed, and though a single tree—an olive, a yew, a sequoia, a sacred fig—may live a millennium or more, the wheat fields around Wallington were reminders that even seeds for annuals or practices like farming could outlast a regime, a dictator, a pack of lies, and a war against science. Lies mutate more freely than seeds, and there are new crops of those as well.

V

Retreats
and
Attacks

*Sir Joshua Reynolds,* The Honorable Henry Fane (1739–1802) with Inigo Jones and Charles Blair, *1761–66.*

# ONE

# Enclosures

In the year 1936, an Englishman planted roses. Doing so was part of making a garden, and gardens are one way that culture does nature. That is to say, a garden is an ideal version of nature filtered through a particular culture, whether it's as formal as a Japanese rock and sand garden or an Islamic paradise garden with a central fountain—or as haphazard as a lot of ordinary private gardens are, arising as they do from limited space, time, budget, and planning. A garden is what you want (and can manage and afford), and what you want is who you are, and who you are is always a political and cultural question. It's true even of vegetable gardens—of whether you plant cabbages or chiles— though more so with pleasure gardens.

The Scottish artist and garden maker Ian Hamilton Finlay once wrote, "Certain gardens are described as retreats when they are really attacks." The gardens of Orwell are sown with ideas and ideals and fenced around by class and ethnicity and nationality and the assumptions therein, and there are plenty of attacks hovering in the background. Gardens have been defended as apolitical spaces—famously, at the end of Voltaire's philosophical satire *Candide*, the title character retreats to "tend his garden," a decision that has often been framed as a withdrawal from the world and politics. It appears to be a conclusive one, since there is no indication that Candide is just recharging preparatory to returning to the fray.

In Voltaire's youth, the gardens of European aristocrats were full of nature laid out in geometrical arrays and trees trimmed into cones and other formal shapes, nature obedient to a Cartesian order. Versailles was the superlative version, a garden radiating out from the monarchical center of power in the great Grand Canal that, seen from the palace, seemed to stretch almost to the horizon, and long straight avenues lined with classical statues and trees. Nature had been conquered. Imagined as an untidy or incoherent realm, it had been given a strict order and discipline by the absolute authority of the king. It was unnatural nature, and proud of it.

The gardens of the English aristocracy in the second half of the eighteenth century took on an aesthetic of naturalness—often of a carefully landscaped, designed, and laboriously executed naturalness that celebrated the aesthetics of the natural world while presuming to groom and improve it. The same kind of laborious earthmoving and outdoor plumbing as at Versailles might be employed, but to make serpentine streams and rolling terrain that hid the handiwork behind it. Nature was supreme except that English taste and money were her master. Even so, the new garden style constituted a revolution in aesthetics. If gardens looked more and more like the unmanipulated natural world, that natural world could be admired more and more as a site of aesthetic pleasure, and while the landscape gardens were for an elite, the natural world was far more open to all.

Even so, those naturalistic gardens were also a counterrevolution. They were arguments of sorts that the English aristocracy and the social hierarchy were themselves natural, that the aristocrats' power and privilege was rooted in the actual landscape, even as the humbler dwellers in the landscape were uprooted in the enclosure acts and driven to industrial labor in cities or to emigration. The process of enclosing the commons began in the Middle Ages in England but peaked between 1750 and 1850 with a series of parliamentary enclosure acts. These acts gave to powerful individuals land that had long been collectively farmed, grazed, and administered, erasing villages and villagers and their self-determination and prosperity. Historian of the commons Peter Linebaugh notes that in England and Wales, "between 1725 and 1825 nearly four thousand enclosure acts appropriated more than six million acres of land, about a quarter of cultivated acreage, to the politically dominant landowners. . . . It got rid of open-field villages and common rights and contributed to the late eighteenth century's crisis of poverty."

These measures transformed the rural working class into an uprooted, dispossessed population who would swell cities as the Industrial Revolution's labor force. Linebaugh lists enclosure, slavery, and mechanization as a trinity of brutally transformative forces at work in the eighteenth and nineteenth centuries. The peasant poet John Clare lived through the transformation in Northamptonshire and wrote of it as it had been when

> *Unbounded freedom ruled the wandering scene*
> *Nor fence of ownership crept in between*
> *To hide the prospect of the following eye*
> *Its only bondage was the circling sky.*

And then after its destruction, "scared freedom bade goodbye" and "all sighed when lawless law's enclosure came." Enclosure was to its time what privatization was to the neoliberal era, a dispossession of the many for the benefit of the few and an assault on the idea of both literal commons and the common good.

The argument in favor of enclosure was supposed to be efficiency and productivity. Arthur Young's 1804 report on agriculture in Hertfordshire notes of a farmer a few miles from Wallington, "Mr. Forster, a gentleman very intelligent in husbandry, at Royston, lamented the great inconvenience of open-fields, pleading strenuously for a general enclosure. He cannot sow turnips in the open-field without leave from the parish flock-master, and pays 1s. 6d. an acre to the shepherd for not eating the crop." In other words, the community made the decisions. Enclosure undermined the power of that community as it impoverished rural laborers and enriched landowners.

They enclosed it legally and literally: Young's book includes several pictures illustrating techniques of plashing—of weaving young plants together so that they would grow into impenetrable hedges bordering the enclosed fields. But in villages near Wallington the farming society resisted enclosure and defended open-field agriculture into the nineteenth century, and Young himself came to believe that enclosure impoverished and destroyed.

While disrupting an old rural culture, the aristocracy positioned themselves as grounded in nature and the countryside. Art historian Ann Bermingham writes, "Nature, with its various representations in painting, poetry, letters, manners, dress, philosophy, and science, became a supreme social value and was called upon to clarify and justify social change. One now did something in a certain way because it was more 'natural.'" Defining the social order as natural and the aristocracy as rooted in the natural world justified the British aristocracy as they expanded their power and wealth even as the French decapitated and drove out their aristocracy after the 1789 revolution.

The idea of nature as a touchstone of all that is true and good has lasted into our time.

A telling detail was the aesthetic of openness as aristocratic English gardens evolved from contained and exuberantly unnatural creations to naturalistic landscape gardens covering far more ground. Bermingham points out that as enclosure made the surrounding countryside look increasingly regimented and artificial, these gardens came to look "increasingly natural, like the preenclosed landscape." Yet the means to limit who could actually access these Edenic expanses also defined them. One was the ha-ha, a ditch around the premises that formed a barrier without interrupting the vista, so that the property seemed to have no end. The ha-ha let you have it both ways, feeling illimitable from inside while keeping others out.

Nevertheless in Orwell's time the natural world was often imagined as outside the social and the political. The German playwright Bertolt Brecht famously wrote in a 1939 poem,

*Ah, what times are these, when*
*a conversation about the trees is almost a crime*
*For it encompasses silence about so many injustices.*

And the French photographer Henri Cartier-Bresson said something similar earlier in the 1930s: "The world is going to pieces and people like Adams and Weston are photographing rocks!" He apparently imagined trees and rocks as outside the political sphere, as not vulnerable to human impacts, and saw California modernists' photographs as apolitical retreats. Many of their contemporaries were photographing the social impact of the Dust Bowl in the central United States—the world literally falling to pieces as topsoil blew away in vast dust storms—and the federal government was planting rows of trees as windbreaks to try to halt the erosion. All art is propaganda, Orwell noted, and nature is political. So are gardens. Flowers. Trees. Water. Air. Soil. Weather.

I write this a couple of days after a news agency reported of Australia, "More than 25.5 million acres of land—an area the size of South Korea—have been razed by the wildfires across the country in recent weeks, according to the latest data, with the southeast particularly hard hit." Among the Australian places burned were swathes of the Gondwanaland forests, the oldest forests in the world, places that had been wet and stable for a hundred million years. People are dying in the defense of the Amazonian rainforest, and what role tree planting and forests will play in countering climate chaos is fiercely debated, as is the definition of a forest as, ideally, a complex ecosystem of many life forms of many ages, not a monocrop tree plantation. The cutting down of trees or the preservation and planting of them are political battles.

I write this as workmen are cutting holes in my own house and I can see the great redwood beams with which it was built at the end of the nineteenth century, from trees that were who knows how ancient when they were logged, probably from primeval forests where ferns and birds and plant communities flourished under the canopies and up in the crowns of these behemoths, while fungal networks (more rhizomatic than rhizomes) connected their root systems. I write this with clean power produced by wind and sun, an option you can choose where I live, because people organized against the power company, and because engineering transformed solar and wind into effective, affordable technologies in the first two decades of the twenty-first century in one of the most overlooked revolutions of all time. I write this in a house whose water travels 160 miles from a snowmelt-filled reservoir inside a national park in the Sierra Nevada, as a result of a battle to protect the place that John Muir and his Sierra Club lost more than a century ago.

I know that even the desire to garden, to be in the country, to rusticate, is culturally determined and rooted in class, or at least the forms it takes are. Orwell acknowledged this in a 1940 essay, in which he said of his generation, "Most middle-class boys grew up within sight of a farm, and naturally it was the picturesque side of farm life that appealed to them—the ploughing, harvesting, stack-thrashing and so forth. Unless he has to do it himself a boy is not likely to notice the horrible drudgery of hoeing turnips, milking cows with chapped teats at four o'clock in the morning, etc., etc."

I learned that from the Latina muralist Juana Alicia, a legendary figure in the San Francisco Bay Area and a student in the first class I ever taught, when I was in my twenties. It was a graduate seminar at the San Francisco Art Institute about landscape and representation. Midway through the class, Juana, who lived near me and sometimes rode home with me, mentioned that she had been a farmworker as a child and young woman in California, and she had been crop-dusted with pesticides while picking lettuce while pregnant, and that all the agrarian landscape images I showed reminded her of that. It was the kindest rebuke ever and one of the most effective.

She reminded me what my Black neighbors had taught me earlier that decade, that the yearning to be more rugged, more rustic, more rough, more scruffy, is often a white and a white-collar yearning, and that those who have only recently escaped agricultural work, maybe sharecropping or slavery or migrant labor, who have survived being treated as dirty or backward, are often glad to be polished and elegant. You have to feel securely high to want to go low, urban to yearn for the rural, smooth to desire roughness, anxious about artificiality to seek this version of authenticity. And if you see the countryside as a place of rest and respite you're probably not a farmworker.

By the nineteenth and twentieth centuries, appreciation of nature was often exhibited as a sign of refinement and even virtue. Of course Stalin loved his gardens and greenhouses at his dachas and the Nazis conflated ideas about racial purity and the protection of nature, particularly of forests, and not a few of the early American conservation groups promoted eugenicist views. There might be virtuous ways to love nature, but the love of nature is no guarantor of virtue.

# Two

# Gentility

The artist Sir Joshua Reynolds, a towering figure in the England of his time, painted his largest work in the early 1760s, and it is so huge—more than eight feet high, almost twelve wide—that the Metropolitan Museum of Art must take it out of its frame to remove it from the gallery in which it is usually displayed. It shows, at nearly life-size, three men in a landscape, two at a table in city clothes, and one standing a little apart in more countrified garb. The picture is bisected by a bit of architecture that includes a classical head and torso so twined about and shrouded in greenery it is easy to miss despite its pallor. This architecture that is also nature that is also classical reference helps convey a very particular notion of gentility and groundedness. The landscape beyond is an ideal one for that moment: stands of frothy trees, curve of hills, body of tranquil water, and beyond that water, more hills, more trees. No fences, farms, houses, walls, roads, other people, just unpeopled nature rolling into the distance.

Sitting on the left, behind the table, is a serious, plain man, older in appearance than the other two. Nearer the center lounges a pale man whose legs, clad in silk stockings and white breeches, are crossed. A hound who shares his languid pose rests its head on his thigh. The ruffles of his shirt raise themselves from the open top of his waistcoat like the wings of some tatted butterfly. The seated men and dog turn their heads toward the figure who stands alone and apart on the right side of this painting, which with its own more open background almost feels like a separate realm. His red coat and green waistcoat contrast with the others' muted colors, just as his tall boots with spurs suggest a man of more action than the other two, though he too has ruffles fluttering between his waistcoat buttons. His face is slack with what looks like boredom or disdain, making him look older than he was—only twenty in 1763.

He is Charles Blair, Orwell's great-great-grandfather. The lounging man at the center is Henry Fane. Both men's status changed between when Reynolds began and completed the painting. In 1762, Fane became the Honorable Henry Fane when his father became the eighth Earl of Westmorland after a distant relation died without heir. The same year, Blair married Henry Fane's sister Mary and became the son-in-law of an earl. Art historian Katharine Baetjer declares, "As it has not been possible to discover any achievements that he then had to his credit, we can only assume that the picture constitutes a particularly monumental celebration of traditional ties of family and friendship," noting elsewhere, "A younger son should not have been important enough in dynastic terms" to be the subject of such a vast and expensive painting. (The fee to Reynolds was two hundred pounds, an immense sum at the time; Reynolds was his era's society portrait maker of choice and grew rich churning out these paintings.) Perhaps Blair had something to do with commissioning this painting that portrays him on quite literally equal footing with this more aristocratic young man, though it stayed in the Fane family until it was found badly decayed in one of their lumber rooms, restored, and eventually sold to another parvenu, Junius Morgan, who gave it to the Metropolitan Museum in 1887. (Morgan's money came from banking, specifically the bank that mutated into JPMorgan Chase.)

The money that qualified Blair to link himself to the daughter of an earl came from Jamaica, which is to say it came from sugar. Sugar in that era was both an extraordinarily valuable crop—British exports from Jamaica, mostly sugar and rum made from sugar, were worth five times the exports from the thirteen colonies—and the result of extraordinarily brutal slave labor. Enslaved Africans were the majority population in Jamaica and the white minority kept them in thrall through punitive cruelty and quite literally worked them to death and bought replacements dragged over from Africa. All the while, the Britons feared that the Africans might rebel, and that fear became their justification for more brutality.

Though mostly kept from literacy and a sympathetic audience, enough of those who were enslaved in the West Indies told their stories that we have a few views from their perspective. In Bermuda, for example, Mary Prince was at age twelve sold away from her family and familiar world to a cruel couple. Her new owner taught the child how to perform various household tasks. "And she taught me (how can I ever forget it!) more things than these; she caused me to know the exact difference between the smart of the rope, the cart-whip, and the cow-skin, when applied to my naked body by her own cruel hand. . . . I lay down at night and rose up in the morning in fear and sorrow; and often wished that like poor Hetty I could escape from this cruel bondage and be at rest in the grave." Hetty was the kind fellow slave who, while pregnant, had died after being beaten "till she was all over streaming with blood." Mary Prince was sold more times, and one owner took her to England, where she eventually achieved freedom and a voice with the publication of her account in 1831.

In her letter from late 1936, Eileen Blair described a visit to her new in-laws in a house that was "very small & furnished almost entirely with paintings of ancestors. The Blairs are by origin Lowland Scottish & dull but one of them made a lot of money in slaves & his son [ ... ] who was inconceivably like a sheep married the daughter of the Duke of Westmorland (of whose existence I never heard) & went so grand that he spent all the money & couldn't make more because slaves had gone out. So his son went into the army & came out of that into the church & married a girl of 15 who loathed him & had ten children of whom Eric's father, now 80, is the only survivor & they are all quite penniless but still on the shivering verge of gentility as Eric calls it in his new book which I cannot think will be popular with the family." Orwell said almost nothing about this ancestry, though his protagonist in *Coming Up for Air* marries, unhappily, a woman from this kind of background: "For generations past her family had been soldiers, sailors, clergymen, Anglo-Indian officials, and that kind of thing. They'd never had any money, but on the other hand none of them had ever done anything that I should recognize as work. Say what you will, there's a kind of snob-appeal in that."

The word *gentility* means of gentle birth, of aristocratic origin, and it is related to the words *genteel* and *gentle* as in *gentleman*, words that describe both social class and an idea of refinement or rather conflate them as though they were always found together. The two words have a cousin in *gentile*, as in one who is not a Jew. *Gentry, gentility, gentiles, gentlemen*—and then eventually *gentleness*: the word also came to mean kindness and mildness in the sixteenth century. At the root of them all is *gen-*, from a proto–Indo-European word that means to give birth, to beget. Among the linguistic descendants of this root word are the English language's *generation, generative, genuine, genealogy, generous, genitals, genesis, degenerate,* and later, *genes, genetics,* and *genocide.*

These three men were portrayed as genteel, at home and at ease in the natural landscape. The man standing so confidently in an English countryside—or Reynolds's idealized version thereof—was the owner of plantations and slaves, which did not appear in this painting. Or in other terms, the elegance of the men and their temperate-zone landscape of leisure is underwritten by labor in a brutal industry in the tropics. The business became famous as the triangle trade, in which British goods were traded for human beings from Africa who were taken to the Americas where sugar and rum were taken in. Asian trade goods were also part of the system, which was more circular than triangular and ugly at every stage. Brutality begot a luxury that was itself concentrated sweetness. Like cotton and tea and the ceramic dishware still called china, sugar was one of the new substances that the colonial era brought to Britain, and it went from a rare luxury to a staple, and so that quintessentially English thing, a cup of tea, could be made with Indian tea and Caribbean sugar, served in Chinese porcelain.

The Reynolds painting is what was called a conversation piece, a genre depicting affluent people at ease, often out of doors—acting naturally, you could say. In other conversation pieces, a black servant or slave appears, sometimes a black male child wearing the padlocked collar of a slave. In the versions I have encountered, these black figures are not named, and the paintings are often titled as though only the white family group was depicted. They are obliterated, not blotted out like those airbrushed out of Soviet photographs in the Stalin era, but never invited in.

Even in Orwell's time, as Brecht's poem and Cartier-Bresson's comment suggest, landscape was seen as a space outside politics, as a refuge from it—but in recent decades, it is as though a wall was breached and politics came rushing in. Or rather scholars talk about what lay outside the paintings, the novels, gardens and parks and estates, and how that had always given meaning to what was within. It's almost the opposite argument of Lawrence Weschler's "Vermeer in Bosnia," in which the serenity of Vermeer's paintings helps a war-crimes-tribunal judge slog through his days and years of listening to perpetrators' and victims' tales of atrocity. In that case, the retreat is a refuge from which one goes forth to deal with the reality of cruelty and injustice and suffering; in this, the gardens and country homes are escapes for people avoiding facing suffering and their own complicity in it. Garden retreats, garden attacks.

In his 1993 book, *Culture and Imperialism*, Edward Said wrote an influential chapter about Jane Austen's *Mansfield Park*. Her 1814 novel is about the desire to belong to the class and place of the Bertrams, an affluent family inhabiting a country estate somewhere in southern England. In this most humorlessly prim of her novels, some of Sir Thomas Bertram's children fall out of the walled garden that is gentility, and Sir Thomas's niece Fanny Price, born into poverty, clambers into it through her diligent propriety. And behind it all, Said points out, are the Antigua sugar plantations and slave labor that pay for the family's luxury and leisure. Sir Thomas and his oldest son go to the Caribbean to manage their possessions, but in so doing they exit the novel's stage. The island and its plantations and slaves and system of production are beyond the scope of the novel and so the financial foundation of it all and the human beings behind that foundation, or buried under it, remain unseen and unimagined.

In 2013, English Heritage, the governmental entity preserving and presenting Britain's historic landscape, published the anthology *Slavery and the British Country House*, whose introduction notes, "It is only in the last 20 years that the relationship between landed wealth, British properties and enslaved African labour began to emerge." The book describes the wealth pouring into Britain from afar and how it was spent on building grand houses on grander grounds. "Both the merchants and the members of Britain's landed elite who were involved in the proliferation of country houses from the late 17th century (the latter to consolidate their status and the former to gain entry into that elite) increasingly utilised notions of gentility, sensibility and cultural refinement in part to distance themselves from their actual connections to the Atlantic slave economy."

One of its authors notes, "Across Britain as a whole, the slave-compensation data suggest that in the 1830s 5 to 10 percent of all British country houses would be expected to have been occupied by slave owners and that in some localities and even some regions the figure would be much higher." The profound confinement of slavery and the labor-intensive sugar plantations haunt places so superficially antithetical they serve almost as alibis: the landscapes of scenic beauty that seem to have nothing to do with manipulation, labor, production, and politics. In that sense, the apoliticalness of nature was itself a political production.

# THREE

# Sugar, Poppies, Teak

The plantation owner Charles Blair married Lady Mary Fane, whose father, before he set off to enjoy his earldom, had been a merchant in Bristol, a city immersed in the slave trade. He too was painted by Reynolds in the early 1760s, as a stout, confident white-wigged figure in so much dull reddish velvet he looks a bit like a sofa stood upright in a murky green landscape. Mary Fane's mother, Elizabeth Swymmer Fane, was herself an heiress to sugar plantation and slave-trading wealth.

As Eileen Blair noted, Charles Blair and Mary Fane Blair's descendants lost the Jamaica fortune, apparently in part when slavery was abolished in the British Empire in 1833. A register for the Blairs' West Prospect plantation gives the names of some of the 133 enslaved people there in 1817: Big Nancy, Abigail, Maryann, Charity, Daphne, Hannah, Louisa, Lucky, Sam, Ross, Philip, Johnny, Yorkshire, Dorset, Dublin, Galway. The English and Irish place-names are a particularly crass way to rename displaced Africans. Harry Blair, age 20, and Sarah Blair, age 33, are among the minority listed with a surname—in this case a surname that raises questions about whether their owner had also been their father.

When Eric Blair chose the name George Orwell, he distanced

himself from the Blairs but covered himself in Englishness twice over. Saint George was England's patron saint, and King George V was on the throne at the time. As a schoolboy, Orwell had been stuffed with enough Greek and Latin to know the name's origin in words for earth and for work, so that it meant farmer, earthworker. Thus Virgil's *Georgics*, his epic poem of agriculture. *Orwell* was an old English word that has, of course, a well in it, which is sometimes thought to also mean spring, and one translation is "spring by a pointed hill." Another source notes that *oran* or *ora* means a border, brink, edge or margin, and the meaning is "well beside the brink." There are also Urwells and an old parish of Orwell in Scotland, whose name is said to be of Gaelic origin and meant "yew wood." All the meanings make it a landscape feature. Orwell is said to have gotten it from the River Orwell in Suffolk, near his parents' home. The name has the added ambivalent charm of sounding a bit like "or," as in alternately, and "oh well," as in resignation, a sigh, a shrug.

Orwell cultivated a loathing for Scots in his cranky youth, which may be another reason he chose to appear in public out from under the family name; that he chose to retreat to Scotland in the last years of his life is one sign he got over it. But Blair is a Scottish name. Charles Blair, whose inheritance in Jamaica consisted of land and human beings, married Mary Fane, and they had another Charles Blair, who in turn had a youngest son named Thomas Richard Arthur Blair. This grandson of the man dominating the Reynolds painting, this grandfather of the man at the center of this book, went into the church and spent time in India and, apparently, Tasmania. In his thirties, while traveling to and fro from India, the minister Thomas Blair married fifteen-year-old Frances Catherine Hare, whom he met in the Cape of Good Hope in what is now South Africa. They were citizens of empire more than of England.

Orwell's father, the youngest son of this youngest son, was born in 1857, christened Richard Walmesley Blair, and raised mostly in Dorset in southern England. Richard Blair also married late, midway through a stagnant career in India. He worked in opium production in India until his retirement in 1912, mostly as a subdeputy opium agent for the British government. Orwell was born in the small farming town of Motihari in the state of Bihar at the center of the north Indian opium industry. Not much is known about how his family lived during the time he, his mother, and his older sister resided with his father. A photograph of him as a disgruntled-looking but plump baby being held up by a dark-skinned woman swathed in white is a reminder that colonial posts were appealing to Britons of modest means partly because they offered a chance to lead a more luxurious, elite life, complete with cheap and abundant servants, than did the mother country.

Richard Blair oversaw the farming of poppies and production of the drug in a process that impoverished, coerced, and sometimes brutally punished the Indian peasants doing the growing and refining. Much of the opium thus produced was, of course, foisted upon China as a counterbalancing commodity for the many goods from that country Britain craved, and a couple of opium wars were fought in the middle of the nineteenth century over China's resistance to this substance that had addicted and undermined so many of its people. "England's national flower is the red Tudor rose. But the prickly truth is that the English owe much of their wealth to another blood-red flower; the poppy," a contemporary writer notes. The protagonist of

Orwell's *Burmese Days*, an English teak merchant in Burma, declares, "We Anglo-Indians could be almost bearable if we'd only admit that we're thieves and go on thieving without any humbug."

Orwell is descended from colonists and servants of empire who lived off the fat of others' land and labor. His mother, Ida Mabel Limouzin Blair, grew up in Burma, where her French father was a teak merchant and shipbuilder. Teak forests near a coast, fields of sugarcane on an island, and opium poppies in the center of a continent, landscapes of labor and exploitation stretched around the world, often and maybe usually invisible to their distant beneficiaries. I don't believe in ancestral guilt, but I do believe in inheritance, and Orwell came from people who benefited from the imperial enterprise and the domestic hierarchies and who sometimes held real power. Perhaps the most telling thing for me is how easy it was to trace his ancestry back for generation after generation. The very traceability is about people who were entered into the record, who were recognized, official. They were in the picture.

There are aristocrats, commoners, members of Parliament, a regicide—Colonel Adrian Scrope who was hung, drawn, and quartered for signing the death warrant for Charles I. There are writers—the minor poet Nicholas Rowe, the minor playwright Francis Fane, and, so far as I can tell, Frances Manners, who was included in the first British anthology of women writers, *The Monument of Matrons* of 1582. There are slave owners and there's distant kinship through his grandmother, Frances Hare Blair, with William Wilberforce, the leader of the antislavery movement in Parliament. Some of this was inscribed in the family Bible Orwell inherited, along with the silver and some of the paintings Eileen Blair mentioned. Family Bibles and silver—for me whose Irish Catholic and Eastern European Jewish ancestors passed along no heirlooms and were largely barred from public life and whose records fade out after a few generations—stir something that might once have been envy but is now just a sense of distance.

# FOUR

# Old Blush

The roses are perfect, rootless, seasonless, timeless, floating across fields of lilac or pale green or yellow ochre, forever blooming, their petals just so, the shadows of each petal clear on the petal beneath it, borne aloft in a realm without thorns, soil, slugs, aphids, without death and decay. They are unbound by gravity, often clustered like celestial phenomena, a rose nebula, a rose galaxy, a rose supernova, sometimes garlanded with ribbons or rising out of sprays of smaller flowers.

They are the chintz and calico roses that became popular in 1984, when Ralph Lauren and other designers began using nostalgic floral prints in their clothing and houseware lines. A fashion writer at *The Washington Post* reported in March 1985, "Handing out the credit— or, if your taste does not tend toward oversized cabbage roses, the blame—is not a simple matter. Some think Ralph Lauren launched the current chintz blitz by using the material last year for both home furnishings and clothes." That's when they caught my eye and stirred a longing in me, a kind of desire to possess not just the roses or whatever pillowcase or jacket they were on but to taste what they seemed to promise: a certain kind of comfortableness, confidence, solidity, and rootedness that was inseparable from a particular kind of Anglophilia.

The roses promised more than themselves. They were covetable as living roses are not, because they would endure, while part of the beauty of flowers is their evanescence. They weren't the only kind of flower imagery that prompted my desire; in my youth, I craved the antique Chinese piano shawls whose peony petals were picked out in perfect satin stitch, and I could succumb to Hiroshige's famous plum blossoms, to the images on old American seed packets and some of the humble printed cottons that had been flour sacks remade into rural American clothing and quilts, but the roses that showed up in 1984 wafted in trailing distinct associations.

I don't know how we knew that these were not just about roses and flowers and fabric but about country houses and heritage and status, at a juncture in American history where a certain egalitarian ideal and confidence about the future was slipping away and the Reagans were in the White House modeling their own versions of upscale elitism for the few and dismantling the safety nets for the many. The aesthetic of the fabrics Lauren and others proffered was nostalgic, looking backward. The desire that arose in me for these floral fabrics was a gently nagging desire for something more and other than the items themselves, for some moment of arrival in a state of being and a realm for which they were only ornaments. They were tickets to a sort of complacent confidence that both allured and repulsed.

In wanting them I wanted more than them or something other than them, I wanted what they meant, and then I came to loathe that promise too. When I had the chance to acquire one of them, it seemed too fussy, too sentimental, too cloying to wear or own. These rose-strewn clothes and cushions and linens were like the sweets you both crave and are a little sickened by even before you bite into them. They beckoned from afar with promises about the place they belonged to, which was a place I never did or would. Perhaps their distance was in time: they beckoned from a never-never land of an idealized past, the past of the pastoral and paradise. But paradise is a walled garden, defined in part by what it shut out.

The word *nostalgia* comes from *nostos*, to return home, and *algia*, pain, grief, but the fabrics gave me a kind of longing to return to something that was never my home, nor my ancestors', and they must have done the same to Ralph Lauren, the Bronx-raised son of Jewish immigrants who started out in the 1960s with a line of men's ties under the name Polo and built a multibillion-dollar global empire selling clothing and furnishings, or rather selling a vision of crashing the gates to join the gentry by aping their costumes and decorations.

It is less that these things are authentically desirable than that our desires have been pruned and trained and cultivated so as to turn toward them the way a sunflower tilts to the sun, and the force of that desire is authentic even if its origin is manipulated. Lauren's advertisements were like stills from movies about flawlessly tall, lean, affluent, golden-white people eternally at leisure, always in poshly pleasant settings. One of his early coups was dressing Robert Redford for the film *The Great Gatsby*, itself about a parvenu among the moneyed elite, and his Safari line started in 1984 was said to have been influenced by the production of the 1985 film *Out of Africa*, which turned Danish aristocrat Isak Dinesen's story of her plantation life in Kenya into a series of tableaux of beautifully dressed beautiful imperialists (including Redford as the big-game-hunting son of an English earl) in beautiful settings, indoors and out.

His goods and visions were about the empire, but the empire was always about people seeming to dominate things that had overtaken and transformed them. Lauren made explicit what was implicit in these textile images: their ties to a particular sector, one that he had no qualms trying to enter or, rather, to reinvent with himself as at the center of an empire invoking safaris, polo, aristocracy, heritage, devaluing its putative essence by reinventing it as surface.

Polo was a Persian and Indian game before the British picked it up. Calico comes from the coastal Indian city of Calicut, from which Europeans exported spices as well as the light cotton fabric. The word *chintz* first appeared in English in seventeenth-century records of the East India Company and seems to come from a Hindi word meaning spray or sprinkle. Chintzes were made by elaborate processes of hand painting and woodblock printing on cotton, and the Indian technique had a huge impact in Europe as it came into fashion in the early eighteenth century. In that moment, the London-based novelist Daniel Defoe noted, "chints and painted calicoes, which before were only made use of for carpets, quilts etc., and to clothe children of ordinary people, become now the dress of our ladies."

The early patterns were distinctly Indian, with twining, sinuous plants whose blooms seemed idealized and abstracted, and with bold borders around each shape. Then an English industry adapting the Indian techniques arose, and chintz became an English thing. The ribbon-stripe chintz made by Richard Ovey in England in 1801 is not so far from the fabric of the Ralph Lauren floral smocks of 1984; fuchsias and other flowers mix with big roses in garlands entwined with pink-and-green striped ribbons, in an aesthetic more naturalistic than the Indian floral images with their clear margins and formal style. The contrasts were lower, the lines were softer, the edges less defined. By the mid-nineteenth century, exported fabrics—made with cotton imported from the slave plantations of the United States—had become a huge part of Britain's international trade.

Even the models for all those English chintz roses were likely new breeds crossed with the roses that came from China, roses that had, as most European roses did not at the time, the capacity to bloom and bloom for months rather than in one burst. The seventeenth-century poet Robert Herrick's famous lines "Gather ye rosebuds while ye may / Old time is still a-flying" are about the old varieties of roses that bloomed briefly in the spring. When roses came to bloom into the summer and autumn the sic transit gloria mundi/vanitas moral of European roses was undermined. Women were still urged to marry young, but roses bloomed on through the summer and beyond.

The rose geneticist Charles C. Hurst wrote in 1941, "The introduction of the China Rose to England towards the end of the eighteenth century caused a complete revolution in the garden Roses of Europe, America and the Near East. . . . The ancient Roses, for the most part, flowered only once a year, in the early summer, while the modern Roses bloom continuously from early summer to late autumn. In a favourable climate like the Riviera they may flower all the year round, since they are potentially perpetual. Recent research shows that this habit of continuous flowering is due to the action of a Mendelian recessive gene introduced into our modern Roses by the China and Tea Roses, already cultivated in China for a thousand years or more."

Four Chinese roses introduced to England between 1792 and 1824 came to be known as the China stud roses, as though they were racehorse studs, like the Arabian stallions who came over a century earlier and, bred to English mares, begat the Thoroughbred. Though the roses were Chinese and at least one was cultivated in Sweden before Britain, they were named after Englishmen: Slater's Crimson China, Parsons' Pink China, also known as Old Blush, Hume's Blush Tea-Scented China, and Parks' Yellow Tea-Scented China. The roses I had run into at Orwell's Wallington home, blooming in early November, were undoubtedly descended in part from these Chinese roses, as are nearly all garden roses now grown in the west.

When Princess Diana died and Elton John sang about her as "England's rose" and mountains of floral tributes piled up in front of the gates of Buckingham Palace, the roses people pictured and the ones they offered up were also probably partly Chinese, and the same is true of those propagated by David Austin, the famous rose breeder who died in 2018 after six decades of producing roses that had both the fragrance and old forms of earlier roses with the repeat flowerings of floribunda and hybrid tea roses. He called them all English roses and gave them English names drawn from literature, society, and history, including Ancient Mariner, the Wife of Bath, Thomas à Becket, and Emily Brontë, along with those of various aristocrats, horticulturalists, and Shakespeare characters from Falstaff to Perdita, and the Brooklyn-born pharmaceutical opioids profiteer Mortimer Sackler. It could be said on the one hand that Sackler would be better represented by a poppy, and on the other that peddling opiates was at the heart of the British Empire (and was Orwell's father's life work).

On my way to England to research this book, I looked at the snack menu on British Air, which included Jaffa cakes, soft cookies with a layer of marmalade capped by dark chocolate, and though I didn't order them there, just seeing them mentioned made me begin to crave them. I bought some in the airport shop. Then, coincidentally enough, the London Review of Books that I had brought with me had a piece about Jaffa—"It happens twice a year. The beach between Tel Aviv and Jaffa fills with Palestinians from the West Bank. For many children this is the only time they get to visit the seaside, even though their homes in the Occupied Territories may be no more than twenty or thirty kilometres away."

Later I drifted into Fortnum & Mason's vast food and upscale housewares emporium in central London on a hot August day and found it thronged with people who seemed to be foreigners buying up tea and biscuits in ornamental tins and other appurtenances of "Englishness," a thing that we recognized and desired, at least those of us crowded into the store. I wasn't sure if the act of acquiring was one of submission or conquest or a nebulous mixture of both, and I too bought some tea and went to a similarly thronged Liberty of London and bought some floral fabric.

Britain—the mythical place bathed in an afterglow of empire, not the conflicted contemporary actuality—seemed to be a place in which all of us, even me growing up in California, had received too much instruction, and also a collage of innumerable pieces of elsewhere. It was the person in the room you were supposed to pay attention to and know all about, the one who was supposed to define what mattered and how things should be. When I got older and learned more about class and imperialism and the British-ruled Ireland my mother's grandparents fled, I didn't exactly get over Anglophilia but I did get a dose of Anglophobia to counter it. But anything I felt was nothing compared to what Jamaica Kincaid did, and wrote of with such vehement eloquence.

# FIVE

# Flowers of Evil

Kincaid, who grew up in Antigua, when the small Caribbean island was still a British possession, speaks as if all that was unspoken in that genteel Britain had gathered to form a voice of tremendous force. She wrote, "I cannot tell you how angry it makes me to hear people from North America tell me how much they love England, how beautiful England is, with its traditions. All they see is some frumpy, wrinkled-up person passing by in a carriage waving at a crowd. But what I see is the millions of people, of whom I am just one, made orphans: no motherland, no fatherland, no gods, no mounds of earth for holy ground, no excess of love which might lead to the things that an excess of love sometimes brings, and worst and most painful of all, no tongue."

That is, in place of a mother tongue of her own, she had the English language, though she made of it a prose style all her own, proceeding with sentences made up of fury and precision, relying as much as possible on rhythmic repetitions and words of few syllables. Her sentences twist, spiral, cover ground, mounting up into complex arguments about flowers, gardens, nature, racism, colonialism, and rage. She wrote like no one else as an avid and expert gardener with a genuine love of plants and aesthetics and a scathing perspective on all the issues that garden walls do not shut out.

She had come to New York as a young woman in the late 1960s, worked as a nanny, been so wittily outspoken that she caught the ear of a man who brought her to *The New Yorker*, where she became a staff writer. The magazine's house style was that of white men such as E. B. White and John McPhee, who wrote in a spare, brisk voice that was supposed to be an apex of clarity and literary goodness, a style that seemed to imply that whatever the writer said was what all reasonable people would agree with, that their particular orientation was a universal one, and that common sense was both a highest good and a settled matter.

Kincaid also wrote in a style that was clear and direct, but she was aware that many people did not agree with her, notably many white people. Sentences such as "Almost as if ashamed of the revulsion and hostility they have for foreign people, the English make up for it by loving and embracing foreign plants wholesale" are brisk declarations of war, or rather recognitions of old wars in many forms, including botany, gardens, names, and ideas of the beautiful and the just. Wars against her, among others. She didn't spare Americans: "The great Abraham Lincoln, a president I am so deeply attached to I grow roses named in his honor in my garden, was a racist but he abhorred slavery and that's good enough for me, being that I am most blessedly descended from the enslaved."

She eventually settled in Vermont, though she regularly announced how much she hated snow and cold and winter. There she planted an ambitious garden, and she often wrote about it, and about ordering plants for it and losing herself in garden catalogues. She could describe the pure pleasure of gardens and plants in detail and the nature of the emotions, desires, and moods they stirred, of sitting admiring a flowerbed she'd made, of which roses she considered hideous and which exquisite.

But her recurrent theme when she wrote of plants and gardens was displacement, people uprooted, culture imposed, plants transplanted and transformed, pasts forgotten and invented, old names taken away and new ones stuck on arbitrarily. She wrote, "I do not know the names of the plants in the place I am from. . . . This ignorance of the botany of the place I am from (and am of) really only reflects the fact that when I lived there, I was of the conquered class and living in a conquered place; a principle of this condition is that nothing about you is of any interest unless the conquerer deems it so. For instance there was a botanical garden . . . but as I remember, none of the plants were native to Antigua."

Colonialism meant knowing too much about the colonizers and their place, too little about one's own people and their places. She wrote in that essay, titled "Flowers of Evil," about the floating gardens of the valley of Mexico—what is now Mexico City—and about Cortez's invasion and the cocoxochitl plant that came back to Europe and was named after a Mr. Dahl of Sweden and hybridized into innumerable showy varieties of dahlia, its origins forgotten. Elsewhere, she wrote most ferociously of all about daffodils.

In her 1990 novel, *Lucy*, the title character is, as she was, a young immigrant from the Caribbean, working as a nanny for a woman whose blithe obliviousness about their differences and penchant for blurring the employer/employee relationship annoy her. The conflict only one of them is aware of reaches its climax when the employer makes her go admire the daffodils coming out in early spring in the wintry Northeast of the United States. Lucy recalls being obliged, while at

Queen Victoria Girls' School in her colonized island, to memorize Wordsworth's poem about daffodils, recounts a nightmare about these flowers she had never seen, in which they obliterate her, and then relates, "I had forgotten all of this until Mariah mentioned daffodils, and now I told it to her with such an amount of anger I surprised both of us." And then they come upon the daffodils in the park: "I did not know what these flowers were, and so it was a mystery to me why I wanted to kill them." Or not, since they had tried to kill her.

A few years later Kincaid declared again, "I do not like daffodils, but that's a legacy of the English approach: I was forced to memorize the poem by William Wordsworth when I was a child." And then she came back to them again: "In my child's mind's eye, the poem and its contents (though not its author) and the people through whom it came were repulsive. . . . And so for me, 'I Wandered Lonely as a Cloud' became not an individual vision coolly astonishing the mind's eye but the tyrannical order of a people, the British people, in my child's life."

She wrote that last bit when she had planted 2,000 daffodil bulbs to go with the 3,500 she had already planted. Perhaps she had reached the point at which the meanings imposed on her could be countered by the meanings she imposed herself. Plants are malleable in many ways. They grow, evolve, adapt, decay; they also take on meanings we ascribe to them, from Christmas trees to victory wreaths, spiritual lotuses to erotic orchids. Daffodils and the English language meant different things to someone born to them. Orwell's diary for March 13, 1940, notes, "As a result of the frost all kinds of cabbages, except a few Brussels sprouts, are completely destroyed. The spring cabbages have not only died but entirely disappeared, no doubt eaten off by the birds. The leeks have survived, though rather sorry for themselves. . . . All the rose cuttings have survived except one. Snowdrops are out & some yellow crocuses, a few polyanthi trying to flower, tulips & daffodils showing, rhubarb just sprouting, ditto peonies, black currants budding, red currants not, gooseberries budding."

In planting that garden in Wallington, in planting roses in the garden, Orwell was rooting himself in a particular soil, and also in ideas and traditions and lineages that whether he loathed them or not were his and were all around him. Or perhaps in his downwardly mobile choices and his production of a significant portion of his own food by the sweat of his own brow, and his grazing of his goats upon the village common, he was trying to step out of them. They were not entirely escapable, and even the form that escape took was full of deeply rooted ideas about rural idylls and the pastoral ideal. Nor was he oblivious to those influences.

That year he planted the roses, he wrote, "In order that England may live in comparative comfort, a hundred million Indians must live on the verge of starvation—an evil state of affairs, but you acquiesce in it every time you step into a taxi or eat a plate of strawberries and cream." Though strawberries and cream, unlike tea with sugar, were actually homegrown offerings. But a decade later he returned to the subject, saying to his fellow Britons, "You have got to choose between liberating India and having extra sugar. Which do you prefer?"

# VI

# The Price of Roses

*Rose production near Bogotá, Colombia, 2019.*

# ONE

# Beauty Problems

The man who planted roses in 1936 wrote about flowers often. In his novels set in England he scattered descriptions of flowers amid the meadows, ponds, lanes, and other rustic backdrops (and descriptions of tropical flowers, as well as temperate-zone flowers gone gigantic, were scattered through *Burmese Days*). In his diaries, there were lists of flowers to buy, reports on the cultivation of domestic flowers, and mentions of wildflowers spotted. In one of his *Tribune* essays in 1944, he deplored "the rapid disappearance of English flower names. . . . Forget-me-nots are coming more and more to be called myosotis. Many other names, red-hot poker, mind-your-own-business, love-lies-bleeding, London pride, are disappearing in favor of colourless Greek names out of botany textbooks." He felt so strongly about these flower names that he made the same complaint all over again two years later, in one of his best-known essays, "Politics and the English Language."

Five years after he planted those roses in Wallington, he declared in his wartime essay "The Lion and the Unicorn: Socialism and the English Genius" that "a minor English trait which is extremely well marked though not often commented on . . . is a love of flowers. This is one of the first things that one notices when one reaches England from abroad, especially if one is coming from southern Europe. Does it not contradict the English indifference to the arts? Not really, because it is found in people who have no aesthetic feelings whatever." And then he went on to classify flowers among hobbies, and hobbies among the characteristics of people who valued liberty and private life, but he had opened a door for a room he hadn't gone into, or perhaps a door onto something larger than a room. If you do go through this door marked aesthetics and Orwell, you wander toward the very center of his life's pursuits.

The door cracks open a little. What about those with a love of flowers but no aesthetic feelings whatsoever? In this passage, Orwell declares the love of flowers is not necessarily aesthetic, if aesthetic means purely visual pleasure. Does it? He describes the growing of flowers as a hobby and lists as other examples of English hobbyists "stamp-collectors, pigeon-fanciers, amateur carpenters, coupon-snippers, darts-players, crossword-puzzle fans," activities of wildly varying utility and antiquity. But the love of flowers extends beyond those who garden, and so for some flowers are a thing to produce and tend, for others they are something to enjoy in meadows or gardens or vases without other action. What is it that they love when they love flowers?

Flowers are of course deployed to mean erotic, romantic, ceremonial, and spiritual things, as garlands draped across altars and hung around the necks of winning racehorses, and all the rest. But before a flower is used to do something else, to honor a human occasion, it is in itself an occasion for attention. We say that flowers are beautiful, but what we mean by the beauty of a flower is something more than appearance, which is why real flowers are so much more beautiful than artificial flowers (but perhaps images of flowers reference the real and all its resonances as imitation flowers do not). That beauty lies in part in what it references or connects to, as life and growth incarnate, as the annunciation of the fruit to follow. A flower is a node on a network of botanical systems of interconnection and regeneration. The visible flower is a marker of these complex systems, and some of the beauty attributed to the flower as an autonomous object may really be about the flower as a part of a larger whole.

I have often thought that much of the beauty that moves us in the natural world is not the static visual splendor that can be captured in a picture, but time itself as patterns, recurrences, the rhythmic passage of days and seasons and years, the lunar cycle and the tides, birth and death. As harmony, organization, coherence, pattern itself is a kind of beauty, and some of the psychic distress of climate change and environmental disruption is in the shattering of this rhythm. The order that matters most is not spatial but temporal. Sometimes pictures convey this, but the habit of seeing in pictures encourages us to lose sight of the dance. Indigenous people who were sometimes despised for not appreciating nature in the English rustic tradition often appreciated it as orderly patterns in time, not as static pictorial pleasure. That is, they might be more inclined to celebrate, for example, key moments in the temporal march of the sun through the year than an exceptionally pretty sunset.

In the introduction to the thick Everyman's edition of Orwell's *Collected Essays*, John Carey declares, "He almost never praises beauty and when he does he locates it in rather scruffy and overlooked things . . . the eye of the common toad, a sixpenny rosebush from Woolworth's." I'd argue that he praises beauty often, and those overlooked things become means of broadening the definition of beauty, finding versions that are not elite or established, finding loveliness in the quotidian, the plebeian, the neglected. That quest makes beauty itself insubordinate to convention. Even *Nineteen Eighty-Four*'s grimness is peppered with moments of reprieve in the things his lonely rebel admires, craves, enjoys, most notably an ordinary landscape and a glass paperweight encasing a bit of red coral.

Winston Smith calls the paperweight he finds in a junk shop a beautiful thing, and it becomes significant in the narrative. We are told, "It was a queer thing, even a compromising thing, for a Party member to have in his possession. Anything old, and for that matter anything beautiful, was always vaguely suspect." Suspect as a sign of the consciousness and pleasure the party sought to eradicate, as the experience Orwell praises in "The Lion and the Unicorn" when he describes hobbies as a private activity that totalitarianism seeks to starve. That essay opens with the famous line "As I write, highly civilized human beings are flying overhead, trying to kill me." Like a searchlight, the context casts his concerns in dramatic light and shadow; that context is always present in his work. The paperweight exists in the context of the Thought Police; the hobbies and questions about beauty exist in the context of the Blitz.

The word *beauty* is one of those overly roomy words, frayed around the edges, ignored through overfamiliarity, often used to mean purely visual beauty. But the kinds of beauty that the *Oxford English Dictionary* enumerates include many that are not visual, including "that quality of a person or thing which is highly pleasing or satisfying to the mind; moral or intellectual excellence," an admirable person, an impressive or exceptionally good example of something.

In her book *On Beauty and Being Just*, the scholar Elaine Scarry notes that among the complaints about beauty is that contemplation of it is passive—"looking or hearing without any wish to change what one has seen or heard." It's a definition startling in its simplicity. What one does not wish to change can be the desirable condition realized, and it's where aesthetic and ethical standards meet. She contrasts that with "looking or hearing that is prelude to intervening in, changing, what one has seen or heard (as happens in the presence of injustice)." Those obsessed with productivity and injustice often disparage doing nothing, though by *doing nothing* we usually mean a lot of subtle actions and observations and cultivation of relationships that are doing many kinds of something. It's a doing something whose value and results are not so easily quantified or commodified, and you could even argue that any or every evasion of quantifiability and commodifiability is a victory against assembly lines, authorities, and oversimplifications. It is perhaps not a coincidence that Jenny Odell's book *How to Do Nothing: Resisting the Attention Economy* begins in a public rose garden in Oakland, California.

"Looking or hearing without any wish to change what one has seen or heard." Perhaps Orwell's domestic diaries are accounts of this; their brief narratives of working and growing and minor events don't involve much desire for things to be other than what they are. Narratives—fiction, myth, fairy tale, journalism—tend to be about what happens when something goes wrong: the politician is corrupt, the river is polluted, the workers are exploited, the beloved has been lost. Even the most sedate children's books have their mild crises of loss, misunderstanding, and missed connection to explore. What exists "without any wish to change" is static; it's before the story begins, before the fall from grace, or after it is concluded with reunion, rectification, or some other form of repair. But every account of what has gone wrong contains at least implicitly, as a value and a goal, what it would mean if things had gone right. And the narrative is often driven by the desire to defend and restore the just, the fair, the good.

The tension exists even in nonnarrative art. The artist Zoe Leonard was bashful about making beautiful images during the AIDS crisis and said so to fellow artist and activist David Wojnarowicz, who replied, "Zoe, these are so beautiful, and that's what we're fighting for. We're being angry and complaining because we have to, but where we want to go is back to beauty. If you let go of that, we don't have anywhere to go." So beauty can be both what one does not wish to change and where one wishes to go, the compass or rather North Star for change. Leonard reflects on their interchange: "You know, we were all just too busy for beauty. We were too angry for beauty. We were too heartbroken for beauty. I felt like an asshole with these picture[s] of clouds, but David was right. You go through all of the fighting not because you want to fight, but because you want to get somewhere as a people. You want to help create a world where you can sit around and think about clouds. That should be our right as human beings." You could argue that if we go too long without sitting around and thinking about clouds we might forget how to do so or why, that we could so shrivel en route we'd be unable to reach that destination.

The woman who wrote in to upbraid Orwell for talking about roses seemed to think that paying attention to that which does not need to be changed is idleness, dissipation, and distraction. Those focused on injustice, on those things that the more we contemplate them the more we want to change them, tend to think of contemplation of what we don't want to change as akin to shirking one's duty or dodging awareness of what we do want to change. I've talked about it as, instead, regeneration of the energy to face destruction, but Scarry suggests it might also matter as a study of the templates of the desirable and the good. What is the goal of social change or political engagement? Can studying what good already exists or has existed be part of the work? There is, of course, a meaningful difference between the dour (and widespread) position that we are forever starting from scratch because everything is contaminated or corrupt and the position that the good exists as a kind of seed that needs to be tended more energetically or propagated more widely.

# Two

# In the Rose Factory

As the airplane descended I could see the greenhouses already, glowing like enormous lanterns across the Colombian savanna in a pitch-black night. They were what I had come to see, though there was no guarantee I could get into one; many had tried to enter and failed, and they were usually shrouded in secrecy. What came from them everyone saw as it poured into the United States; how it was produced was the secret. We landed at the airport in Bogotá, and my companion, Nate Miller, found us a taxi. It took us through the outskirts of the great sprawl of that city and through miles of boulevards lined with concrete buildings.

Like other Latin American cities I'd visited, Bogotá felt both monumental and flimsy, majestic and precarious. The city's architecture seemed improvisational. Buildings of various styles and solidity jostled one another on the avenues, heavily armed policemen stood on street corners, and security guards also bearing automatic weapons glowered at the entrance to businesses and restaurants. Walls were topped with razor wire, windows had iron grilles over them, doors had many locks apiece.

The taxi driver let us off on a cobblestone street that sloped uphill toward what I'd see in the morning were the steep green mountains hemming in the city's eastern edge. We arrived so late at night I cannot remember how we came by the key to the flat we had rented for a week from the uncle of one of Nate's friends. I went to sleep in a bedroom with whitewashed plaster walls, twelve-foot ceilings, and a massive wooden bed made up with worn and dirty sheets and a pile of grubby blankets, near a window with two layers of wooden shutters with immense iron bolts inside the window onto the street that had, additionally, an iron grille outside it.

We went out in the morning for coffee, and in the daylight I got a better look at the handsome old Candelaria district we were staying in and saw, as well, the deep poverty of the people in the street tending tiny snack stands, sometimes just a few handfuls of pastries or sweets from which the profit must have been infinitesimal. Later, we'd see men opening up their hands to show raw emeralds dug from the Colombian earth and bargaining with other men at the emerald trading corner; craftswomen sitting on the ground displaying traditional beaded necklaces on blankets spread out before them; an old woman dancing to a small music player, walking with grave dignity the steps of a dance as though she was utterly alone in a somber world, but with a hat out for money.

Nate had grown up in San Francisco and after college taken a job with an international labor-rights group in Colombia, where organizing for and joining unions can be dangerous and where an American was an eyewitness less likely to be killed himself and maybe able to prevent others from being killed. He had rounded out his time there with an investigation of labor conditions in the flower industry that culminated in a substantial report released in the United States. He had come to love the country and its people and formed strong friendships, and it wasn't hard to convince him to spend an extra week taking me around Bogotá's flower-growing outskirts before he went off to see his godson and namesake on the coast.

He left his union-organizer job in New York to board a flight that would bring him to the same Texas airport that my flight out of San Francisco did, so we could fly to Colombia together. Nate, whom I've known since the end of his teens, is idealistic, enthusiastic, gregarious, tall, thin, with curly hair shorn short on the sides, glasses that make him a little owlish, skin so brown that he is often taken for some other race than white. Between that and his fluent Colombian-accented Spanish, he would blend in everywhere we went, while I with my pallor and lack of all but the most primitive Spanish would stand out.

That first morning, he found us a bus, one of the unofficial small buses that the poor ride around Bogotá and beyond, and we went off to the flower-growing periphery of the city. People poured on and off the crowded bus. The driver stopped at various checkpoints to hand other men some money. We passed construction workers in bright blue with neon green safety vests napping on the verdant meridians of boulevards and vendors of luridly colored roses hawking their wares and washers of windshields darting in and out of traffic at every stop. Stray dogs wandered through this bustle, universally ignored.

Reaching the countryside meant reaching the greenhouses, the kind I'd seen glowing as we landed the night before. They were huge, each the size of a sports field, with walls and roofs of clear plastic sheeting grown dusty and opaque with time, not standing alone but in formations of a dozen or a score at a time. Most were partly hidden behind hedges and walls, and guards stood at the gates. Through the still-clear bits you could see flowers. The weather of the savanna around Bogotá, several thousand feet above sea level and only three hundred miles north of the equator, is mild and constant, and the equatorial year-round twelve hours of daylight mean that the growing season never ends.

Decades ago, the flower industry in Colombia was promoted as the replacement for another agricultural export crop, coca leaves, and the cocaine made from them. The substitution was a failure—coca cultivation continues in remoter places—but a vast flower industry with its own problems has grown up in Colombia, which raises 80 percent of the roses sold in the United States, along with many other kinds of flowers for export. The first air shipment of flowers for the United States took off in 1965; by the time Nate wrote his report, the country was the world's second largest exporter of flowers, and the industry, which employs about 130,000 Colombians, was the leading source of jobs for women in the country. A similar industry in Kenya and Ethiopia supplies the European flower market.

Nate mentioned, as we walked through a small town and caught another bus that dropped us off on a highway lined by plastic greenhouses for miles, that most of the workers had been independent farmers a generation ago. A process analogous to the British enclosures of the eighteenth and nineteenth centuries had made many of them landless workers in industrialized agriculture. Here and there in the countryside, we saw small farms with cows and patches of various crops being grown, but the flower industry and its greenhouses made a sort of plastic ring around Bogotá, from whose airport most of the harvest left.

I had emailed the Rainforest Alliance, which was supposed to certify that flowers were grown to high environmental and labor standards, and somehow, just before we left, they had arranged for us to visit one of the farms, but this was so startling a development that we didn't quite believe it would happen. In his years of research Nate had never gotten inside, and neither had a Bogotá cinematographer I met later, and not for lack of trying. In my email, I had said I was writing a book about roses and mentioned I was traveling with a companion, and they presumably hadn't looked me up, which might have set off a small alarm, or asked my companion's name, which would've set off large alarms. So on that first day we wandered around the highway lined with greenhouses and asked at a few of them if we could just take a peek, to no avail, and we caught a taxi to some other of the farms and tried them too, with the same result.

The next day we took a rough little taxi to the home of an employee from the Rainforest Alliance. He lived in a beautiful building high on the eastern rim of the city, and his luxurious hired car and driver took the three of us along the elevated periphery of tall trees and wealthy homes to the US-owned Sunshine Bouquet Company. Even before we pulled up at the well-guarded, hedge-shrouded entrance to Sunshine Bouquet's rose farm, or rose factory, it was clear to us that Nate knew a lot more about the industry than he did, though we didn't inform him of that. He was a well-dressed man with excellent English he dispensed as pleasantries and business platitudes, and if I'm not mistaken, he had never been to a rose farm either.

We were escorted to a sort of boardroom from which you could see a lunchroom with workers already in it—most start work very early in the morning—and told a few things that confirmed that the managers here were proud of their enterprise and somehow thought that we would be impressed. We were then sent off with a boss and two upper-ranking workers named Carolina and José, each wearing the same kind of coveralls as most of the other workers, inscribed with slogans across the back.

Hers said,

> *Cuando se trabaja en equipo,*
> *el éxito y los triunfos de se celebran equipo*
> [When you work as a team,
> you celebrate success and triumph as a team]

His said,

> *El esfuerzo y la pasión satisface nuestra labor*
> [Effort and passion make us feel satisfied in our work]

These slogans appeared on the backs of other workers' uniforms, as did some other slogans:

> *Sunshine bouquet, el mejor lugar para ser feliz*
> [Sunshine Bouquet, the best place to be happy]
> *Queremos crecer junto contigo*
> [We want to grow together with you]
> *La actitud depende de ti.*
> *Lo demás queremos que lo aprendas aquí.*
> [The attitude depends on you.
> The rest we want you to learn here.]

The slogans were in that genre often called Orwellian, which is to say they were ominous in their insincerity and unsettling in their contradictions and their imposition on workers who seemed unlikely to agree wholeheartedly with them or to be wearing them by choice. But it wasn't coveralls I'd come to see. It was roses and the labor that produced those roses. And soon enough we were in one of the dozens of greenhouses. Each such structure consisted of metal scaffolding with huge sheets of plastic attached to it, designed so that the sheets could in warm weather be opened up for ventilation and shut tight in cooler weather.

We entered the greenhouse from a door at the center and found ourselves on a broad path to the opposite door. This was flanked on either side by rosebushes taller than my head stretching in rows to the far walls, each plant so close to the next that they made up a dense hedge in which individual plants were not readily distinguishable, each row so close to the next that anyone passing between them, as we soon did, had to sidle. The thorns were never far away. Strands of twine stretched from wooden posts held the stems in place, and there was a sense of crowding, of compression, of repetition, and almost of confusion from so many roses in so many rows stretching so far that vanishing point perspective came in and you could see roses and poles and support beams getting smaller and smaller in the distance that was still inside the plastic greenhouse.

They get 104 roses per year from each square meter, our guides told me. Along the central aisle stood narrow carts in which the cut roses were laid in orderly stacks. The flowers in each planted row were all the same color, in various stages of openness, and the name of each variety was at the head of the row. Iron Pink. Constellation. Billabonga. Privilege. Pink Floyd. Pop Star. Icon. Billionaire. Halloween. Rejected roses and trimmings were piled up in bins.

They were nearly all varieties of hybrid tea rose, and their lines were sharper and straighter than old-fashioned roses. The closed flowers came to a sharp point, a few petals peeling crisply away from the bud, folding back to form straight lines and more sharp points.

The old-fashioned roses' incurving petals are often rounder, gentler, and they achieve their full expression when the flower is open. They look demure, while modern roses often look brash, as if an introverted flower became extroverted. Most commercial roses won't ever open fully and they're marketed as buds, a sort of pointed pellet of tight-packed petals at the end of a long stem, a dozen of them looking a little like a quiver of gaudy arrows.

The workers have a slogan, "The lovers get the roses, but we workers get the thorns." A rose is beautiful, but a greenhouse with thousands upon thousands of roses, a place producing millions per year, with stems and leaves and petals all strewn on the floor and heaped together in bins as byproduct, was not. Insofar as these roses were beautiful, their beauty was meant to occur somewhere else, for someone else, a continent away. Some of them were grown in paper bags to protect the petals from light, and we saw a row of rosebushes whose stems culminated in brown sacks, like divas backstage with their hair in curlers.

From this complex, we were told, as we paced and stopped and inspected and listened, they sent six million roses to the United States for Valentine's Day and another six million for Mother's Day. Across the Colombian flower industry, those two holidays translate into enormous pressure on workers, longer hours, and exhaustion. But the shipments go out almost daily year-round. Refrigerator trucks carrying four hundred boxes of roses apiece race from the Sunshine Bouquet site to the airport, where they're loaded onto 747 airplanes and flown to Miami for distribution across the United States by more trucks. Each box, they told us, holds 330 roses, and one 747 can hold 5,000 boxes, or 1.65 million roses. The idea of an immense airplane whose sole freight was roses burning its carbon and rushing high over the Caribbean to deliver its burden to people who would never know of all that lay behind the roses they picked up in the supermarket was maybe as perfect an emblem of alienation as you could find. Could roses be more uprooted? "It is only very rarely, when I make a definite mental effort, that I connect this coal with that far-off labour in the mines," Orwell had written of the stuff he burned at home, and it was even more rarely that anyone connected the roses to the toil in these greenhouses. They were the invisible factories of visual pleasure.

# THREE

# The Crystal Spirit

Long ago, I got into an argument with some other writers over the question of what constitutes a good book. One of them was smitten with a book that was a gracefully written and cleverly structured narrative, and others got on board with the idea that these grounds were enough. It did have formal graces, and to my eyes it was also a book whose derogatory and distorted representation of a marginalized group and general cruelty made it at least as ugly as it was beautiful. Orwell had noted in his essay on Jonathan Swift, "It is true that the literary quality of a book is to some small extent separable from its subject-matter. Some people have a native gift for using words, as some people have a naturally 'good eye' at games. It is largely a question of timing and of instinctively knowing how much emphasis to use."

The book the others lauded manipulated its material and misled its readers in ways that violated journalists' and historians' standards. This corruption of the source material seemed to prioritize the author's art making over any obligation to the people it was about, or to the people who might read it with a desire to know the world better, or to the historical record, as if the lives of others were raw material with which writers could do what they liked. I've always considered it a challenge as well as an obligation to work within the facts and believe a nonfiction writer can find the necessary latitude without twisting and distorting them.

None of the others seemed to share my sense that this was not a set of ethical issues separate from an aesthetic success but part of the work of art's aesthetics. Beauty is not only formal, and it lies not only in the superficial qualities that are appealing to the eye or ear; it lies in patterns of meaning, in invocations of values, and in connection to the life the reader is living and the world she wants to see. A dancer's gesture may be beautiful because it is a precisely executed move by a highly skilled artist-athlete, but even a gracefully executed kick of a child is ugly. The meaning subverts the form, and elegance of form is always capable of being corrupted by what meaning it delivers. "The first thing that we demand of a wall is that it shall stand up," Orwell wrote in his critique of the painter Salvador Dalí. "If it stands up, it is a good wall, and the question of what purpose it serves is separable from that. And yet even the best wall in the world deserves to be pulled down if it surrounds a concentration camp." Form cannot be separated from function. And the beauty—or the hideousness—can be in meaning, impact, implications, rather than appearance.

The lone dissident near Tiananmen Square in Beijing who on June 5, 1989, stood in front of a long row of tanks to stop them from crushing the student uprising was a slight, nondescript figure in a white shirt and black trousers with droopy plastic shopping bags in each hand. While facing the tanks, he swung one arm, stiff-armed, awkwardly, and scuttled to stay in front of the lead tank. But dangerous confrontation with far superior power epitomizes what we mean by a beautiful gesture. He was apparently willing to risk everything on behalf of an ideal and a group of idealists. The word *integrity* means moral consistency and commitment, but it also means something whole and unbroken, uninjured, and it's a quality found in many beautiful things. The book I loathed broke faith and broke fellowship.

Orwell was passionate about the beauty of gestures and intentions, ideals and idealism when he encountered them, and it was to defend them that he spent much of his life facing their opposites. A passage in *Homage to Catalonia* describes one of his most vivid encounters with such things: "In the Lenin Barracks in Barcelona, the day before I joined the militia, I saw an Italian militiaman standing in front of the officers' table. He was a tough-looking youth of twenty-five or six. . . . Something in his face deeply moved me. . . . With his shabby uniform and fierce pathetic face he typifies for me the special atmosphere of that time."

And then he describes how the whole city had something of that spirit: "Waiters and shop-walkers looked you in the face and treated you as an equal. Servile and even ceremonial forms of speech had temporarily disappeared. . . . Down the Ramblas, the wide central artery of the town where crowds of people streamed constantly to and fro, the loudspeakers were bellowing revolutionary songs all day and far into the night. And it was the aspect of the crowds that was the queerest thing of all. . . . There was much in it that I did not understand, in some ways I did not even like it, but I recognized it immediately as a state of affairs worth fighting for."

Years later, he still remembered that soldier and wrote a poem about him that presumed the young soldier was dead, forgotten, buried under lie upon lie. But he concluded:

*But the thing that I saw in your face*
*No power can disinherit:*

*No bomb that ever burst*
*Shatters the crystal spirit.*

These qualities—you could call them heroic or noble or idealistic—
were the beauty he found in Spain, along with the hideousness of a
corrupted war, the stench, privation, and chaos of the trenches, and the
impact of almost dying of a gunshot wound, then being hunted like a
rabbit. In the poem, lies are themselves murderous, smothering,
though something survives beyond death. The coexistence of opposites
and their clash occurs often in Orwell's work, generating the tensions
he explores, hedgehogs and prophets, lilacs and Nazis, toads and atom
bombs, beautiful old books and memory holes.

They are the parties to the conflicts that absorbed him, and sometimes the one is the counterweight to the ominous ugliness of the
other. In 1941, leaving London during the Blitz, a day after visiting
the underground bomb shelters in the subways and a church crypt, he
wrote, "At Wallington. Crocuses out everywhere, a few wallflowers
budding, snowdrops just at their best. Couples of hares sitting about
in the winter wheat and gazing at one another. Now and again in this
war, at intervals of months, you get your nose above water for a few
moments and notice that the earth is still going round the sun."

From the same root as *integrity* comes the word *disintegration*, literally the loss of the integrity that holds things together, and the
Spanish Civil War could be, as the poem implies, thought of as a long
assault on many kinds of integrity. There's a peaceful disintegration
familiar to gardeners, the transmutation of the no-longer living into
food for new life, and then there's forced and violent disintegration.
Nuclear explosions on film, for example, unfolding like some monstrous time-lapse bloom, and forest fires have moments of sublimity:

there is often beauty of a sort in violence and destruction. Nine years after he led the Manhattan Project to develop the first atom bombs, including the ones dropped on Japan in 1945, the physicist J. Robert Oppenheimer was asked, as part of an interrogation to see whether he had communist sympathies, if he objected on moral grounds to development of the far more powerful hydrogen bomb. His answer echoed Orwell's comment about walls: "Even if from a technical point of view it was a sweet and lovely and beautiful job, I have still thought it was a dreadful weapon."

The contemporary world is full of things that look beautiful and are produced through hideous means. People die so that this mine may profit, that these shoes may be produced as cheaply as possible, that that refinery may spew these toxic fumes in the course of producing its petroleum. I have often thought about this disconnection as a lack of integrity that's pervasive in modern life.

Once, the trees from which wood came, the fields from which grain came, the springs, river, well, or rain from which drinking water came would have been familiar; every object would appear out of somewhere, from someone or something known to the user, and producers and consumers would be the same people or people who knew one another. Industrialization, urbanization, and transnational markets created a world where water poured out of faucets, food and clothing appeared in stores, fuel (in our time if not in Orwell's with the coal chutes and sooty air) was largely invisible, and the work that held all this together was often done by people who were themselves invisible. There were undeniable benefits—a more stimulating and various material and mental life—but they came at a cost.

The places, plants, animals, materials, and objects that had once been as well-known as friends and family had become strangers, as had the people who worked with these materials. Things appeared from beyond the horizon, from beyond knowing, and knowing was an act of volition instead of a part of everyday life. Orwell had taken up that act of volition when he went to England's north to see the coal industry and the poverty of the region that kept the country running, when he talked about the exploitation of India to produce England's living standards. Edward Said's critique of *Mansfield Park* is not just that it is all propped up by slave labor but that this knowledge is avoided, in Jane Austen's society as well as in her novel and its characters. They do not know who and what they are, and their ignorance is an ugly attempt to cover up ugliness.

I came of age in the 1980s, when a number of progressive campaigns were designed specifically to make visible what had been invisible, as a means to make both producers and consumers more accountable. Activists tried to make audiences imagine and understand their connections to distant sweatshops and rainforests, to apartheid in South Africa, nuclear testing in the Nevada and Kazakhstan deserts and nuclear weapons stationed in Germany, clearcutting in North America's Pacific Coast old-growth forests and the Amazon rainforest, and dirty wars and death squads the US government supported in Central America. Distance was a form of invisibility when it came to how things were made, though exploitation can happen in local agriculture or the back of a restaurant. This activism urged us to integrate this knowledge of the conditions of production into what we saw when we looked at the results. It was, in a way, an attempt to regain what had been lost, to strenuously rebuild the knowledge that had once been built into everyday life.

With roses the contradictions are particularly pointed. Roses are supposed to be emblems of love, romance, a gift given to convey affection or adoration, and they often carry a sense of lightness, of pleasure and joy, of leisure and abundance of the kind a flower garden is supposed to convey. "Say it with flowers" was a widely used florists' advertising slogan, and flowers were only supposed to say tender, loving things. In Virginia Woolf's novel *Mrs. Dalloway*, Mr. Dalloway buys great bunches of red and white roses for his wife as a means of saying "I love you" when he is reticent about saying those words aloud.

When we give them to each other we intend to hand each other not only a dozen roses but the associations that come with them. What do we hand each other when historic meaning and current reality are in open conflict? A rose worker had told Nate, "Today, a flower is not produced with sweetness but with tears. Our product is used to express beautiful feelings throughout the world, but we are treated very poorly." I don't know how I'd learned long ago that the conditions that produced the roses for sale in supermarkets and florists were disturbing, but they had made these roses, for me, items where the tension between what something looks like and what it means as a product of labor and industry was particularly strong.

# FOUR

# The Ugliness of Roses

How many aspects of a thing can you strip away before it ceases to be what it is called; when does something cease to be itself and become something else; when does meaning fall apart or definition stretch until it shreds? Later in my tour of the rose farm I was taken into a long room in which hundreds of bouquets of roses of all colors in glass cylinders were lined up on long steel tables. They were being tested for longevity and their names were written on labels in front of each bouquet, like place cards at a formal dinner. Sophie, Mandala, Titanic, Tibet (a white rose), Escimo (another white rose), Bikini, Freedom, Porvenir, Priceless, Lady Night, Diplomat, Light Orlando, Malibu, Classic Cézanne, Confidential, Mother of Pearl. Their mostly English names were further reminders that they were destined to travel.

What was startling was what was not there. There was almost no smell from the thousands of roses in the low-ceilinged room. Scent is a kind of voice, a way in which flowers speak—"caresses floating in the air," the poet Rainer Maria Rilke called it. Say it with flowers; these were mute. We did encounter one fragrant row of yellow roses in the greenhouse, but these flowers were bred for appearance and durability, the two things that made them profitable (and though roses are often thought of as fragile, they are tough flowers compared to many so delicate and short-lived they could not be mass-produced and shipped internationally). Scent wasn't bred out on purpose but it wasn't sought out, either.

The old celebration of roses is as much about what meets the nose as the eye. Shakespeare declared, "The rose looks fair, but fairer we it deem / For that sweet odour which doth in it live." There are vernacular expressions about scent too—stop and smell the roses, come out smelling like a rose. The premise of all these is that roses smell. Extracting rose scent has been an art since at least the thirteenth century BC when Persians, Babylonians, and Greeks produced scented oils. The Persians are said to be the first to advance to distilling the scent, and those ancient methods are still in use in contemporary home distilleries in Iran. These perfumers would have no use for a 747's load of 1.65 million roses without much scent.

Lack of scent was among the more minor reasons the visit was unsettling, though. After the greenhouse came the workroom, a vast chilly structure in which roses came in from the greenhouses and went out as packaged bouquets, some already labeled with the price tag and name of the far-off supermarket for which they were destined. It was a factory whose product happened to be roses, a rose factory. The floors were wet and leaves, thorny stems, and petals were strewn across them. The workers, mostly young, mostly moving fast, wore rubber boots and gray coveralls or work shirts emblazoned with the slogans. Some wore rubber gloves as well.

There were perhaps 150 people at work in the frigid air. I felt like an intruder on their daily ordeal, and I was embarrassed to be with their bosses for how it implied that I approved of the system and aligned myself with its managers and was, with them, watching them in ways that could be intimidating and oppressive. The work seemed too relentless to interrupt, and because any question Nate and I might ask was impossible to answer honestly without risk, there seemed to be no point in speaking to the workers beyond greetings and thanks.

The roses had been grown, but the bouquets were assembled on a production line like any other mass-produced product. Men rolled big carts laden with roses across the room, and other workers, male and female, unloaded the roses wrapped in mesh rectangles and, after sorting them for color, stem length, and other qualities, loaded them onto a sort of frame like a monstrous comb the length of the room. The roses were lined up between the teeth of the comb, and on the other side, other workers took out the roses, a few at a time, to gather a bouquet, sort them for quality and homogeneity, roll them up so that all the rosebuds—they were always buds, not open roses—were level, and chop their stems to make them even in length. Others were busily stripping off some of the leaves, and yet others filled buckets with water and wheeled some of the finished bouquets away to a room just above freezing where they were sorted for shipping. Some of the bouquets ended up on actual conveyer belts, those emblematic structures of the Fordist factory.

At the end of our visit we were given a choice between some of the must luridly unnatural looking bouquets of roses I have ever seen, white roses with each petal tinged with hot pink, mixed with baby's breath and sprays of some sort of bright berry. Nate and I each chose one of the least repulsive, because it seemed too complicated to refuse them. I carried mine as a badge of shame. It marked me as someone who'd bought into the lure of cheap roses and the idea that these were beautiful, in a part of the world where nearly everyone knew what ugliness they arose from.

I knew it better myself after the next day's outing. We went back to the little town we'd visited the first day and up a quiet side street to a shady office where Beatriz Fuentes ran the Casa de Las y Los Trabajadores de las Flores, a labor-rights organization for flower workers. A sturdy woman in a brown sweater with her long hair pulled back into a braid, she greeted Nate warmly, and then we sat down. She began by telling me (in Spanish, with Nate translating) her own story. She had gone to work in the industry when she was seventeen, in 1997, as the industry itself was in change. It had been a paternalistic system, in which the owner provided gifts and goods for the workers—she mentioned lunches, milk from a cow on site, an annual feast—but suddenly things changed. The traditional treats and rewards stopped. "They came in and started talking about efficiency, productivity, and whatnot. So, they turned upside down the way we used to work."

Workers ceased to be employees and became subcontractors and temporary employees, so that no worker acquired the rights of a long-term employee, even after decades with one company. Those who were sick, injured, speaking up for their rights, or organizing were easy to fire under this system. There were also no pay raises. Most workers make about $256 a month, and overtime is the only way to earn more. Nate had written in his report, "During peak seasons, for example the weeks and months leading up to Mother's Day and Valentine's Day, employees reported that work weeks can exceed 100 hours. Women, many of whom are single heads-of-households, are exposed to numerous toxic chemicals that have been linked to higher rates of birth defects."

The other major change Beatriz noted was the arrival of engineers who came in and studied the workers, detailing how many times this one went to the bathroom in a shift, how long that one took to pick flowers from a row. All that information went into new regulations requiring the workers to maximize productivity and minimize freedom of movement. The workplaces were modernized, as we had seen at Sunshine Bouquet, and workers began to be assigned to a single task all day. Workers were disposable parts in a vast, relentless machine, and the machine sped up so that each worker now must do several times what they might have done thirty years ago.

Beatriz told us that in the greenhouses, "on this side, they sent two or three cutters and made them cut all day long, cutting and cutting with the scissors. And behind them there was a woman, we call her the 'skater,' who would pick up the flowers, count them, tag them, and bring them up. But that meant one would only be cutting, cutting, cutting, and cutting all day long. That gave way to another problem that emerged when the companies came in: occupational diseases due to repetitive functions. Just as we had to use scissors to cut during harvest, the women in the rooms had to sort, and they contracted bursitis, tendonitis, and rotator cuff problems."

Beatriz herself had pain in her arm after a dozen years of cutting flowers. "I went to my general health practitioner, who asked me several questions, ran tests on me, and ultimately determined that I had developed carpal tunnel syndrome and tendonitis due to my activities cultivating flowers." With that diagnosis she was sent to her employer's medical program, where "at thirty-one years old, I was told that I had tendonitis and carpal tunnel syndrome because of excessive motions related to peeling potatoes, ironing my kids' clothes, and washing dishes."

Three other women joined us, each of whom had been working for a quarter century or more for the major flower producers and still worked there, despite painful and incapacitating chronic injuries as a result of the work. I could see it in the careful way they moved. They talked about sexual harassment, about a woman fired for staying home to take care of a sick baby, of their struggle to unionize workers to gain rights and protections for them.

Beatriz in 2004 managed to help organize a union in the company she worked at, but noted, "The flower companies have always had anti-union policies. Since I've been in this sector, I've seen at least fifteen flower companies shut down, and all of them for the same reason: when workers decide to organize and fight for their rights, the companies prefer to shut down and file for bankruptcy, so as not to give us the right of association."

The problems were not just human. The four women explained that the thirsty industry was consuming the groundwater. "We're running out of water. And we must remember that a flower is sixty percent water. Each flower you get is sixty percent water and forty percent solid. What we're exporting is also huge amounts of water. In addition, people think that in the Bogotá savanna we breathe clear air, and that's a lie, because the air in this savanna and in all of these municipalities is highly contaminated. It's sixty years' worth of chemicals, fungicides, and the like. And those fungicides have killed butterflies, other insects, worms, many insects living here. This is to say that the problem with floriculture is not only social and labor related, it's also environmental. So, in floriculture the social- and labor-related issues are important, and that's what we do here, but the environmental aspect is terrible. They have ruined the water, the animals, the flora, the air, everything!"

Was the ugliness in the roses for being produced in such a way or in us for failing to see it? Had the roses become lies of a sort, seeming to be one thing but being in truth another? Were they now emblems of deceit, a kind of counterfeit rose signifying formal beauty rather than their own conditions of production? Much of Orwell's work was about ugliness of various kinds, but what he found hideous serves as a negative image of what he found beautiful.

# FIVE

# Snow and Ink

For Orwell, so much of both the ugliness and the beauty was in language. He was passionately committed to language as a contract crucial to all our other contracts. Words should exist in reliable relationship to what they describe, whether it's an object or an event or a commitment. (And by being honest about ambivalence, ambiguity, confusion, conflictedness, or lack of reliable information, you can be clear even when your subject is not, as he was in *Homage to Catalonia* when he stated he did not know the truth of some situations and could only report what he'd seen in others.) Another word for broken contracts is lies.

Lies gradually erode the capacity to know and to connect. In withholding or distorting knowledge or imparting falsehood, a liar deprives others of the information they need to participate in public and political life, to avoid dangers, to understand the world around them, to act on principle, to know themselves and others and the situation, to make good choices, and ultimately to be free. The liar drives a wedge between what he or she knows and what the victim of the lie knows, though the lied-to person or people may be entirely convinced, confused, or suspicious. Or they may be aware they are being deceived, in which case they may or may not know the nature of the deception or what it endeavors to conceal. Authoritarians often coerce people to go along with what they know are lies, making them reluctant coconspirators who may be deceiving yet other parties. Knowledge is power, and the equitable distribution of knowledge is inseparable from other forms of equality. Without equal access to the facts, equal capacity in decision-making is impossible.

Just as lying tries to prevent some kinds of information from getting out, so other kinds of abuse of power try to prevent facts, information, perspectives from getting in, by forming classes of people whose voices and testimony will be excluded by law, or by discrediting or intimidating them, or by perpetuating their subordinate status. Much of my own work in recent years has tried to call attention to inequality of voice—to how sexual and gender violence, as well as racism, have been perpetrated in part by silencing some voices, often by threat and violence but also by systemic devaluation, including portrayal of those voices as untrustworthy, unqualified to speak, and unworthy of being heard or even allowed into the places where voices determine how our lives shall be lived in what kind of a world.

Devaluing voices allows a society to be officially against something it in practice tolerates or encourages, by pretending it doesn't exist. One of Orwell's most significant blind spots is around gender, around how marriages and families can become authoritarian regimes in miniature, down to the suppression of truths and promulgation of lies that protect the powerful. This is replicated in workplaces, schools (where he recognized it well), public life, and other parts of private life, reinforced by laws, customs, and culture. He was part of an age that was (with some notable exceptions) strategically oblivious to inequalities we have since worked hard to recognize. Or some of us have, while others have striven mightily to preserve the old order and its suppressions and exclusions.

One can charge Orwell himself with silencing in that, in all his book reviews and literary essays, there is little consideration of women writers. Most of his essays considering movements and tendencies in the literature of his time are exclusively about men, though plenty of women were at work then. In his 1940 essay on Henry Miller, he says, "Miller is writing about the man in the street, and it is incidentally rather a pity that it should be a street full of brothels." A pity not for the women in those brothels, who seem doomed to remain a blurry background, but for the narrative he's criticizing and perhaps the man who is the inevitable subject. Orwell was better at recognizing racism, in his writings about India, Burma, imperialism and colonialism, and anti-Black discrimination in the United States, among other things.

In recent years, the term *gaslighting* for the attempt to undermine someone's perceptions has migrated from private life, where it's most often about a man bullying a woman into losing confidence in her own perceptions, into what demagogues do to whole societies. Sissela Bok, in her landmark book on lying, writes, "Deceit and violence— these are the two forms of deliberate assault on human beings. Both can coerce people into acting against their will. Most harm that can befall victims through violence can come to them also through deceit. But deceit controls more subtly, for it works on belief as well as action." As withheld information, a lie is a sort of shield for the liar; as falsity it is a sword. It matters whether or not people believe the lies, but unbelievable lies wielded by those with power do their own damage. To be forced to live with the lies of the powerful is to be forced to live with your own lack of power over the narrative, which in the end can mean lack of power over anything at all. Authoritarians see truth and fact and history as a rival system they must defeat.

Orwell's writing life started out with an ordinary loathing of hypocrisy and evasiveness. The Spanish Civil War sharpened this into a focus on the power of lies in political life that only grew stronger in his 1940s essays and in *Animal Farm* and in what is perhaps the twentieth century's most significant book about systematic lying, *Nineteen Eighty-Four*. His baptism by propaganda during the war in Spain trained his gaze on those near at hand, on the corruption within what was supposed to be his own side as well as that of the putative enemy.

That side was the left and the intelligentsia in what was supposed to be the free world, when they acquiesced to the extraordinary dictatorship of lies that was Stalin's USSR and its outposts and supporters around the world. If communism was intended to distribute power universally, the Soviet Union's leadership hoarded that power by withholding information, whether it was the truth about the Ukraine famine or scientific facts, and wielded that power as a weapon in show trials, forced confessions, erasures, and rewritings of recent history. The Soviet Union forced ordinary people to become liars themselves, repeating things they didn't believe, submitting to things they knew to be untrue. (The slogans the rose workers were obliged to wear had a tang of this coercion.)

Another crucial aspect of any regime of lies is the unequal distribution of the privacy that protects our thoughts and actions. The powerful become unaccountable because their actions are concealed and misrepresented, while ordinary people are deprived of privacy through surveillance and encouraged to inform on one another to the authorities. Such betrayals violate not only literal privacy but loyalty to private relationships over the state. Pavlik Morozov, the boy who in 1932 denounced his father to local authorities in the Urals, resulting in that father's execution, was made into a hero after whom innumerable branches of the Soviet children's organization the Young Pioneers were named. This has its echo in *Nineteen Eighty-Four*'s Tom Parsons, the neighbor of Winston Smith whose daughter turns him in for thoughtcrime and who is so well indoctrinated that he ruefully commends his child from his prison cell.

In the Soviet Union and its satellites, false allegations were an easy means of revenge; the regime of lies encouraged and rewarded liars. This and the constant surveillence made people fearful to communicate their real thoughts, hopes, and experiences to others. Capitalist nations also have shameful histories of violating their citizens' right to privacy and concealing illicit and immoral government acts; in the United States the anticommunist era came closest to this pall of suppression and invasion of private life and belief as it mirrored what it claimed to oppose (but the rise of government surveillance of citizens in the post-9/11 era runs a close second).

Eventually, under totalitarianism, the regime of lies breaks down the psyches of many who live in its grasp, convincing them to abandon the search for truth and accuracy in their own thoughts and words as well as those of others. Sometimes this takes the form of intellectual surrender, a cowed willingness to believe everything it is convenient to believe, sometimes cynicism, a refusal to believe anything and an assertion that everything is equally corrupt. Hannah Arendt famously wrote, "The ideal subject of totalitarian rule is not the convinced Nazi or the convinced Communist, but people for whom the distinction between fact and fiction (i.e., the reality of experience) and the distinction between true and false (i.e., the standards of thought) no longer exist." Charting that distinction was one of Orwell's central tasks, and you can invert Arendt to say that the potent enemy of totalitarianism is she who is passionate and clear about the distinction between fact and fiction, truth and falsity, and stands on the reality of her own experience and capacity to bear witness to it.

Arendt and Orwell were engaging in parallel diagnoses with her *Origins of Totalitarianism* and his *Nineteen Eighty-Four.* In her 1951 book, Arendt speaks of the loneliness that this begets, as "man loses trust in himself as the partner of his thoughts and that elementary confidence in the world which is necessary to make experiences at all. Self and world, capacity for thought and experience are lost at the same time." In his 1946 essay "The Prevention of Literature," Orwell writes that lies are "integral to totalitarianism, something that would still continue even if concentration camps and secret police forces had ceased to be necessary." To have total power is to have power over truth and fact and history and to reach for it over dreams and thoughts and emotions. He continues, "From the totalitarian point of view history is something to be created rather than learned. A totalitarian state is in effect a theocracy, and its ruling caste, in order to keep its position, has to be thought of as infallible. But since, in practice, no one is infallible, it is frequently necessary to rearrange past events in order to show that this or that mistake was not made, or that this or that imaginary triumph actually happened. . . . Totalitarianism demands, in fact, the continuous alteration of the past, and in the long run probably demands a disbelief in the very existence of objective truth."

Totalitarianism is impossible without lies. So it is significantly a language problem and a storytelling problem that can be fought to some extent with language—with the language of history that is not manipulable by the regime, independent journalism uncovering the current situation, logic and scientific method demanding a basis for statements, with the language of ideas that invite people to find their own concepts and principles and to look at the world critically, with the commitment to honor the contracts that words make. With the language of love and fellowship that builds back relationships and drives away loneliness. With the poetry that captures nuance of experience and unexpected alignments. All these things require either the freedom to do them safely or the courage to do them when they are dangerous.

Orwell continues, "But to be corrupted by totalitarianism one does not have to live in a totalitarian country. The mere prevalence of certain ideas can spread a kind of poison that makes one subject after another impossible for literary purposes. Wherever there is an enforced orthodoxy—or even two orthodoxies, as often happens—good writing stops." Good writing here arises from freedom; specifically freedom to tell the truth. Words at their best uncover things and show them clearly. At their worst, they do the opposite, and he took up the problem in another of his 1946 essays, "Politics and the English Language," writing that "the inflated style is itself a kind of euphemism. A mass of Latin words falls upon the facts like soft snow, blurring the outlines and covering up all the details." The essay is not only about outright lies but about circumlocutions, evasions, the capacity of vague and misleading language to hide or excuse crimes and corruption. He was as concerned with the acquiescence to and promulgation of lies by his literary and journalistic colleagues and by their use of language as a tool of deceit and concealment as he was with that of politicians.

His hatred of sloppy language was partly an aesthetic thing, but he was clear how readily it became a means of justifying or concealing atrocity. "In our time, political speech and writing are largely the defence of the indefensible. Things like the continuance of British rule in India, the Russian purges and deportations, the dropping of the atom bombs on Japan, can indeed be defended, but only by arguments which are too brutal for most people to face, and which do not square with the professed aims of political parties. Thus political language has to consist largely of euphemism, question-begging and sheer cloudy vagueness."

Although he denounces stale metaphors in this essay, he uses fresher ones himself, and as is so often the case with metaphors, they come from the natural world. First comes the image of muffling snow blurring what lies beneath it, an image of whiteness, then comes one of darkness: "When there is a gap between one's real and one's declared aims, one turns as it were instinctively to long words and exhausted idioms, like a cuttlefish squirting out ink." Snow, ink, it's an elegant turn in a furious essay. And then, "But if thought corrupts language, language can also corrupt thought." *Corruption* means both to subvert something ethically and to enter a state of decay and putrefaction, and it comes from the Latin *rumpere*, meaning to break. Corruption is breakage and disintegration. Thus the ugliness that is the breaking of contracts and the loss of the integrity of things—of science, of history, of knowledge, of relationships, of meaning, perhaps of minds, bodies, places, ecosystems too.

He saw some of this capacity to connect and perceive in individual words, which is why the English of *Nineteen Eighty-Four* is being shrunk by the authorities into Newspeak. Smith's colleague at the Ministry of Truth, whose task it is to shrivel the language, declares, "Don't you see that the whole aim of Newspeak is to narrow the range of thought? In the end we shall make thoughtcrime literally impossible, because there will be no words in which to express it." Each word is a set of relationships, direct and indirect, a species in an ecosystem. The death of a word thins out a language and the possibilities of thought. Eventually the system collapses into ruins as thinking becomes impossible, the way an ecosystem collapses when key species become extinct.

In the novel's appendix about Newspeak, Orwell describes how the word *free* was shrunk to mean only free from, as in "this dog is free from lice." "It could not be used in its old sense of 'politically free' or 'intellectually free,' since political and intellectual freedom no longer existed even as concepts, and were therefore of necessity nameless." It's not only a loss of particular words but of the complexity, nuance, shade, evocation of words. As he'd written elsewhere, in another of his similes drawn from the natural world, "The imagination, like certain wild animals, will not breed in captivity," and Newspeak was a cage for thoughts.

"Politics and the English Language" addresses language that is too loose, blurring, evading, meandering, avoiding. *Nineteen Eighty-Four* depicts language when it is too tight, too restrictive in vocabulary and connotation, when some words have been murdered and others severed from too many of their associations. Somewhere in between is the possibility of a language that is clear but evocative, in which the speaker or writer's explorations invite those of the listener or reader, in which there is something a little wild in language, and the wild and the free overlap. That integrity, those honored contracts, those endeavors to reach out and make whole through the use of words that connect, empower, liberate, illuminate are the beauty to which he is most committed and the one he most celebrates, in the writing of others and in his own efforts as a writer.

Such beauty does not necessarily resemble the visual splendor that the word most commonly references. He took all this on in his 1946 essay "Why I Write." One motive, he said, was "perception of beauty in the external world, or, on the other hand, in words and their right arrangement. Pleasure in the impact of one sound on another, in the firmness of good prose or the rhythm of a good story. Desire to share an experience which one feels is valuable and ought not to be missed." When he was young, he noted, "I wanted to write enormous naturalistic novels with unhappy endings, full of detailed descriptions and arresting similes, and also full of purple passages in which words were used partly for the sake of their own sound." He lost his affection for the color purple: "And looking back through my work, I see that it is invariably where I lacked a political purpose that I wrote lifeless books and was betrayed into purple passages, sentences without meaning, decorative adjectives and humbug generally."

The ethical purpose sharpened the aesthetic means, he makes clear, and politics saved him from insignificance. "In a peaceful age I might have written ornate or merely descriptive books, and might have remained almost unaware of my political loyalties. As it is I have been forced into becoming a sort of pamphleteer." But pamphleteer was neither a bad job nor one without aesthetic demands and pleasures: "What I have most wanted to do throughout the past ten years is to make political writing into an art. . . . I write . . . because there is some lie that I want to expose, some fact to which I want to draw attention, and my initial concern is to get a hearing."

And then comes the cluster of sentences that has long served me as a credo: "But I could not do the work of writing a book, or even a long magazine article, if it were not also an aesthetic experience.

Anyone who cares to examine my work will see that even when it is downright propaganda it contains much that a full-time politician would consider irrelevant. I am not able, and do not want, completely to abandon the world view that I acquired in childhood. So long as I remain alive and well I shall continue to feel strongly about prose style, to love the surface of the earth, and to take a pleasure in solid objects and scraps of useless information." What might be considered irrelevant is a series of pleasures and personal commitments, akin to the roses in "bread and roses." (The view acquired in childhood might be the broad, untamed interest in many things, notably the love of the surface of the earth in the next sentence.)

Clarity, precision, accuracy, honesty, and truthfulness are aesthetic values to him, and pleasures. In 1937, when he was in Spain fighting for his ideals, Eileen Blair wrote to the publisher of *The Road to Wigan Pier*, "The word my husband particularly wants changed is in Chapter I, the last paragraph but one. In the manuscript the sentence is: 'For the first time in my life, in a bare patch beside the line, I saw rooks copulating.' According to my husband, Gollancz and he altered *copulating* to *courting*, but he wishes the phrase to read '. . . I saw rooks treading,' because he has seen rooks courting hundreds of times. Of course if by any chance Gollancz changed his mind and left *copulating*, that would be better still, but I expect there is no hope of that." It's about scrupulousness even in small matters.

Clarity, honesty, accuracy, truth are beautiful because in them representation is true to its subject, knowledge is democratized, people are empowered, doors are open, information moves freely, contracts are honored. That is, such writing is beautiful in itself, and beautiful in what flows from it. There are more conventional kinds of beauty in Orwell's work—natural landscapes from Burmese forests to British meadows, all those flowers, the golden eye of the toad. But this beauty in which ethics and aesthetics are inseparable, this linguistic beauty of truth and of integrity as a kind of wholeness and connectedness, between language and what it describes, between one person and another, or between members of a community or society, is the crucial beauty for which he strove in his own writing.

# VII

# The River Orwell

*Vernon Richards,* Orwell and Son, *1945.*

# ONE

# An Inventory of Pleasures

In the year 1936, a young writer planted roses. A decade later a wearier, wiser man set out to make another garden on a more ambitious scale, and in the ten years between the small garden in Wallington in southern England and the one that grew into a small farm on the Isle of Jura off the west coast of Scotland, his life had changed many times and he had grown immeasurably as a writer.

He'd become haggard during the war years. Eileen had moved to London for government jobs—first at the Press and Censorship Bureau of the Ministry of Information, then at the Ministry of Food—and he had joined her later. From 1941 to 1943, he worked for the BBC, writing scripts, working with a staff, recruiting writers and others to join in conversations, all for programs to be broadcast in India. The new job meant giving up his garden and much of his time to write; the new salaries made them comparatively affluent for the first time in their married life. They lived in London for most of the war, going back to Wallington for the occasional weekend and lending out the cottage to friends who had been bombed out or wanted a holiday.

John Morris, who worked with him at the BBC, thought he resembled "one of those figures on the front of Chartres Cathedral; there was a sort of pinched Gothic quality about his tall thin frame.

He laughed often, but in repose his lined face suggested the gray asceticism of a medieval saint carved in stone and very weathered. . . .
His most striking features were his luxuriant and unruly hair and the
strange expression in his eyes, a combination of benevolence and fanaticism; it was as though he saw more (as indeed he did) than the
ordinary mortal." Others talk about his wheezing and fatigue from
even minor exertion. He was running down. Or his body was.

His literary work was ramping up, and the fable published in August 1945 as *Animal Farm: A Fairy Story* was his first commercial success. He'd written it during the war with Eileen's encouragement and
input. They were away from home when their top-floor flat in London
was smashed up by a German bomb on June 28, 1944, but the manuscript of the book was among the belongings that were scattered and
coated with dust. "This Ms. has been blitzed which accounts for my
delay in delivering it & its slightly crumpled condition, but it is not
damaged in any way," he wrote to T. S. Eliot at the publishing house
Faber and Faber, one of the many editors to reject the book.

A few weeks before the bombing, they had adopted a baby to realize his longtime desire for children—she was more ambivalent, and
her own poor health might have been a factor. Christened Richard
Horatio Blair, the child was sweet-natured and thriving, and they
were soon both devoted to and delighted by him. But it was she who
stopped everything to tend to the child (he was devoted when present
but often absent). Less than a year later, while he was in Germany
reporting on the end of the war, Eileen died. She had been ill for some
time. Perhaps the wartime rationing and meager diet took a toll on
her; Orwell also blamed her years of long hours of office work. They
both smoked prodigiously (at one point she said if they smoked less
they could afford a larger flat).

Her main trouble appears to have been uterine fibroids or something of that kind that caused chronic blood loss and anemia and sometimes acute pain. (Her uterine bleeding, his pulmonary hemorrhages: they were a bloodily unhealthy couple, and she had delayed seeing doctors lest she get a diagnosis she needed to report when they were questioned about their fitness to adopt the baby.) She went in for surgery and wrote poignantly loving, self-effacing letters to her husband, worrying about the expense rather than herself. Midprocedure, she died on the operating table, on March 29, 1945, apparently due to the anesthesia. She was thirty-nine.

The Orwell of 1946 is an astonishment. Eileen's death was preceded by that of his widowed mother in March 1943 and followed by that of his older sister in May 1946. His own health was declining, and with every justification to sink into grief and exhaustion, he was instead prolific and full of plans, including for an ambitious novel—at that point titled *The Last Man in Europe*—and for a new life in one of the remoter parts of the British Isles, the Isle of Jura in the Hebrides, which he had visited briefly in the summer of 1944. While complaining that in order to make a living he was "smothered under journalism," he produced essays and reviews at a heroic rate, often four a week that winter and spring.

Among them is a cluster of essays celebrating familiar comforts and pleasures. They were written between late 1945 and May 1946, when he set aside journalism and moved to Jura to begin the novel that would eventually be titled *Nineteen Eighty-Four*. There's a practical explanation for those essays: these domestic and idyllic subjects were, for an overworked writer, the ones that required little or no reading or other research, only reverie. They could be dismissed as lightweight, but there are traces of them in the heavyweight novel he was working toward, and just as pleasure in "the surface of the earth" and "solid objects and scraps of useless information" shows up in his most scathing political work, so politics shows up in many of these essays. The choice of widely accessible, low-cost, and free pleasures and the savoring of everyday life in postwar Britain was itself political, as was the focus on the natural world as a major source of meaning and value. (The same season he wrote an essay making the case that books were not unaffordable luxuries for ordinary people, in part by comparing the cost of books and cigarettes.) Political and moral: he may have been endeavoring to cheer up others—and himself—by turning toward these things he relished.

At the start of this run he wrote "In Defence of English Cooking," published in the *Evening Standard* in mid-December. He takes extravagant pleasure in the recollections and the names: "First of all, kippers, Yorkshire pudding, Devonshire cream, muffins and crumpets. Then a list of puddings that would be interminable if I gave it in full: I will pick out for special mention Christmas pudding, treacle tart and apple dumplings. Then an almost equally long list of cakes: for instance, dark plum cake (such as you used to get at Buzzard's before the war), short-bread and saffron buns." He praises marmalade, haggis, and suet pudding, and "bread sauce, horse-radish sauce, mint sauce and apple sauce; not to mention redcurrant jelly, which is excellent with mutton as well as with hare."

The day before he published this piece about roasts, puddings, and sauces he wrote down "Politics and the English Language" in his payments book. He started the new year with the fierce "The Prevention of Literature" in *Polemic* and, on January 5, a piece on the pleasures of junk shops, which he differentiated from antique shops for their dusty obscurity, their broken items of no value, and their proprietors, who tended to be enigmatic figures with little interest in sales. He noted that their "finest treasures are never discoverable at first glimpse; they have to be sorted out from among a medley of bamboo cake-stands, Britannia-ware dish-covers, turnip watches, dog-eared books, ostrich eggs, typewriters of extinct makes, spectacles without lenses, decanters without stoppers, stuffed birds, wire fire guards, bunches of keys, boxes of nuts and bolts, conch shells from the Indian Ocean, boot trees, Chinese ginger jars and pictures of Highland cattle."

Lists are a form of collecting, an inventory of what is available at least to the imagination, and sometimes a reaching for assurance that there is some kind of abundance beyond the privation at hand. In his 1939 novel *Coming Up for Air*, his protagonist muses that "there's a kind of peacefulness even in the names of English coarse fish. Roach, rudd, dace, bleak, barbel, bream, gudgeon, pike, chub, carp, tench. They're solid kind of names. The people who made them up hadn't heard of machine-guns, they didn't live in terror of the sack or spend their time eating aspirins, going to the pictures, and wondering how to keep out of the concentration camp."

People in harsh circumstances—war, expeditions, prisons and other institutions—sometimes plunge into daydreams and conversations about what feasts they'd devour or what other everyday pleasures they'd seek; they make lists as a means of feeling a sense of control over the future. Orwell's essays in the form of inventories, written at the end of a war with rationing still in effect and food still scarce and drab, may have arisen from such conditions. Among junk-shop treasures he listed glass paperweights "that have a piece of coral enclosed in the glass, but these are always fantastically expensive." Just such a paperweight would be purchased by Winston Smith and become one of *Nineteen Eighty-Four*'s central symbols (and a junk-shop proprietor is a crucial figure in the novel). He described the appeal of these shops to "the jackdaw inside all of us, the instinct that makes a child hoard copper nails, clock springs, and the glass marbles out of lemonade bottles. To get pleasure out of a junk shop you are not obliged to buy anything, nor even to want to buy anything."

On the twelfth of January he published an essay on the proper way to make a cup of tea, about which he had strong opinions: water straight from a boiling kettle, loose tea in abundance, from India and not China if possible, in a ceramic or china teapot, and most controversially, and adamantly, the tea in the cup first, and not the milk. No sugar. On the nineteenth he published a piece about "Songs We Used to Sing"; in this phase of his writing life, he gave serious attention to nonsense poetry, fairy tales, popular songs, nursery rhymes, gag postcards, "good bad books," and other elements of popular culture. (He turned "Little Red Riding Hood" into a radio script that the BBC broadcast that summer.) Earlier in the year, his publisher Fredric Warburg—who had published *Animal Farm* when several others had rejected the allegorical tale—wrote that Orwell had a nursery rhymes project and "plans to throw up his journalism from the beginning of May until November, and to retire to the Hebrides for six months to write a novel."

Susan Watson, whom he'd hired to help him with Richard, recalled that when Aunt Nellie came to visit, aunt and nephew looked over the latter's extensive collection of Donald McGill's cheerfully ribald postcards with delight. His long 1941 essay on the postcards and their variety of lowbrow humor argued that they "give expression to the Sancho Panza view of life," to the comedy of survival, and then shifts into his own quixotic note: "When it comes to the pinch, human beings are heroic. Women face childbed and the scrubbing brush, revolutionaries keep their mouths shut in the torture chamber, battleships go down with their guns still firing when their decks are awash. It is only that the other element in man, the lazy, cowardly, debt-bilking adulterer who is inside all of us, can never be suppressed altogether and needs a hearing occasionally."

"It is foully cold here and the fuel shortage is just at its worst," he wrote in a letter that winter, suggesting that his pleasures were all in the imagination. Nevertheless, his next essay was in praise—or defense—of the British climate: "There is a time to sit in the garden in a deck chair, and there is a time to have chilblains and a dripping nose." It was a list of often small and subtle pleasures, urban and rural, month by month: April's "smell of the earth after a shower," May's "pleasure of not wearing underclothes," June's "cloud-bursts. The smell of hay. Going for walks after supper. The back-breaking labour of earthing up potatoes," and July's "going to the office in shirt sleeves. The endless pop-pop-pop of cherry stones as one treads the London pavements" all the way to November's "raging gales" and "smell of rubbish fires." February, he admitted, "is a particularly detestable month with no virtue except its shortness. But in fairness to our climate one ought to remember that if we did not have this period of damp and cold, the rest of the year would be quite different." The same kind of vivid detail about the state of being embodied and what is felt, smelled, tasted, seen, heard enlivened his novels, and the same sense of fairness also runs through all his work.

In detestable February he proceeded, with the same strictness he'd applied to a proper cup of tea, to describe the perfections of an imaginary pub named the Moon Under Water. He celebrated it via another list: "The grained woodwork, the ornamental mirrors behind the bar, the cast-iron fireplaces, the florid ceiling stained dark yellow by tobacco-smoke, the stuffed bull's head over the mantelpiece—everything has the solid, comfortable ugliness of the nineteenth century." It's quiet enough to talk, never rowdy, serves draft stout, has glass and pewter mugs, a garden where families can come on summer evenings, and the barmaids know everyone's name. Domestic scenes like this recur in the season's essays, and in this one it's easy to see that without an injection of political urgency elsewhere in his work, he could have become a curmudgeon mourning the good old days.

His writing that season wasn't all reverie and pastoral. He penned a four-part analysis of the political situation early that year, wrote about starvation across continental Europe, reviewed Yevgeny Zamyatin's dystopian novel *We* and the American novelist Richard Wright's *Black Boy*, argued by letter with the author of a book about Burma, tried to help the refugee writer Victor Serge get published, became vice chair of the anarchist-oriented Freedom Defence Committee at the behest of George Woodcock, and with a public letter to *The Manchester Guardian* stood up for some Indian passengers who had been badly treated on a passenger ship. That is to say, his usual political life continued even while he wrote these idyllic essays.

Sometimes the past was deployed to condemn the present—this was his conservative side, mourning declines and disappearances. A diatribe against modern "pleasure spots" advocates for nature and all the things that make human beings puny in the face of natural forces, and it points out the unnatural forces that were launched in the summer of 1945 with the first nuclear explosions: "But meanwhile man's power over Nature is steadily increasing. With the aid of the atomic bomb we could literally move mountains: we could even, so it is said, alter the climate of the earth by melting the polar ice-caps and irrigating the Sahara." Atomic bombs would even find their way into the April 12 essay on toads.

The piece on climate appeared on February 2, the piece on the ideal pub on February 9, a piece on pacifism on February 10, the well-known essay "Decline of the English Murder" on crime fiction—celebrating old murder stories and excoriating more brutal new ones—on February 15. And then on February 21 the *Manchester Evening News* noted that his regular piece would not appear due to illness. He had had another lung hemorrhage, and in March another such notice appeared to explain another canceled column.

In February he had written to a friend that he needed to go to Wallington to pack up the cottage and terminate that era of his life, "but I have been putting it off because last time I was there it was with Eileen and it upsets me to go there." Though on March 14, he wrote a letter to George Woodcock stating that he was still sick in bed, a day later he wrote a longer letter, proposing marriage to a young woman he didn't know very well, confiding to her, "There isn't really anything left in my life except my work and seeing that Richard gets a good start. It is only that I feel so desperately alone sometimes. I have hundreds of friends, but no woman who takes an interest in me and can encourage me." She was one of several young women who rebuffed his forlorn, awkward advances in that period.

The toad in April 12's "Some Thoughts on the Common Toad" serves as a portrait of the artist as an exhausted but motivated amphibian, described throughout in the singular, with a masculine pronoun. "At this period, after his long fast, the toad has a very spiritual look, like a strict Anglo-Catholic towards the end of Lent. His movements are languid but purposeful, his body is shrunken, and by contrast his eyes look abnormally large. This allows one to notice, what one might not at another time, that a toad has about the most beautiful eye of any living creature." He builds up strength by eating insects and "goes through a phase of intense sexiness." Orwell describes the creatures' indiscriminately orgiastic mating and adds that "the spawning of the toads . . . is one of the phenomena of Spring which most deeply appeal to me" but notes that "many people do not like reptiles or amphibians." By the time the essay has turned the last corner and arrived at its conclusion, he's contemplating the people who don't like him and his own pleasures: "How many a time have I stood watching the toads mating, or a pair of hares having a boxing match in the young corn, and thought of all the important persons who would stop me enjoying this if they could. But luckily they can't."

In a letter to another woman friend that spring, he wrote, "I'm going down to Wallington tomorrow to sort out the furniture and books, and then I hope Pickford's man will come along and tell me when he can remove the stuff. I've also got to buy a lot of stuff. This kind of thing is a complete nightmare to me, but I've no one I can shove it on to." There were real lists and inventories to produce as well as the literary ones scattered in the essays of 1946. Almost exactly a decade after he'd moved to Wallington, he had overcome his dread of returning. That plunge into the past gave him the material that went into "A Good Word for the Vicar of Bray," which appeared in *Tribune* two weeks after the essay in praise of toads.

The ebullient essay that had made such an impact on me so long ago, that had led me to the cottage in Wallington and the roses blooming there, and to writing this book, was the result of a widower's expedition to revisit the scenes of his married life and end that era. "Recently, I spent a day at the cottage where I used to live, and noted with a pleased surprise—to be exact, it was a feeling of having done good unconsciously—the progress of the things I had planted nearly ten years ago," he wrote. He noted in another letter that the visit wasn't as painful as expected, except when he found old letters, and that he'd wandered up the road to "the little disused reservoir in the village where we used to catch newts, and there were the tadpoles forming as usual." But a paragraph later, he said he looked forward to Jura and described far grander waters and beasts: "There are bays of green water so clear you can see about 20 feet down, with seals swimming about."

The domestic diary he restarted took note of what was blooming where as he went from London to his sister Marjorie's funeral in Nottinghamshire and onward to stay near Edinburgh with friends from the Spanish Civil War, and then to Jura. On May 22, on his way there, he stopped to tend Eileen's grave near Newcastle: "Polyantha roses on E's grave have all rooted well. Planted aubretia, miniature phlox, saxifrage, a kind of dwarf broom, a house-leek of some kind, & miniature dianthus. Plants not in very good condition, but it was rainy weather, so they should strike." This might be one of the most poignant images of Orwell: a widower stooped over his young wife's grave, in a place where he had few connections, digging and planting on a gray, damp day.

The essay "Why I Write" was published in June but must have been written earlier. Once he was in Jura his days were filled with the toil of making a home in the long-uninhabited farmhouse, starting a garden, shooting rabbits, fishing, and otherwise doing everything but writing, aside from the domestic diary that was also a collection of lists—of fish caught, tasks accomplished, things planted, weather reported, wildlife observed, equipment secured, of facts in the immediate past and intentions for the immediate future. He had found Barnhill, as the isolated farmhouse was known, through his wealthy friend David Astor. It was a large place with four bedrooms and outbuildings situated in a gentle depression in the magnificent rolling landscape, a short walk from the eastern shore of Jura, facing the Scottish coast.

Some called his migration to this remote location suicidal or masochistic, and many who've written about him seem to consider living in London an eminently reasonable thing to do and living on a Scottish island unreasonable. They seem to assume that reasonability meant eking out as long a life as possible rather than living it as fully as possible. Orwell had all along tended to choose the latter over the former. And the air of London, filthy with coal smoke, was itself deadly in ways rarely acknowledged in his lifetime, particularly for someone with his underlying pulmonary conditions. Before the now-famous Great Smog that killed thousands of Londoners in 1952, there were periodic air pollution crises with smog so dense it stopped daily life outdoors and sometimes indoors, including one in January 1946, while he and Richard lived there, and another in 1948 that killed hundreds. The postwar city was also full of ruins and rubble: German bombing had damaged 1.7 million buildings and destroyed more than 70,000 altogether.

As far back as the summer of 1940, he had written in his diary, "Thinking always of my island in the Hebrides, which I suppose I shall never possess nor even see." Moving to the island was the realization of a dream, underwritten by sales from his dystopian fable. Jura's air was fresh, and its summer weather often pleasant and mild, though Orwell continued smoking his dank tobacco, burning peat, and using a paraffin stove to heat his writing room, none of which helped his failing lungs. But he spent a lot of time outdoors once he was there. When he returned to London in November, he reported that the city was colder than Jura and more short on fuel.

In moving to the island, Orwell was anxious to find a place where his son could run free and to get out of London literary life and back into literary productivity. He was a fond and devoted father. Susan Watson recalled that he boasted that "during the bombing he was looking after Richard on his own and was proud that he had only missed one bottle because of the greater necessity of going down to the air raid shelter. Some people thought that after Eileen's death he would give Richard up, but he never once thought of this." In making the move, he may also have been anticipating a future in which atomic wars made a city like London a target, and he'd just lived through years of bombings there. He also liked the distance from the highly regulated postwar state. He wrote to a friend that he didn't have a license for the rifle he used on rabbits because "there's no policeman on this island!"

Once he was established, he and the people who clustered around him—Richard; Watson as Richard's nanny until his grim, hardworking younger sister, Avril Blair, drove her off; various guests; eventually some other helpers with the farmwork—seem to have eaten well on vegetables from the garden, fresh milk and butter first from the crofter a mile away and then from their own cow, eggs from their hens, rabbits he shot, fish caught almost daily from a small motorboat he acquired, crabs and lobsters from traps, and occasionally a celebratory goose from the flock they raised. You could cut your own peat from the bogs, and Orwell did. Thanks to the food rationing that had begun during the war (but wouldn't end until the 1950s), they were chronically short on flour and bread and always urging guests to bring some. At one point, Richard Blair said in a recent talk about his and his father's time in Jura, they had sixteen acres under cultivation.

Orwell's letters encouraging his friends to visit were comic for their repeated instructions: "I'll tell you about how to do the journey. It isn't really a very formidable one except that you have to walk the last 8 miles." Coming after train, bus, and ferry rides, those eight miles were over a road too rough for most vehicles even when dry, and impossible when wet, and Orwell walked it often, sometimes loaded with luggage or furniture, and sometimes traveled it on a motorcycle whose repair was another of his recurrent tasks. There was no electricity, and the nearest telephone was more than a dozen miles away. He seems to have been enjoying himself. That June, he sowed seed in an ambitious vegetable garden. He planted flowers later that year, including lupines, pansies, primroses, and tulips; later on came roses again. In July, he ordered half a dozen apple trees and six other fruit trees, including two morello cherries. He was planting a future again, or at least hope for one.

I had myself hoped to visit the place, but the 2020 pandemic put an end to my plans. I had to settle for writing to the proprietor of Barnhill. When I asked her whether anything remained of his efforts, Damaris Fletcher, part of the same family that owned it in Orwell's time, replied, "The 'garden' at Barnhill is not fenced off so many seasons of deer and wild goats forage right up to the windows. . . . The one plant that has miraculously survived from Orwell's time in the house is the azalea in front of the kitchen window." She also noted, "Actually the Great Man was a tad romantic about what he might grow on the boggy peaty soil with a very short growing season. It is possible to garden on Jura but I often think of the garden my mother-in-law made at Ardlussa. It has 10 foot brick walls surrounding it and protecting it from marauding animals and the cold winds and all the soil had been brought from the mainland from when boats came to collect slate from the quarry and filled the hold with a cargo of best soil for the garden on the return trip." Orwell's confidence in the longevity of both the garden and the gardener might have been misplaced, or perhaps it was a gesture of defiance or a gamble.

That spring of the abundant essays, he had thought a lot about domesticity, coziness, and privacy. He opened February's "Decline of the English Murder" with an evocation of the imaginary reader on a Sunday afternoon, on the sofa by a fire, after a roast and pudding "driven home, as it were, by a cup of mahogany-brown tea, have put you in just the right mood" to read about murder. In a January piece decrying plans for ultramodern housing, he had insisted that people "want day nurseries and welfare clinics, but they also want privacy. They want to save work, but they want to cook their own meals. . . . A deep instinct warns them not to destroy the family, which in the modern world is the sole refuge from the State." Privacy and personal relationships as strongholds of the self would become a central theme in *Nineteen Eighty-Four*.

His friend Sir Richard Rees wrote afterward, "One of the chief memories that I retain of this strenuous and self-martyrising man is the atmosphere of coziness which he managed to diffuse. After one of the frequent disastrous expeditions in Jura—returning on foot, for example at midnight in a misty drizzle having left the truck containing drums of indispensible lamp-oil bogged down somewhere in the hills—one would find that he had come down from his sick-room, stoked up the kitchen fire and made preparations for supper, not merely with efficiency, but with a comforting, hospitable, Dickensian glow." And despite all the distractions, he got the first fifty pages of his new novel written by the time he left Jura that fall. Or rather he complained that that's all he had written, but to write fifty pages he had to have laid the groundwork for a book as a whole.

# Two

# "As the Rose-Hip to the Rose"

In his memoir *Speak, Memory*, Vladimir Nabokov, who was a passionate lepidopterist as well as a novelist, says, "It is astounding how little the ordinary person notices butterflies" and recounts a moment when he asked a hiker descending a trail if he'd seen any. "'None'" says the hiker, "descending the trail where, moments before, you and I had been delighting in swarms of them." You see what you're looking for, and after that encounter with the roses at his cottage, and plunging into a lot of his other work, I went back to the novel I had read many times before.

Rereading a significant book is like revisiting an old friend: you find out how you've changed when you encounter them again; you see differently because you're different. Some books grow, some wither upon reacquaintance, or because you're asking different questions you find different answers. What struck me this time around was how much lushness and beauty and pleasure are in *Nineteen Eighty-Four*. They're endangered, furtive, corrupted, but they exist. It's mostly remembered as a novel about Big Brother, the Thought Police, the memory hole, Newspeak, torture, and the other aspects of a brilliantly realized vision of maximum totalitarianism. Those were what was new and startling in the book when it appeared, and they mattered as threats to what Orwell and his protagonist value.

What they value is also, of necessity, present in the book. Winston Smith is far from exemplary or heroic, but he does resist. That resistance consists not of activity that will overthrow the regime—though he aspires and eventually volunteers to do so—but thoughts and acts that violate its precepts. Those precepts are rooted in controlling consciousness and culture, not just actions and infrastructure. So Smith works at having an interior life with memories, thoughts, emotions, reason, independent-mindedness, true solitude, and true connection. And at establishing evidence of an objective reality to which he wishes to swear a kind of loyalty, because he is forever trying to piece together a reliable sense of the past, even though his job at the Ministry of Truth is to alter it. He desires the life of the mind and the senses, beauty, history, nature, pleasure, and sex, and the privacy and freedom in which all those things flourish. His romance with a woman (that is in some way also with these qualities) drives the plot of the book.

If there is a plot. As the book opens, Smith begins a diary in the beautiful old book with creamy paper and marbled covers he had bought in a junk shop in a proletarian district of what was once London. It's a relic of the past, both in its lush materials and its invitation to private thought and private record keeping, because hope, introspection, and memory are also imperiled in the regime. As he begins to write, with an inkwell and an old-fashioned pen, he reflects that "he was already dead." And then, "Now that he had recognized himself as a dead man it became important to stay alive as long as possible."

But he doesn't do that. He decides instead to live as fully as possible, pursuing a series of dangerous actions—keeping a diary of subversive thoughts, skipping obligations, engaging in solitary wandering, a love affair, a venture into political resistance—as the novel progresses. But he's a condemned man from the outset. His only freedom lies in what he says and does along the way. The Buddhist parable about the person who, having fallen over a cliff while being chased by a tiger, grasps a strawberry plant that is coming loose, and whose death in a fall is inevitable, advises savoring the strawberry. Orwell seemed to be doing that with his new life in Jura; Winston Smith did that with his pursuit of pleasures and liberties.

Another thing that was striking on rereading it is what a dreamy book it is, how far it is from a conventional realist novel that plays by the rules of probability and believability. In the book's third chapter, Smith has a dream of his mother and younger sister who disappeared in the chaos that preceded the present order—he dreams of them often—and then he dreams of a place. "Suddenly he was standing on short springy turf, on a summer evening when the slanting rays of the sun gilded the ground. The landscape that he was looking at recurred so often in his dreams that he was never fully certain whether or not he had seen it in the real world. In his waking thoughts he called it the Golden Country. It was an old, rabbit-bitten pasture, with a foot-track wandering across it and a molehill here and there." It's a classic Orwell landscape, full of unexceptional beauty.

In the dream, a dark-haired young woman appears, and "with what seemed a single movement she tore off her clothes and flung them disdainfully aside." He admires the gesture: "With its grace and carelessness it seemed to annihilate a whole culture, a whole system of thought, as though Big Brother and the Party and the Thought Police could all be swept into nothingness by a single splendid movement of the arm." And then a hundred pages later he's met the dark-haired Julia, who gives him intricate directions to a meeting spot outside London that matches up perfectly with the Golden Country of his dreams, down to the molehills. There, she sweeps off her clothes "with that same magnificent gesture by which a whole civilization seemed to be annihilated."

It's dream and nightmare all the way through, with the agents of the state understanding his mind and deeds and fears better than even their surveillance technology makes possible. Or rather dream, nightmare, and long informative digressions on the workings of the world of *Nineteen Eighty-Four*. Inserted into the text is a lengthy excerpt of the forbidden book by the demonized Goldstein, a discourse on Newspeak at the end of the book, and shorter disquisitions woven in about the politics and practices of the time and place in which Winston and Julia live. This time around, I thought the three elements should not blend, but they do, magnificently. Often they do so because the novel slips imperceptibly from an experience of Winston's to an exposition of some piece of his world, and then back into reverie and dream.

Women's gestures are one of the recurrent motifs, the lover's erotic gesture of abandon and opening, the mother's gesture of drawing in and protecting. It's a book of powerful women, with powers antithetical to its sinisterly powerful men, even down to the affectionate, sixtyish drunk, surname Smith, he meets in the Ministry of Love's prison who puts an arm around him and speculates that she could be his mother. Near the narrative's beginning, Winston attends a movie theater where he sees footage of a lifeboat full of refugee children being mowed down by machine guns. In that boat, a woman tries to shelter her small son with her arms, though of course her arms can't stop bullets. The gesture returns when he dreams of his mother again: "The dream was still vivid in his mind, especially the enveloping protecting gesture of the arm in which its whole meaning seemed to be contained."

He thinks of his mother: "It would not have occurred to her that an action which is ineffectual thereby becomes meaningless. If you loved someone, you loved him, and when you had nothing else to give, you still gave him love." Things that matter for their own sake and serve no larger purpose or practical agenda recur as ideals in the book. The thrush in the Golden Country sings for no perceptible purpose, and listening to it he falls out of fear and out of thought into pure being.

And though the Golden Country, where Winston and Julia first make love, is a powerful place, the book finds its heart in the bedroom above the junk shop in the prole district where Winston bought the journal and then a glass paperweight with a bit of coral in it. Like the thrush, the paperweight is something he values because it exists for its own sake, outside of some larger scheme of utility. Uselessness is itself a kind of resistance, or rather what is deemed useless serves subtler purposes. The paperweight he brings back to place on the table in the bedroom has its own power as a lens onto another world: "a little chunk of history that they've forgotten to alter. It's a message from a hundred years ago, if one knew how to read it." And it's the world they've made: "The paperweight was the room he was in, and the coral was Julia's life and his own, fixed in a sort of eternity at the heart of the crystal."

There's another kind of enchantment out the window of that bedroom. On three occasions he looks out and sees "a monstrous woman, solid as a Norman pillar, with brawny red forearms and a sacking apron strapped about her middle. . . . One had the feeling that she would have been perfectly content, if the June evening had been endless and the supply of clothes inexhaustible, to remain there for a thousand years, pegging out diapers and singing rubbish." Each time they see her she's hanging out diapers and singing, in a magnificent cockney-accented contralto, the same song. It's drivel, we're told, but its rhymes about love, yearning, loss seem subversive for their celebration of personal attachment and memory, and the voice and its emotional force transcend the song's content.

Early on, he reflected that tragedy such as his mother's "belonged to the ancient time, to a time when there were still privacy, love, and friendship, and when the members of a family stood by one another without needing to know the reason." The song and the singer celebrate at least a banal version of that love. The song: she remembers and cherishes and mourns, or at least sings of those things. The diapers: she tends new life that constitutes a kind of hope for the future and a gesture of care in the present. The regime seeks to eradicate hope and memory and history and human relations, to create an unchanging present in which it wields absolute control, not only of external events but internal life. Love is subversive. Memory is subversive. Hope is subversive. Even perception is subversive. "The Party told you to reject the evidence of your eyes and ears. It was their final, most essential command." And later science, evolutionary history, the fossil record, the ancientness of the earth are all denied by a torturer who announces, "We make the laws of nature."

Perhaps she has been, will be there for a thousand years. The washerwoman is a revelation, an elemental life force, a divinity of sorts, a fertility goddess. As his idyll winds to its brutal conclusion, he sees her one last time after reading Goldstein's book to Julia in their mahogany bed. Julia has gone to sleep as he reaches a passage promising to reveal the central secret of the regime. He pauses, both frustrated and reassured by a book that has thus far only confirmed what he already knew, falls asleep himself, and upon waking hears her singing once again.

This time around he goes to the window and sees her, at work in in a fresh, rain-washed world, more deeply. "It struck him for the first time that she was beautiful. It had never before occurred to him that the body of a woman of fifty, blown up to monstrous dimensions by childbearing, then hardened, roughened by work till it was coarse in the grain like an over-ripe turnip, could be beautiful. But it was so, and after all, he thought, why not? The solid, contourless body, like a block of granite, and the rasping red skin, bore the same relation to the body of a girl as the rose-hip to the rose. Why should the fruit be held inferior to the flower?"

It's a moment, it seems, for the author as well as his protagonist, of recognition of another kind of beauty, of a toughness that is life and perpetuates life, of survival and endurance as beautiful in themselves. And it's a moment when metaphor mends disconnection, when what he has learned of flowers and fruit and the passage of time in the botanical world becomes equipment to understand humanity. Winston muses, "She had had her momentary flowering, a year, perhaps, of wild-rose beauty and then she had suddenly swollen like a fertilized fruit and grown hard and red and coarse, and then her life had been laundering, scrubbing, darning, cooking, sweeping, polishing, mending, scrubbing, laundering, first for children, then for grandchildren, over thirty un-broken years. At the end of it she was still singing." He thinks of the thrush that sang in the Golden Country, of things that exist for them-selves, in celebration, feels a "mystical reverence" for the singer. Then the Thought Police break in, and the idyll is over. That it ends on this vision of beauty and awe seemed significant this time around.

The rest of the book narrates Winston's destruction and his pitiful afterlife. But he has found what he sought. At various points, Winston thinks that "if there is hope . . . it lies in the proles." Winston's reduction through brainwashing and torture into a defeated, obedient wraith isn't a prophecy of doom. The book doesn't rest its case on his fate; it bets on the washerwoman and what she represents, as vitality and generosity and fecundity. Or so it seemed to me.

Margaret Atwood has made a different case for why *Nineteen Eighty-Four* is not quite the dystopia it is often taken for. "Orwell has been accused of bitterness and pessimism—of leaving us with a vision of the future in which the individual has no chance, and where the brutal, totalitarian boot of the all-controlling Party will grind into the human face, for ever," she wrote in *The Guardian* in 2003. She rests her case on the final section of the book, the appendix on Newspeak cast as a historical document, noting that "the essay on Newspeak is written in standard English, in the third person, and in the past tense, which can only mean that the regime has fallen, and that language and individuality have survived. For whoever has written the essay on Newspeak, the world of *Nineteen Eighty-Four* is over. Thus, it's my view that Orwell had much more faith in the resilience of the human spirit than he's usually been given credit for." She borrowed this device to suggest in the mock-scholarly afterword to her novel *The Handmaid's Tale* that the regime at the heart of it would likewise perish.

Horror doesn't have to be permanent to matter. The Soviet Union collapsed in 1991, but it caused the deaths of tens of millions and the suffering and destruction of far more, and some of its brutality lives on in the current Russian government (which is energetically rehabilitating Stalin, rewriting history, and killing off dissidents). Joy doesn't have to and can't be permanent either. Winston Smith pursues pleasure and joy and finds them, and is then tortured and brainwashed to make him a person incapable of those things. It's significant that he also pursues truth and meaning and that these also matter to him, these are also crushed by the regime.

He has been defeated; he has managed to live first, and though those victories are fleeting they are victories. Are there victories that are not temporary? There's another story implicit in the book, one in which Winston Smith breaks no rules, takes no chances, finds no joys, makes no love. It's a story in which there is no torture, no prison, or rather in which those things exist but they control him more effectively by how he obeys the regime in order to steer clear of them than by being applied to him directly after he rebels.

In the Golden Country, after Julia and Winston have made love for the first time, he reflects, "In the old days, he thought, a man looked at a girl's body and saw that it was desirable, and that was the end of the story," but in their time it is a political act, a blow against the regime, a victory. A fleeting one, and one for which they will pay dearly. *Nineteen Eighty-Four* is a warning about present as well as potential dangers, in defense of all the things Orwell valued, and on this reading of the book I noticed them too. A warning is not a prophecy: the former assumes that we have choices and cautions us about the consequences; the latter operates on the basis of a fixed future (and of course the novel was about atrocities and perils in the present, as well as what they might become if taken to their logical end). As the novelist and speculator on utopias and dystopias Octavia Butler put it, "The very act of trying to look ahead to discern possibilities and offer warnings is in itself an act of hope."

Orwell completed the novel as tuberculosis was slowly killing him, and it's often proposed that Winston Smith's appalling physical deterioration in prison mirrored his own from the disease and its harsh treatments. You could say that the tuberculosis bacteria had made a garden of his lungs and were flourishing there, feeding on him as though the soft tissue of his lungs was fertile topsoil. The disease had been rampant in the nineteenth century and into the twentieth— John Keats, Emily Brontë, Henry David Thoreau, Paul Laurence Dunbar, Anton Chekhov, and Franz Kafka are among the writers who died of it. As Orwell was dying, medical science was just beginning to develop the antibiotic treatments that can cure it. Refined versions of those medicines have diminished its impact in wealthier nations, though it still kills more than a million annually and is one of the world's leading infectious diseases. Healthy people's immune systems are often able to stall the progression of the disease or destroy the bacilli altogether. Orwell was not such a person.

After a winter in London, he went back to Barnhill from April through December 1947, and his sister Avril stayed on after his departure to tend the animals and the garden—or rather farm, because it had grown in scale. That fall, he had finished a draft of the novel while his health deteriorated, and on Christmas Eve he went into a hospital near Glasgow for seven months. TB bacilli are hungry for oxygen, and so as part of his treatment, the doctors tried to reduce his left lung's access to air. They crushed the left phrenic nerve that controls breathing and began a routine of pumping his abdomen full of air every few days to keep pressure on the deflated lung.

Though stuffed with as much food as he could eat as part of the regimen, he grew increasingly gaunt. His body was disintegrating, losing the integrity of organ function, of the cell walls, veins, arteries, capillaries whose ruptures produced all that blood. Corruption was overtaking him. He feared that Richard might catch the disease from him: "After I was certain what was wrong with me," he wrote to Eileen's brother's widow on New Year's Day, 1948, "I tried to keep him out of my room, but of course couldn't do so entirely."

With the help of his friend David Astor in getting an export license and his newfound wealth, he obtained a supply of streptomycin, a new drug being used to treat TB in the United States, not yet available to patients in Britain. Perhaps because his doctors had no experience with the medicine, he took a high daily dose that made his skin turn red and flake off, his hair and nails come out, and ulcers appear in his mouth that bled in the night so that his mouth was glued shut with dried blood every morning. After fifty days of dosing, he stopped, and the symptoms disappeared. He gave away the rest of the imported medicine, and it is said to have saved two women from the disease.

In late summer 1948, he returned to the island for the rest of the year and immediately resumed a domestic diary, which begins with a report on the oats and hay and "roses, poppies, sweet williams, marigolds full out, lupins still with some flowers. . . . A lot of apples on some of the 1946 trees, but not much growth. Strawberries superlatively good." The chickens, pig, and cows were doing well, and they had acquired a horse named Bob, but this diary, unlike the earlier ones, noted his own condition. Sometimes too unwell even to keep up the diary, he stayed through Christmas Eve. That day he wrote his last domestic-diary entry, ending, "Snowdrops up all over the place. A few tulips showing. Some wallflowers still trying to flower." A little more than a week later, he was taken away to the sanatorium in the Cotswolds in which he spent the first nine months of 1949.

That September, as his condition further deteriorated, he was transferred to University College Hospital in London. His last diary recounts what he called death dreams: "Sometimes of the sea or the sea shore—more often of enormous, splendid buildings or streets or ships, in which I often lose my way, but always with a peculiar feeling of happiness & of walking in sunlight. Unquestionably all these buildings etc. mean death." *Nineteen Eighty-Four* was published in Britain and the United States a few weeks before his forty-sixth and final birthday, June 25, 1949. Widely reviewed, it made a powerful impression on critics and readers, and its sales and impact have never ceased. It was attacked furiously by communists who still supported the USSR, socialists who saw it as an attack on the Labour government then in power, and misapprehended by conservatives then and ever after as a book aligned with their views.

He tried to set the record straight with a statement addressed to the head of the United Auto Workers in the United States that got published in *Life* magazine: "My novel *Nineteen Eighty-four* is *not* intended as an attack on socialism, or on the British Labour party, but as a show-up of the perversions to which a centralized economy is liable, and which have already been partly realized in Communism and fascism. I do not believe that the kind of society I describe necessarily *will* arrive, but I believe (allowing of course for the fact that the book is a satire) that something resembling it *could* arrive. I believe also that totalitarian ideas have taken root in the minds of intellectuals everywhere," and he noted that the book was set in England to emphasize that totalitarianism could triumph anywhere. A few days later he made plans about pigs for Jura, in a letter to his friend Richard Rees.

In that private hospital room in London, he died from a massive lung hemorrhage in the small hours of the night on January 21, 1950, which is to say he drowned in his own blood. He died with a fishing pole in his room. A few months earlier, wearing a velvet smoking jacket purchased for the occasion, he had married the young magazine editor Sonia Brownell. They had plans to fly, with his newfound affluence from book sales, in a private plane to a sanatorium in Switzerland. There he hoped that he could get some fishing in. The fishing pole, like the trees and roses he planted, the son he adopted, and maybe the marriage he embarked upon from a hospital bed, seems like a gesture of hope, not that the future was certain, but that it was worth reaching for.

Among the few essays he wrote in his last years was a long, thoughtful piece about Mahatma Gandhi, who had been assassinated in January 1948, a few months after he had helped drive the British out of India. The essay appeared in January 1949. Essays are often explicit where novels are implicit, and "Reflections on Gandhi" restates some of the principles of *Nineteen Eighty-Four*. Orwell found alien and a little alarming what he saw as the inflexible absolutism and asceticism of Gandhi and his transcendent spirituality. He found in these qualities a kind of abstraction and a sense that the end justifies the means that were to him too close to the ideological fanaticism he'd devoted his life to opposing. The essay may not be an accurate reading of Gandhi, but it is a clear measure of his own views and priorities.

The antithesis of transcendent might be rooted and grounded, and Orwell was attached to the ordinary joys and pleasures and the love of the things of this world and not the next. He wrote another one of his credos in the essay: "The essence of being human is that one does not seek perfection, that one *is* sometimes willing to commit sins for the sake of loyalty, that one does not push asceticism to the point where it makes friendly intercourse impossible, and that one is prepared in the end to be defeated and broken up by life, which is the inevitable price of fastening one's love upon other human individuals. No doubt alcohol, tobacco and so forth are things that a saint must avoid, but sainthood is also a thing that human beings must avoid. . . . Many people genuinely do not wish to be saints, and it is probable that some who achieve or aspire to sainthood have never felt much temptation to be human beings."

That is, he saw the willingness to suffer and accept suffering and one's own flaws and others as part of being human and the price paid for the joys also included. The commitment to the things of this world could also be the focus of a spiritual discipline, a willingness to sacrifice, and a warmth he saw Gandhi as lacking. In some sense, perhaps his unsaintly martyr Winston Smith became fully human through his misadventures, and his recognition of the beauty of the washerwoman was part of that, a new capacity to see imperfect and unidealized beauty. "Our job," Orwell declared in the Gandhi essay, "is to make life worth living on this earth, which is the only earth we have."

He asked that roses be planted on his grave. When I checked, a few years ago, a scrappy red rose was blooming there.

# THREE

# The River Orwell

F ar from Suffolk's coastline, in the flat countryside of East Anglia, the slender River Gipping gathers volume from tributary streams and flows toward the sea. In the town of Ipswich, at the Stoke Bridge, its name changes and it becomes the eleven-mile-long River Orwell (or twelve or nine, depending on the source). The bridge and the name change mark roughly where the freshwater river ends and the tidal river mixing fresh water and salt water begins, if most of its length should be called a river at all rather than a long estuary. It is not quite the same waterway it was in the early 1930s when an ambitious young writer is said to have plucked his surname from it. Thanks to sea-level rise driven by climate change, it may become a longer river as the point at which saltwater intrusion moves upstream, or not, since the rising North Sea is also gnawing hungrily at the Suffolk coast. Those rising oceans also increase the frequency and reach of floods, and a two-hundred-metric-ton £70 million flood barrier lurks underwater in the Orwell, intended to protect Ipswich into the early twenty-second century.

When I spent an afternoon meandering near the bridge that marks where the Gipping becomes the Orwell, Ipswich seemed a weary town in which many buildings no longer served the purposes for which they were built, and what had once been an important seaport seemed to be in its afterlife. There was a window display about the last sailing ships to come up to the port, bringing wheat from Australia in the 1930s, a great pale blue octopus with chains for arms painted on an abandoned industrial building, more graffiti in the skate park on the Gipping side of the bridge, and a shape like a phantom tree from where ivy had been torn off the wall of another old riverside building.

The Orwell widens out past Ipswich to join the Stour as they meet the North Sea. The deepwater port they form was for more than a millennium important for trade and for incoming and outgoing invasions and coastal defense. In the year 885, King Alfred confronted invading Danes there, but further fleets of Danes managed to sail up the Orwell, destroy Ipswich, and establish a Danish kingdom. It was a port from which military invasions were launched, pilgrims embarked, and trade ships sailed and landed, carrying wool, salt, and cloth and bringing books and wine from the continent.

The broad span of the modern Orwell Bridge crosses the river just upstream from the Orwell Country Park, an expanse of forest sloping down to the river's pebbled strand. When I visited the park, the acorns were pale green on the oaks, a line of dark green seaweed showed where high tide was, and storm-tossed men's underwear loaded with gravel among the smooth pebbles bore witness to other events. Sam had joined me briefly on my explorations, and when we were on that river's edge, he wondered whether the word *Orwellian* should perhaps mean something other than ominous, corrupt, sinister, deceitful, a hypocrisy or dishonesty so destructive that it is an assault on truth and thought and rights.

Not many writers become adjectives, and even Joycean or Shake-spearean don't circulate the way that Orwellian does. A quick search for the word at *The Washington Post* produced 754 results, including "an Orwellian corporate bureaucracy of censors"; "Orwellian tactics of information suppression"; "an Orwellian test for immigrants"; "Or-wellian assaults on objective reality"; "Orwellian language to obscure evil"; even "Orwellian doublespeak," in which the word *doublespeak* seems to come from *Nineteen Eighty-Four*'s neologism *doublethink*. The word was particularly useful for describing and deploring the Chinese government's current attempt to create total social control and supervision for all its citizens while imprisoning, sterilizing, raz-ing the mosques of, and otherwise committing genocide against the Uighur Muslims of western China.

I have not performed the popular feat of connecting phenomena Orwell described and deplored to the crimes and travesties of our own times, not least because the task is too easy and the relevant top-ics too abundant and obvious (and even so, the differences between our troubles and the absolutist and austere tyranny of *Nineteen Eighty-Four* are also meaningful). The age of Trump and climate de-nial are of course over-the-top Orwellian; since before the year 1984, editorialists have reached for the novel to describe corrosive politics, including Ronald Reagan's bland euphemisms for class and race war and Tony Blair and George W. Bush's campaign of deceit to launch wars against that abstraction "terror" that killed perhaps a million nonabstract human beings. That era produced responses such as the website the Memory Hole, named after the desktop pit into which Winston Smith dumped newspaper articles once their account of history had been replaced by a more expedient version.

Even more than that, Silicon Valley, in whose shadow I dwell, has become a global superpower. The unprecedented wealth of the few corporations that have achieved dominance comes from managing the flow of information as the locks, weirs, and floodgates manage the River Orwell, and from amassing more information on each of us than Big Brother, the KGB, Stasi, and the FBI ever dreamed of, too often with our willing cooperation as our phones track our movements and social media platforms and retail websites compile dossiers on us that are sold to yet other corporations. Their impact includes the swaying of public imagination in the 2016 elections that brought on first Brexit and then Trump, as well as the rise of a demagogue in Brazil and genocide in Burma. New technologies around facial recognition and DNA tracing have further extended institutional power and eroded privacy. I doubt his critiques will cease to be relevant in the next several decades, and so *Orwellian* is too handy a term to abandon, but Sam had a point.

Orwell's signal achievement was to name and describe as no one else had the way that totalitarianism was a threat not just to liberty and human rights but to language and consciousness, and he did it in so compelling a way that his last book casts a shadow—or a beacon's light—into the present. But that achievement is enriched and deepened by the commitments and idealism that fueled it, the things he valued and desired, and his valuation of desire itself, and pleasure and joy, and his recognition that these can be forces of opposition to the authoritarian state and its soul-destroying intrusions.

The work he did is everyone's job now. It always was.

# GRATITUDE

I wrote this book in a time of intense crisis, around climate, environment, and nature, around human rights, democracy, media, technology, gender, and race, and around the questions of who would be allowed to speak and who would check the liars. Living for a few years with one foot in Orwell's time often made me think about who did Orwell's work in our own. The political essayists, historians, and journalists, the media and technology critics, the dissidents and whistleblowers, the human rights and climate organizers and defenders of the marginalized and devalued were compelling presences for me all through the years this book took shape, some as public figures I read or listened to, some as friends and acquaintances whose conversations and examples kept me going, some as both. There were so many.

I can name a few with whom I was personally connected: Taj James, Erica Chenoweth, Dahlia Lithwick, Astra Taylor, Marina Sitrin, L. A. Kauffman, Bob Fulkerson, Anna Goldstein, Joe Lamb, Antonia Juhahz, Roshi Joan Halifax, Nancy Meister, Philip Heying, Jessica Tully, Padma Viswanathan, Cleve Jones, Garnette Cadogan, Joshua Jelly-Schapiro, Eyal Press, Christina Gerhardt, Siva Vaidhyanathan, Susan Sheu, Brian Colker, Conchita Lozano and Galicia Lozano Stack, Moriah Ulinskas, Mona Eltahawy, Ayelet Waldman, Natashia Deon, Jaime Cortez, Jonny Diamond and John Freeman at

*Lit Hub* and all my *Guardian* editors, Jarvis Masters, Blake Spalding, Jen Castle, Terry Tempest Williams, Brooke Williams, Caroline Nassif, May Boeve, Bill McKibben, Steve Kretzman, Stephanie Syjuco, Erik Mebust, Thelma Young-Lutunatabua, everyone at Oil Change International, and of course the Auntie Sewing Squad and its inimitable overlord Kristina Wong. They demonstrated again and again why precision and accuracy in language and fact and science and history matter, of what power one voice or the chorus of many ordinary people can have, of how what matters most can be and must be defended, not least by being named and recognized, understood and praised. But I also found relevant to this book and its ideas the defenders and producers of pleasure and joy, beauty and those passages of a life that are not ordinarily productive, not quantifiable in terms of results, those private, musing, meandering moments that also feed us and shape us, which is to say artists, musicians, gardeners, and poets.

Writing a book is a solitary business, or the part that is the actual writing is, and this one was written mostly during the exceptional isolation of the COVID-19 pandemic. But it emerges from conversations, kindness, and friendship from many people. Thanks go first of all, of course, to my dear friend Sam Green. Our ongoing conversations and his endless curiosity and enthusiasm for trees launched me on the initial quest that brought me face-to-face with Orwell's roses. To Dawn Spanyol and Graham Lamb, who welcomed me in, a huge debt of gratitude for their warmth to a stranger and enthusiasm about gardens, writers, and the process of sifting through meanings and possibilities and evidence of the past. (I hope readers will respect their privacy and not pillage their home.) To Rob Macfarlane for so meanders in words and walking over so many years.

Thank you to Nate Miller for an extraordinary week in Colombia poking into the rose-growing industry and for almost two decades of friendship. To Beatriz Fuentes and the Casa de Las y Los Trabajadores de las Flores and her colleagues who spoke with me there, and to Nancy Viviana Piñeiro for translating those interviews.

To Olga Tomchin and Zarina Zabrisky for help with Russian sources and information. To Mauricio Montiel Figueras, for an enchanted afternoon at the Guadalupe shrine in Mexico City, and dear chilanga friend Adriana Camarena for making many Guadalupe connections over the years, including getting me to San Francisco's cathedral before dawn on December 12, 2010, where we saw the archbishop kneel before a Latino immigrant playing Juan Diego and a shower of many-colored rose petals from the cathedral's dome. To Nicola Beauman for the loan of her home in Cambridge, with thanks for the generosity and for the enchantment of the back garden and the book collection there.

To Adam Hochschild, who had a very helpful response to a December 2019 email titled "Do you have time for a fun chat about Stalin?" for his long friendship, his understanding of the Soviet Union, the Spanish Civil War, and left politics in the twentieth century, his books on those subjects, and his extremely helpful reading of a draft of this book. To carla bergman for her response to an early draft and for her friendship and her advocacy of militant joy. To Joe Lamb and planetologist David Grinspoon for taking a look at the scientific parts of the book.

I owe immense thanks to the scholars who collected and edited Orwell's writings, the letters and recollections of his friends, and biographical details about him, and to their perspectives and interpretations, particularly Peter Davison for the twenty-volume edition of Orwell's complete works. I am grateful to Peter Stansky, whose two volumes of Orwell biography demonstrated how much empathy and insight can amplify each other, and whom I had the joy of meeting at his home near Stanford early in this project. More thanks to Amy Elizabeth Robinson for telling me that Peter lived near me and putting us in touch. To Adam Eaker, curator of painting at the Metropolitan Museum, for correspondence and conversation about Sir Joshua Reynolds's painting of Orwell's ancestor and access to the museum's archive of information on it. To Raghu Karnad for the offer to take me to Orwell's birthplace in northern India, with regrets this adventure wasn't possible (and hope it may be at some future point). To Damaris Fletcher for a delightful correspondence about Barnhill. To Michael Mattis and Julie Hochberg for permission to reproduce Tina Modotti's photograph *Roses, Mexico*, and to Caroline Deck at the Phillips auction house, who graciously put me in touch with the new owners.

Thanks to the Berkeley and San Francisco rose gardens and their gardeners and the principles that funded roses for the public. Thanks as well to the farm stand next to the Simón Bolívar statue in San Francisco's United Nations Plaza for supplying me with their scruffy, thorny, fragrant, locally grown roses for more than thirty years.

To my agent, Frances Coady of Aragi Inc., and my editors for this book, Paul Slovak and Bella Lacey, and to the editorial, design, publicity, and marketing staff at Viking—particularly Maya Baran, Sara Leonard, and Allie Merola—and Granta Books and Pru Rowlandson there, for their toil on behalf of *Orwell's Roses*. And to designer Jon Gray for the glorious cover.

And last and never least, to Charles, for the expertise as a pulmonary physician he brought to bear on Orwell's illnesses, and for companionship all through the exploration, the reading, and the writing, the doubting and deciding and wondering.

# NOTES

xi **"The very act of trying"**: Octavia Butler, "A Few Rules for Predicting the Future," *Essence*, May 2000, 165–6.

## PART I: THE PROPHET AND THE HEDGEHOG

### DAY OF THE DEAD

5 **"Their silence is more eloquent"**: Man Ray, *Self Portrait* (Boston: Little, Brown, 1963), pp. 281–82.

7 **"Yet, after this lapse"**: This and following excerpts are from "A Good Word for the Vicar of Bray," in *Smothered Under Journalism*, vol. 18 of *The Complete Works of George Orwell*, ed. Peter Davison (London: Secker and Warburg, 1998), p. 259.

9 **coined the term *cold war***: "You and the Atom Bomb," *Tribune*, October 19, 1945, and in Paul Anderson, ed., *Orwell in Tribune: "As I Please" and Other Writing 1943–47* (London: Politicos, 2006), p. 247.

10 **"Even an apple tree"**: "A Good Word for the Vicar of Bray," in *Smothered Under Journalism*, p. 261.

13 **"the glory of the garden"**: Esther M. Brookes's eight-page self-published brochure *Monks Fitchett—The Road to George Orwell* (1983). Graham had remarked to me of her, "But would you like to know about the real celebrity who lived in this house?" half joking about the major impression she made on the area.

13 **"Cut down the remaining phloxes"**: Peter Davison, ed., *George Orwell Diaries* (New York: Liveright, 2009), pp. 252–53.

### FLOWER POWER

15 **the body symbolizes everything else**: Mary Douglas, *Purity and Danger: An Analysis of the Concepts of Pollution and Taboo* (London: Routledge, 1991), p. 123.

17 **"Your thorns are the best part of you"**: Marianne Moore, *Becoming Marianne Moore: The Early Poems 1907–1924* (Berkeley: University of California Press, 2002), p. 83.

18 **"The agile brain of the warm-blooded birds"**: Loren Eiseley, *The Immense Journey* (New York: Time Inc., 1962), p. 47.

19 **two hundred tons, equivalent to 134 million hips:** "Rose Hip Syrup Supplies on Sale Next Month," *Times* (London), January 15, 1942.

20 **"Most have five petals":** Theophrastus quoted in Jennifer Potter, *The Rose* (London: Atlantic Books, 2010), p. 10; the Pliny the Elder quote is on p. 15.

## LILACS AND NAZIS

22 **"I gave it up partly because the climate":** "Autobiographical Note," written in 1940 for *Twentieth Century Authors*, reprinted in Sonia Orwell and Ian Angus, eds., *Orwell: My Country Right or Left: 1940–1943* (Boston: David R. Godine, 2000), p. 23.

23 **"East Enders, mostly costermongers":** These two quotes are from his hop-picking journal rather than his 1931 published piece. Sonia Orwell and Ian Angus, eds., *Orwell: An Age Like This: 1920–1940* (Boston: David R. Godine, 2000), p. 63.

24 **"What impressed me as much":** Noelle Oxenhandler, "Fall from Grace," *New Yorker*, June 16, 1997, p. 65.

24 **"Swing was really a dance":** Jacques Lusseyran, *And There Was Light* (New York: Parabola Books, 1987), p. 161.

25 **Much of his life, he suffered:** A good account of his medical history is John J. Ross, "Tuberculosis, Bronchiectasis, and Infertility: What Ailed George Orwell?," *Clinical Infectious Diseases* 41, no. 11 (December 1, 2005): pp. 1599–603.

26 **"He was a rebel against his own":** Arthur Koestler in Audrey Coppard and Bernard Crick, *Orwell Remembered* (London: BBC, 1984), p. 169.

27 **"not-too-long country walks":** These quotes are from Jacintha Buddicom, *Eric and Us*, postscript by Dione Venables (Chichester, UK: Finlay Publisher, 2006), pp. 26 and 38.

27 **"We used to go for long, trailing kind of walks":** *Coming Up for Air* (San Diego: Harcourt, 1950), p. 43.

28 **"If you want a picture of the future":** *Nineteen Eighty-Four* (London: Penguin, 2003), p. 307.

28 **"Political language . . . is designed"**: "Politics and the English Language," *Horizon*, April 1946, and in Sonia Orwell and Ian Angus, eds., *George Orwell: In Front of Your Nose: 1945–1950* (Boston: David R. Godine, 2000), p. 139.

28 **"Ask a journalist what a jackboot is"**: As I Please, *Tribune*, March 17, 1944, and in Sonia Orwell and Ian Angus, eds., *As I Please, 1943–1945* (Boston: David R. Godine, 2000), p. 110. He took up the jackboot question again on August 18, 1944, also in *Tribune*: "In spite of my campaign against the jackboot . . . I notice that jackboots are as common as ever. . . . But I am still without any clear information as to what a jackboot is. It is a kind of boot that you put on when you want to behave tyrannically: that is as much as anyone seems to know" (p. 177).

28 **"In the good days when nothing in Woolworth's"**: As I Please, *Tribune*, January 21, 1944, and in *Orwell in Tribune*, pp. 87–88.

28 **"The garden is still Augean"**: Letter to Jack Common, April 16, 1936, in Peter Davison, ed., *George Orwell: A Life in Letters* (New York: Liveright, 2010), p. 60.

28 **"A dead German soldier"**: "Revenge Is Sour," *Tribune*, November 9, 1945, and in *Orwell in Tribune*, p. 258.

30 **"Anyone who cares to examine my work"**: "Why I Write," in *Smothered Under Journalism*, p. 319.

30 **"the weed with a pink flower"**: As I Please, *Tribune*, August 25, 1944, and in *Orwell in Tribune*, p. 181.

30 **"I had brought with me two things impossible"**: Coppard and Crick, *Orwell Remembered*, p. 75.

31 **"He commented on the actions of politicians"**: Coppard and Crick, *Orwell Remembered*, p. 91.

31 **"He knew an awful lot about the countryside"**: Kay Ekevall in Stephen Wadhams, *Remembering Orwell* (London: Penguin, 1984), p. 57.

31 **"If you went with a country walk"**: Coppard and Crick, *Orwell Remembered*, pp. 239–40.

31 **"bored him to death"**: David Holbrook in Wadhams, *Remembering Orwell*, p. 179.

32 **"A happy vicar I might have been"**: "A Happy Vicar I Might Have Been," on the website of the Orwell Foundation, https://www.orwellfoundation.com/the-orwell-foundation/orwell/poetry/a-happy-vicar-i-might-have-been/.

32 **That aunt, Helene Limouzin**: Nellie Limouzin was written about by Darcy Moore at some length in "Orwell's Aunt Nellie," *George Orwell Studies* 4, no. 2 (2020): pp. 30–45.

32 "There was an Aunt Ivy": Buddicom, *Eric and Us*, p. 14.

33 "It will pay the rent": Nellie Limouzin, in *A Kind of Compulsion*, vol. 10 of *The Complete Works of George Orwell*, ed. Peter Davison (London: Secker and Warburg, 1998), p. 314.

34 "Forgive me for not writing": Letter to Brenda Salkeld, in *Orwell: An Age Like This*, p. 119.

34 "marrows & pumpkins, which are swelling": Letter to Eleanor Jaques, in *George Orwell: A Life in Letters*, p. 26.

35 "This age makes me so sick": Letter to Brenda Salkeld, in *Orwell: An Age Like This*, p. 140.

35 "Yes, I remember we went to supper": Pitter in Coppard and Crick, *Orwell Remembered*, p. 70.

36 "I was both a snob and a revolutionary": *The Road to Wigan Pier* (London: Penguin Classics, 2001), p. 130.

37 "the red cows were grazing": *A Clergyman's Daughter* (Oxford: Oxford University Press, 2021), p. 44.

38 "The garden is potentially good": *Orwell: An Age Like This*, p. 214.

40 "He was traditional in a way": Spender in Coppard and Crick, *Orwell Remembered*, p. 262.

40 "I lost my habit of punctual correspondence": Eileen O'Shaughnessy Blair in Peter Davison, ed., *The Lost Orwell: Being a Supplement to "The Complete Works of George Orwell"* (London: Timewell Press, 2006), p. 64.

41 "We have now 26 hens": *George Orwell Diaries*, p. 154.

43 "Outside my work": "Autobiographical Note," in *Orwell: My Country Right or Left*, p. 24.

44 "In a world where '[n]ot merely the validity'": Kunio Shin, "The Uncanny Golden Country: Late Modernist Utopia in *Nineteen Eighty-Four*," June 20, 2017, https://modernismmodernity.org/articles/uncanny-golden-country.

44 "The Party told you": *Nineteen Eighty-Four*, p. 92.

44 "There's probably been nothing else": "Ross Gay Interview at *Jacket Copy*: He Has His Own Orchard!" *Harriet* (blog), Poetry Foundation, https://www.poetryfoundation.org/harriet/2016/02/ross-gay-interview-at-jacket-copy-he-has-his-own-orchard.

45 "I saw a little boy, perhaps ten years old": March 1947 preface to the Ukrainian edition of *Animal Farm*, in *It Is What I Think*, vol. 19 of *The Complete Works of George Orwell*, ed. Peter Davison (London: Secker & Warburg, 1998), p. 88.

46 "the dahlias blackened immediately": *George Orwell Diaries*, p. 249.

46 **"Watching the things of the world come apart"**: Wendy Johnson, *Gardening at the Dragon's Gate* (New York: Bantam Dell, 2008), p. 121.

46 **"The source of his self-regenerative power"**: George Woodcock, *The Crystal Spirit: A Study of George Orwell* (Boston: Little, Brown and Co., 1966), p. 61.

47 **"Joy remakes people through combat"**: carla bergman and Nick Montgomery, *Joyful Militancy: Building Thriving Resistance in Toxic Times* (Oakland, Calif.: PM Press, 2017), pp. 59–60.

PART II: GOING UNDERGROUND

SMOKE, SHALE, ICE, MUD, ASHES

51 **we think of these plants:** Michael Pollan writes in *The Botany of Desire* (New York: Random House, 2001), "We automatically think of domestication as something we do to other species, but it makes just as much sense to think of it as something certain plants and animals have done to us, a clever evolutionary strategy for advancing their own interests" (p. xvi.)

52 **"The modern English literary world"**: *The Road to Wigan Pier*, p. 152.

53 **"The monstrous scenery of slag-heaps"**: *The Road to Wigan Pier*, pp. 14–15.

53 **"a world from which vegetation had been banished"**: This and the next quote are from *The Road to Wigan Pier*, p. 98.

53 **"in the darkness you can see long serpentine fires"**: *George Orwell Diaries* (Wigan Pier section), p. 77.

54 **"some of the older men have their foreheads"**: *George Orwell Diaries*, p. 37.

54 **"Our civilization . . . *is* founded on coal"**: *The Road to Wigan Pier*, p. 18.

CARBONIFEROUS

57 **"After Laurentia had converged"**: "Variscan Orogeny," Geological Society of London, https://www.geolsoc.org.uk/Plate-Tectonics/Chap4-Plate-Tectonics-of-the-UK/Variscan-Orogeny.

59 **In 2009, scientists reported:** Howard J. Falcon-Lang, William A. DiMichele, Scott Elrick, and W. John Nelson, "Going underground: In search of Carboniferous coal forests," *Geology Today* 25, no. 5 (September–October 2009): 181–84.

60 **Georg Feulner theorized that the cold:** Georg Feulner, "Formation of most of our coal brought Earth close to global glaciation," *Proceedings of the*

*National Academy of Sciences of the United States of America* 114, no. 43 (October 24, 2017): 11333-11337. https://doi.org/10.1073/pnas.1712062114.

60 **"All that is solid"**: Karl Marx and Frederick Engels, *The Communist Manifesto: A Modern Edition* (London: Verso, 1998), p. 39.

61 **"The remains of the swamp grass"**: M. Ilin, *New Russia's Primer: The Story of the Five-Year Plan*, trans. George S. Counts and Nucia P. Lodge (New York: Houghton Mifflin, 1931), available online at https://marxists.org/sub ject/art/literature/children/texts/ilin/new/ch06.html.

## IN DARKNESS

63 **"There are still living a few very old women"**: *The Road to Wigan Pier*, p. 30.

64 **"I have to trap without a light"**: *The Condition and Treatment of the Children Employed in the Mines of the United Kingdom* (London: William Strange, 1842), p. 48.

66 **In 1800, Britain mined:** Figures for British coal mining, 1800 to present: Hannah Ritchie, "The death of UK coal in five charts," Our World in Data, January 28, 2019, https://ourworldindata.org/death-uk-coal.

66 **In 2015, the last deep coal mine:** Ritchie, "The death of UK coal."

66 **in 2019, the country went a fortnight:** Jasper Jolly, "Great Britain records two weeks of coal-free electricity generation," *Guardian*, May 31, 2019, https://www.theguardian.com/business/2019/may/31/great-britain-rec ords-two-weeks-of-coal-free-electricity-generation.

67 **"After a few hundred yards of walking"**: *George Orwell Diaries*, p. 47.

67 **"The place where these men"**: *George Orwell Diaries*, p. 71.

68 **"When I am digging trenches in my garden"**: *The Road to Wigan Pier*, p. 28.

68 **His friend Richard Rees ruefully remarked:** Richard Rees quoted in Peter Stansky and William Abrahams, *Orwell: The Transformation* (New York: Alfred A. Knopf, 1979), p. 145.

68 **"The Spanish war and other events"**: "Why I Write," in *Smothered Under Journalism*, p. 319.

69 **"1,000 tonnes of smoke particles"**: "Case Study—The Great Smog," Royal Meteorological Society, www.metlink.org/other-weather/miscellaneous-weather /case-studies/case-study-great-smog/.

69 **three times as many Londoners ultimately died:** The figure of twelve thousand deaths is widely given and appears to originate from Michelle L. Bell, Devra L. Davis, and Tony Fletcher, "A Retrospective Assessment of

Mortality from the London Smog Episode of 1952: The Role of Influenza and Pollution," *Environmental Health Perspectives*, January 2004, pp. 6–8.

69 **800,000 Europeans:** See Damian Carrington, "Air pollution deaths are double previous estimates, finds research," *Guardian*, March 12, 2019, https://www.theguardian.com/environment/2019/mar/12/air-pollution -deaths-are-double-previous-estimates-finds-research. For the 2021 study, see Oliver Milman, "'Invisible killer': fossil fuels caused 8.7m deaths globally in 2018, research finds," *Guardian*, February 9, 2021, https://www.theguard ian.com/environment/2021/feb/09/fossil-fuels-pollution-deaths-research.

71 **about 280 parts per million:** PA Media, "Carbon dioxode levels in atmosphere reach record high," *Guardian*, April 7, 2021, https://www.theguardian .com/environment/2021/apr/07/carbon-dioxide-levels-in-atmosphere -reach-record-high.

## PART III: BREAD AND ROSES

### ROSES AND REVOLUTION

77 **Her purchase made the news:** Auction price reported in Rita Reif, Auctions, *New York Times*, April 19, 1991.

78 **she had laid them on their side:** Patricia Albers, *Shadows, Fire, Snow: The Life of Tina Modotti* (Berkeley: University of California Press, 2002), p. 126.

79 **no one cries over artificial flowers:** Peter Coyote in a public conversation with Michael Pollan and the author at Book Passage, Corte Madera, CA, 2019.

79 **"Lilies that fester":** From Shakespeare's "Sonnet 94," *William Shakespeare's Sonnets*, edited by Thomas Tyler (London: David Nutt, 1890), p. 253.

81 **"Within your womb was lit":** Dante, *Paradiso*, XXXIII, lines 6–9, translated by James Finn Cotter (Amity, NY: Amity House, 1987), p. 610.

83 **"when Mary commanded Juan Diego to gather flowers":** D. A. Brading, *Mexican Phoenix: Our Lady of Guadalupe: Image and Tradition Across Five Centuries* (Cambridge: Cambridge University Press, 2001), p. 357.

### WE FIGHT FOR ROSES TOO

85 **"If you want to know what I liked":** This and other quotes from and information about Todd's encounters in southern Illinois and the birth of the phrase "bread and roses" in Helen Todd, "Getting Out the Vote: An Account of a Week's Automobile Campaign by Women Suffragists," *The American Magazine*, September 1911, p. 611–19.

86 **"As we come marching, marching"**: James Oppenheim, *The American Magazine*, December 1911, p. 214.

87 **"We mean to make things over"**: From the song "Eight Hours," published in 1878, with lyrics by I. G. Blanchard and music by Rev. Jesse H. Jones, included in *The Fireside Book of Favorite American Songs*, edited by Margaret Bradford Boni (New York: Simon and Schuster, 1952), according to https://www.marxists.org/subject/mayday/music/eighthour.html.

88 **"what the woman who labors wants"**: Schneiderman's speech was published under the heading "Votes for Women," *Life and Labor*, September 1912, p. 288.

## In Praise Of

92 **"A correspondent reproaches me"**: As I Please, *Orwell in Tribune*, p. 87.

92 **"Last time I mentioned flowers"**: As I Please, *Orwell in Tribune*, pp. 129–30.

93 **"Is it wicked"**: "Some Thoughts on the Common Toad," *Tribune*, April 12, 1946, and in *Orwell in Tribune*, p. 307 and *Smothered Under Journalism*, p. 239.

93 **in 1939, they reportedly burned:** Daniela Späth/lbh, "Conspiracies swirl in 1939 Nazi art burning," Deutsche Welle (DW), March 20, 2014, https://www.dw.com/en/conspiracies-swirl-in-1939-nazi-art-burning/a-17510022.

93 **"A new art is beginning to arise"**: This and the other Blunt quotation are from Miranda Carter, *Anthony Blunt: His Lives* (New York: Farrar, Straus & Giroux, 2003), pp. 149 and 203.

94 **"As often as possible"**: Lawrence Weschler, *Vermeer in Bosnia* (New York: Pantheon Books, 2004), p. 14.

94 **"the pressure of all that violence"**: Weschler, *Vermeer in Bosnia*, p. 16.

96 **"all art is to some extent propaganda"**: *Orwell: My Country Right or Left*, pp. 239–40.

96 **"There is no such thing"**: "Politics and the English Language," in *George Orwell: In Front of Your Nose*, p. 137.

96 **"because there is some lie"**: "Why I Write," in *Smothered Under Journalism*, p. 319.

97 **"This is the age of machines"**: "Some Thoughts on the Common Toad," in *Smothered Under Journalism*, p. 240.

98 **"dissociate Socialism from Utopianism"**: These quotes are from *Tribune*, December 24, 1943, and in *Orwell in Tribune*, p. 74.

98 **"Once the dream of paradise starts"**: Milan Kundera, interview with Philip Roth, *New York Times*, November 30, 1980.

99 **"all 'favourable' Utopias"**: These quotes are from Orwell writing as John Freeman, "Can Socialists Be Happy?," *Tribune*, December 24, 1943, and in *Orwell in Tribune*, pp. 67 and 68.

99 **"The sexual act, successfully performed"**: *Nineteen Eighty-Four*, p. 78.

100 **"We know only that the imagination"**: "The Prevention of Literature," in *George Orwell: In Front of Your Nose*, p. 72.

100 **"The real objective of Socialism is not happiness"**: "Can Socialists Be Happy?," *Tribune*, December 24, 1943, and in *Orwell in Tribune*, p. 70.

100 **"They wanted to produce a perfect society"**: *Orwell in Tribune*, p. 71.

## BUTTERED TOAST

101 **"And 1936 particularly"**: Woodcock, *The Crystal Spirit*, p. 167.

102 **pawned the family silver**: Anthony Powell, *Infants of the Spring* (Berkeley: University of California Press, 1977), p. 98.

102 **"a disillusioned little middle-class boy"**: Pollitt's review is reproduced at "Harry Pollitt's Review of Orwell's 'The Road to Wigan Pier,'" Scottish Communists, October 5, 2017, https://scottish-communists.org.uk/com munist-party/britain-s-socialist-heritage/110-harry-pollitt-s-review -of-orwell-s-the-road-to-wigan-pier.

103 **"The winter barley was a foot high"**: *Homage to Catalonia* (San Diego, CA: Harcourt Brace & Company, 1980), p. 72.

103 **"On a bullet-chipped tree"**: *Homage to Catalonia*, p. 101.

104 **"One realized afterwards"**: *Homage to Catalonia*, p. 104.

105 **"full of revolutionary sentiments"**: *Homage to Catalonia*, pp. 42–43.

105 **"an artist at the job"**: *Homage to Catalonia*, pp. 42–43.

106 **"With the Communist intellectuals"**: Stephen Spender in Richard Crossman, ed., *The God That Failed* (New York: Harper and Row, 1949), p. 255.

106 **"It is curious, but till that moment"**: "A Hanging," in *Orwell: An Age Like This*, p. 45.

106 **"half-dressed and . . . holding up his trousers"**: "Looking Back on the Spanish War," in *Orwell: My Country Right or Left*, p. 254. He also wrote to Stephen Spender in a letter on April 15, 1938 (*George Orwell: A Life in Letters*, p. 105), that he had attacked Spender as an example of the "parlour Bolshie" before they met but "even if when I met you I had not happened to like you, I should still have been bound to change my attitude, because when you meet anyone in the flesh you realise immediately that he is a human being and not a sort of caricature embodying certain ideas."

107 **"to remind us that we have never read Marx"**: Eileen Blair, letter to Norah Myles, in *George Orwell: A Life in Letters*, p. 95.

## THE LAST ROSE OF YESTERDAY

109 **"almost bare-foot, a little lousy"**: Eileen Blair, letter to her brother Laurence O'Shaughnessy, in *George Orwell: A Life in Letters*, p. 77.

109 **"If the Soviet dictator appeared to support"**: Adam Hochschild, *Spain in Our Hearts: Americans in the Spanish Civil War, 1936–1939* (New York: Houghton Mifflin Harcourt, 2016), p. 47.

111 **"My first thought, conventionally enough"**: *Homage to Catalonia*, p. 186.

111 **Modotti is said to have helped**: Albers, *Shadows, Fire, Snow*, pp. 301–4.

111 **"Being a model Communist"**: Albers, *Shadows, Fire, Snow*, p. 178. Louis MacNeice, another contemporary of Orwell's, wrote, "The strongest appeal of the Communist Party was that it demanded sacrifice; you had to sink your ego" (Carter, *Anthony Blunt*, p. 111).

113 **took her into exile from Mexico**: On Vittorio Vidali, see also Dorothy Gallagher, *All the Right Enemies: The Life and Murder of Carlo Tresca*; Burnett Bolloten, *The Spanish Civil War: Revolution and Counterrevolution*; Paul Preston, *The Spanish Holocaust: Inquisition and Extermination in Twentieth-Century Spain*; and Dominic Moran, *Pablo Neruda*. Moran writes (p. 89), "He had also participated in the kidnapping and horrific slaying of Andreu Nin back in Spain, where he took part in hundreds of Soviet-sanctioned executions of Communist 'dissidents.'"

113 **"Like Mary, Tina became a paragon"**: Albers, *Shadows, Fire, Snow*, p. 287.

114 **"it did not behoove an agitator to dance"**: Emma Goldman, *Living My Life* (New York: Cosimo Classics, 2011), p. 56.

114 **"a rendezvous of Trotskyite and anarchist elements"**: Paz quoted in Albers, *Shadows, Fire, Snow*, p. 299.

114 **"almost a monster"**: Hugh Thomas, *The Spanish Civil War*, rev. ed. (New York: Modern Library, 2001), p. 310.

115 **"Down here it was still the England"**: *Homage to Catalonia*, pp. 231–32.

116 **"fire does not die"**: Pablo Neruda, "Tina Modotti Ha Muerto," translated as "Tina Modotti Is Dead," in Pablo Neruda, *Residence on Earth*, trans. Donald D. Walsh (New York: New Directions, 1973), pp. 325–36.

117 **"she's been in disagreement"**: Victor Serge, *Notebooks* (New York: NYRB Books, 2019), p. 135. On p. 144 he notes that an associate "is convinced that Tina Modotti was 'suppressed.'" Patricia Albers discusses those who believed

Modotti had been poisoned on p. 331 of her biography of the artist and notes that a Mexican report said she had "revulsion at Commissario Carlo's purge activities in Republican Spain." She also cites the anarchist Carlo Tresca, whom Vidali would later be accused of murdering as well, who thought that Vidali had done it. Paul Preston, *The Spanish Holocaust: Inquisition and Extermination in Twentieth-Century Spain*, p. 353: "Both Josif Grigulevich (codenamed 'Maks'), who was briefly Vidali's assistant at the Fifth Regiment, and Vidali himself (codenamed 'Mario') belonged to the NKVD Administration for Special Tasks (assassination, terror, sabotage and abductions) commanded by Yakov Isaakovich Serebryansky. Both Vidali and Grigulevich would later be heavily involved in the first attempt to assassinate Trotsky."

## PART IV: STALIN'S LEMONS

### THE FLINT PATH

121 **Esther Brookes, the schoolmistress:** Esther Brookes in her self-published brochure on the cottage in Wallington, which she called Monks Fitchett.

122 **fields that had been tilled for a thousand years:** See John W. M. Wallace, *An Agricultural History of the Parish of Wallington: Farming from Domesday Onwards* (Wallington UK: Wallington Parochial Church Council, 2010).

125 **"Any point of a rhizome":** The quotes in this passage are from Gilles Deleuze and Félix Guattari, *A Thousand Plateaus: Capitalism and Schizophrenia*, trans. Brian Massumi (Minneapolis: University of Minnesota, 1987), pp. 7 (first two) and 11.

126 **"made to carry some portion of our thoughts":** Henry David Thoreau, *Walden and Other Writings of Henry David Thoreau* (New York: The Modern Library, 1937), p. 203.

128 **"Since the War I have devoted":** Charles C. Hurst, "Genetics of the Rose," *The Gardeners' Chronicle* 84, nos. 35–36 (July 14, 1928).

128 **"the fifty best fragrant roses":** This catalogue is in his papers in the Cambridge University Library.

### EMPIRE OF LIES

131 **"His primary liberty":** John R. Baker, "Science, Culture and Freedom," in *Freedom of Expression: A Symposium* (London: Hutchinson International Authors Ltd., 1945), pp. 118–19.

132 **"the only man on earth"**: Gary Paul Nabhan, *Where Our Food Comes From: Retracing Nikolay Vavilov's Quest to End Famine* (Washington, DC: Island Press, 2011), p. 11.

133 **"neo-Lamarckism"**: J. V. Stalin, "Anarchism or Socialism?" written 1906–7, published in *Works*, vol. 1, *November 1901–April 1907* (Moscow: Foreign Languages Publishing House, 1954), marxists.org/reference/archive/stalin /works/1906/12/x01.htm.

133 **"Socialism is a theory which presupposes"**: Anton Pannekoek, *Marxism and Darwinism* (Chicago: Charles H. Kerr and Company Cooperative, 1913), p. 28.

135 **"Mendelian heredity"**: Julian Huxley, *Soviet Genetics and World Science* (London: Chatto and Windus, 1949), p. 183.

137 **notably the playwright George Bernard Shaw:** His March 2, 1933, letter to *The Manchester Guardian* proclaims, "Particularly offensive and ridiculous is the revival of the old attempts to represent the condition of Russian workers as one of slavery and starvation, the Five-Year Plan as a failure, the new enterprises as bankrupt and the Communist regime as tottering to its fall. . . . We desire to record that we saw nowhere evidence of such economic slavery, privation, unemployment and cynical despair of betterment as are accepted as inevitable and ignored by the press as having 'no news value' in our own countries."

137 **At the time, only a few journalists:** Malcolm Muggeridge did so through a series of articles in *The Manchester Guardian* in 1933, Gareth Jones in a series of articles in 1933 in the *New York Evening Post* and other newspapers.

137 **"the most characteristic product"**: And other quotes, Malcolm Muggeridge writing anonymously in *The Manchester Guardian*, March 27, 1933.

138 **"Like many others who"**: Review of Eugene Lyons's *Assignment in Utopia*, in *Orwell: An Age Like This*, p. 333; originally in *The New English Weekly*, June 9, 1938.

138 **"The formula 2 + 2 = 5"**: Eugene Lyons, *Assignment in Utopia* (New York: Harcourt Brace & Co., 1937), p. 240.

139 **"Execution was the favored solution"**: Adam Hochschild, *The Unquiet Ghost: Russians Remember Stalin* (Boston: Mariner Books, 2003), p. xv.

140 **"We will go into the pyre"**: Vavilov, quoted in Peter Pringle, *The Murder of Nikolai Vavilov: The Story of Stalin's Persecution of One of the Twentieth Century's Greatest Scientists* (London: JR Books, 2009), p. 231.

140 **"You are the Vavilov who fiddles"**: Simon Ings, *Stalin and the Scientists* (New York: Grove Atlantic, 2017), p. 292.

141 **"Wheat Can Become Rye":** *Our Job Is to Make Life Worth Living*, vol. 20 of *The Complete Works of George Orwell*, ed. Peter Davison (London: Secker & Warburg, 1998), p. 214.

### FORCING LEMONS

143 **Churchill or his daughter expressed a wish for lemons:** One account from an attaché is given at https://ww2today.com/5th-february-1945-churchill-roose velt-and-stalin-meet-at-yalta, another in the CIA's journal *Studies in Intelligence* 46, no. 1 (Pittsburgh: Government Printing Office, 2002), pp. 29 and 102.

143 **"He arranged to have a lemon shrub":** Molotov in Zhores A. Medvedev and Roy Aleksandrovich, *The Unknown Stalin* (New York: The Abrams Press, 2004), p. 194, where they also note, "In 1946 he was particularly keen on lemons."

143 **Another high-level official told:** V. M. Molotov and Feliz Chuev, *Molotov Remembers: Inside Kremlin Politics* (Chicago: Ivan R. Dee, 2007), p. 175. The official was Akaki Ivanovich Mgeladze, former first secretary of the Central Committee of Georgia.

144 **"He was unable merely to contemplate nature":** Svetlana Alliluyeva, *Twenty Letters to a Friend*, trans. Priscilla Johnson McMillan (New York: Harper & Row, 1967), p. 28.

144 **"Let them get used to the cold":** From the book *Stalin's Near Dacha* (in Russian). "Сталин. Большая книга о нем" Коллектив авторов под редакцией А.И.Анискина. Глава 16. Эвкалипты и лимоны. *Stalin: A Big Book about Him*, ed. A. I. Aniskin (Moscow: ACT, 2014), p. 324.

144 **"we should all have our heads cut off":** Lewis Carroll, *The Annotated Alice in Wonderland*, with an introduction by Martin Gardner (New York: Bramhall House, 1960), p. 106.

145 **"The really frightening thing":** *Tribune*, February 4, 1944, and in *George Orwell: As I Please*, p. 88.

145 **"Who controls the past":** *Nineteen Eighty-Four*, p. 284.

146 **"Roughly a quarter century":** Nabhan, *Where Our Food Comes From*, p. 176.

## PART V: RETREATS AND ATTACKS

### ENCLOSURES

149 **"Certain gardens are described as retreats":** Ian Hamilton Finlay in many places, including Robin Gillanders, *Little Sparta* (Edinburgh: Scottish National Portrait Gallery, 1998).

151 **"between 1725 and 1825 nearly four thousand"**: Peter Linebaugh, *Stop, Thief!* (Oakland, CA: PM Press, 2013), p. 144.

151 **"Unbounded freedom ruled"**: John Clare, *Selected Poems* (London: Penguin Classics, 2004), p. 169.

152 **"Mr. Forster, a gentleman"**: Arthur Young, *A General View of the Agriculture of Hertfordshire Drawn Up for the Consideration of the Board of Agriculture and Internal Improvement* (London: Printed by B. McMillan, 1804), p. 48.

152 **"Nature, with its various representations"**: Ann Bermingham, *Landscape and Ideology: The English Rustic Tradition, 1740–1860* (Berkeley: University of California Press, 1986), p. 1.

153 **"increasingly natural, like the preenclosed landscape"**: Bermingham, *Landscape and Ideology*, pp. 13–14.

153 **"Ah, what times are these, when"**: From Brecht's poem "An die Nachgeborenen," translated for the author by Professor Christina Gerhardt.

153 **"The world is going to pieces"**: Cartier-Bresson, quoted in Estelle Jussim and Elizabeth Lindquist-Cock, *Landscape as Photograph* (New Haven, CT: Yale University Press, 1985), p. 140.

154 **"More than 25.5 million acres"**: Rachel Elbaum, "Australian crews race to contain blazes ahead of heat wave later this week," NBC News, January 7, 2020, https://www.nbcnews.com/news/world/australian-crews-race-contain -blazes-ahead-heatwave-later-week-n1111656.

155 **"Most middle-class boys grew up"**: "Inside the Whale," in *Orwell: An Age Like This*, p. 503.

155 **Latina muralist Juana Alicia**: Juana Alicia's work can be seen at https:// juanaalicia.com.

## GENTILITY

158 **"As it has not been possible to discover"**: Katharine Baetjer, *British Paintings in the Metropolitan Museum of Art, 1575–1875* (New Haven, CT: Yale University Press, 2009), p. 64.

158 **"A younger son should not have been"**: Katharine Baetjer, *British Portraits in the Metropolitan Museum of Art* (New York: The Metropolitan Museum, 1999), p. 27.

158 **The fee to Reynolds was two hundred pounds**: Baetjer, *British Paintings in the Metropolitan Museum of Art*, p. 65.

159 **"And she taught me"**: Mary Prince, *The History of Mary Prince, a West Indian Slave, Related by Herself* (London: F. Westley and A. H. Davis, 1831), p. 6.

160 **"very small & furnished almost entirely"**: Eileen O'Shaughnessy Blair in *The Lost Orwell*, p. 65.

160 **"For generations past her family"**: *Coming Up for Air*, p. 108.

163 **"It is only in the last 20 years"**: *Slavery and the British Country House*, ed. Madge Dresser and Andrew Hann (Swindon, UK: English Heritage, 2013), p. 13, http://historicengland.org.uk/images-books/publications/slav ery-and-british-country-house/.

163 **"Across Britain as a whole"**: *Slavery and the British Country House*, p. 20.

## Sugar, Poppies, Teak

165 **A register for the Blairs' West Prospect plantation**: https://www.ucl .ac.uk/lbs/estate/view/1789.

166 **"spring by a pointed hill"**: David Mills, *A Dictionary of English Place Names* (Oxford: Oxford University Press, 2011), p. 356.

166 *oran or ora* **means**: Walter W. Skeat, *The Place Names of Suffolk* (Cambridge: Cambridge Antiquarian Society, 1914), p. 114.

166 **"yew wood"**: W. J. N. Liddal, *The Place Names of Fife and Kinross* (Edinburgh: William Green and Sons, 1896), p. 45.

167 **They were citizens of empire**: Among the many guides to Orwell's ancestors are pages 4–9 of Peter Stansky and William Abraham, *The Unknown Orwell* (New York: Alfred A. Knopf, 1972). Gordon Bowker's biography, *George Orwell* (London: Abacus, 2003), pages 3–10, covers the same ground.

167 **"England's national flower"**: Garry Littman, "A Splendid Income: The World's Greatest Drug Cartel," *Bilan*, November 24, 2015, https://www.bilan .ch/opinions/garry-littman/_a_splendid_income_the_world_s_greatest _drug_cartel.

168 **"We Anglo-Indians could be almost bearable"**: *Burmese Days* (New York: Houghton Mifflin Harcourt Company, 1962), p. 39.

168 **There are aristocrats, commoners**: I pieced some of this together from genealogy websites, which allowed me to go a little beyond the published record.

## Old Blush

171 **"Handing out the credit"**: "The Drumbeats of Fashion," *Washington Post Magazine*, March 10, 1985.

174 **meaning spray or sprinkle:** Etymology of *chintz* from Rosemary Crill, *Chintz: Indian Textiles for the West* (London: Victoria and Albert Publishing in association with Mapin Publishing, 2008), p. 9.

174 **"chints and painted calicoes":** Crill, *Chintz*, p. 16.

174 **The ribbon-stripe chintz made by Richard Ovey:** Reproduced in Linda Eaton, *Printed Textiles: British and American Cottons and Linens, 1700–1850* (New York: The Monacelli Press, 2014), p. 108.

175 **"The introduction of the China Rose":** Charles C. Hurst, "Notes on the Origin and Evolution of Our Garden Roses," *Journal of the Royal Horticultural Society* 66 (1941): 73–82.

176 **Brooklyn-born pharmaceutical opioids profiteer Mortimer Sackler:** David Austin, *The English Roses: Classic Favorites & New Selections* (Richmond Hill, ON: Firefly Books, 2008). On p. 190, "'Mortimer Sackler' forms a large shrub that requires plenty of space."

177 **"It happens twice a year":** Yonatan Mendel, "A Palestinian Day Out," *London Review of Books*, August 15, 2019, https://www.lrb.co.uk/the-paper/v41/n16/yonatan-mendel/diary.

FLOWERS OF EVIL

179 **"I cannot tell you how angry":** Jamaica Kincaid, *A Small Place* (New York: Farrar, Straus & Giroux, 2000), p. 31.

180 **"Almost as if ashamed of the revulsion":** Jamaica Kincaid, *My Garden (Book)* (New York: Farrar, Straus and Giroux, 1999), p. 120.

180 **"The great Abraham Lincoln":** Jamaica Kincaid, "Inside the American Snow Dome," *Paris Review*, November 11, 2020 https://www.theparisreview.org/blog/2020/11/11/inside-the-american-snow-dome/.

181 **"I do not know the names of the plants":** Jamaica Kincaid, "Flowers of Evil," *New Yorker*, October 5, 1992, p. 156.

182 **"I had forgotten all of this" and "I did not know what these flowers":** Kincaid, "Mariah," *New Yorker*, June 26, 1989, pp. 32 and 35.

182 **"I do not like daffodils":** Jamaica Kincaid, "Alien Soil," *New Yorker*, June 21, 1993, p. 51.

182 **"In my child's mind's eye":** Jamaica Kincaid, "Garden Inspired by William Wordsworth's Dances with Daffodils," *Architectural Digest*, May 2007, https://www.architecturaldigest.com/story/gardens-article.

182 **"As a result of the frost":** *George Orwell Diaries*, p. 261.

183 **"In order that England may live":** *The Road to Wigan Pier*, p. 148.

183 **"You have got to choose":** "Do Our Colonies Pay?" in *Orwell in Tribune*, p. 301.

## PART VI: THE PRICE OF ROSES

### BEAUTY PROBLEMS

187 **"the rapid disappearance of English flower names":** As I Please, April 21, 1944, in *Orwell in Tribune*, p. 129.

187 **"a minor English trait":** "The Lion and the Unicorn: Socialism and the English Genius," published in 1941 as a small book, and in *Orwell: My Country Right or Left* (Boston: David R. Godine, 2000), pp. 58–59.

188 **"stamp-collectors, pigeon-fanciers":** "The Lion and the Unicorn," in *Orwell: My Country Right or Left*, p. 59.

189 **"He almost never praises beauty":** Carey, introduction to *George Orwell: Essays* (New York: Alfred A. Knopf, 2002), p. xv.

190 **"It was a queer thing":** *Nineteen Eighty-Four*, pp. 109–10.

191 **"looking or hearing without any wish":** Elaine Scarry, *On Beauty and Being Just* (Princeton, NJ: Princeton University Press, 1999), p. 61.

191 **"looking or hearing that is prelude":** Scarry, *On Beauty and Being Just*, p. 61.

192 **"You know, we were all just too busy":** Zoe Leonard in an interview with Anna Blume, Anthony Meier Fine Arts, http://www.anthonymeier finearts.com/attachment/en/555f2a8acfaf3429568b4568/Press/555f2b 29cfaf3429568b5c35.

### IN THE ROSE FACTORY

196 **substantial report released in the United States:** Nate's 2017 report is *Mother's Day in the Flower Fields: Labor Conditions and Social Challenges for Colombia's Flower Sector Employees*, published by the Project for International Accompaniment and Solidarity and by Global Exchange, available at http://pasointernational.org/wp-content/uploads/2017/05/Colombias -Cut-Flower-Industry_-May-2017-PASO-Compressed.pdf.

203 **"It is only very rarely":** *The Road to Wigan Pier*, p. 29.

### THE CRYSTAL SPIRIT

205 **"It is true that the literary quality":** "Politics vs. Literature: An Examination of *Gulliver's Travels*," *Polemic*, September–October 1946, and in *Smothered Under Journalism*, p. 429.

206 **"The first thing that we demand":** "Benefit of Clergy: Some Notes on Salvador Dali," published in June 1944 and then physically cut out of the book it was in for obscenity, in *George Orwell: As I Please*, p. 161.

NOTES

207 **"In the Lenin Barracks":** *Homage to Catalonia*, p. 3.

207 **"Waiters and shop-walkers looked you":** *Homage to Catalonia*, p. 5.

207 **"But the thing that I saw in your face":** "Looking Back on the Spanish Civil War," published 1943, in *Orwell: My Country Right or Left*, p. 267.

208 **"At Wallington. Crocuses out":** *George Orwell Diaries*, p. 330, entry from March 4, 1941.

209 **"Even if from a technical point":** Transcript of *The Trials of J. Robert Oppenheimer*, dir. David Grubin, aired January 26, 2009, on PBS, https://www-tc.pbs.org/wgbh/americanexperience/media/pdf/transcript/Oppenheimer_transcript.pdf.

## THE UGLINESS OF ROSES

213 **"caresses floating in the air":** Rilke, "Les Roses," in *The Complete French Poems of Rainer Maria Rilke*, trans. A. Poulin (Minneapolis: Graywolf Press, 2002), p. 8.

214 **"The rose looks fair":** Shakespeare, "Sonnet 54," *William Shakespeare's Sonnets*, edited by Thomas Tyler (London: David Nutt, 1890), p. 212.

## SNOW AND INK

223 **"Miller is writing about the man":** "Inside the Whale," in *Orwell: An Age Like This*, p. 496.

223 **"Deceit and violence":** Sissela Bok, *Lying* (New York: Vintage, 1999), p. 18.

225 **"The ideal subject of totalitarian rule":** Hannah Arendt, *The Origins of Totalitarianism* (New York: Harcourt Brace & World, 1951), p. 474.

226 **"integral to totalitarianism":** "The Prevention of Literature," published 1946, in *George Orwell: In Front of Your Nose* (Boston: David R. Godine, 2000), p. 63.

227 **"But to be corrupted by totalitarianism":** *George Orwell: In Front of Your Nose*, p. 67.

227 **"the inflated style is itself":** "Politics and the English Language," in *George Orwell: In Front of Your Nose*, p. 136.

228 **"In our time, political speech":** *George Orwell: In Front of Your Nose*, p. 136.

228 **"When there is a gap":** *George Orwell: In Front of Your Nose*, p. 136.

228 **"Don't you see that the whole aim":** *Nineteen Eighty-Four*, p. 60.

229 **"It could not be used":** *Nineteen Eighty-Four*, p. 344.

229 **"The imagination, like certain wild animals":** "The Prevention of Literature," in *George Orwell: In Front of Your Nose*, p. 72.

230 **"perception of beauty in the external"**: "Why I Write," in *Smothered Under Journalism*, p. 318.

230 **"And looking back through my work"**: *Smothered Under Journalism*, p. 320.

230 **"In a peaceful age I might"**: *Smothered Under Journalism*, p. 319.

230 **"What I have most wanted"**: *Smothered Under Journalism*, p. 319.

230 **"But I could not do the work of writing a book"**: *Smothered Under Journalism*, p. 319.

231 **"The word my husband particularly wants"**: Letter to Victor Gollancz, *Facing Unpleasant Facts, 1937–1939*, vol. 11 of *The Complete Works of George Orwell*, ed. Peter Davison (London: Secker & Warburg, 1998), p. 356.

### PART VII: THE RIVER ORWELL

### AN INVENTORY OF PLEASURES

235 **"one of those figures on the front"**: Coppard and Crick, *Orwell Remembered*, p. 171.

236 **"This Ms. has been blitzed"**: *George Orwell: A Life in Letters*, p. 236.

236 **she said if they smoked less**: Bernard Crick, *George Orwell: A Life* (Boston: Little, Brown and Co., 1981), p. 296.

238 **"First of all, kippers"**: "In Defence of English Cooking," in John Carey, ed., *George Orwell: Collected Essays* (New York: Everyman's Library, 2002), pp. 971 and 972.

239 **"finest treasures are never discoverable"**: "Just Junk—But Who Could Resist It?" *Evening Standard*, January 5, 1946, and in *Smothered Under Journalism*, p. 18.

239 **"there's a kind of peacefulness"**: *Coming Up for Air* (Boston: Houghton Mifflin, 1969), p. 87.

239 **"that have a piece of coral"**: "Just Junk—But Who Could Resist It?," *Evening Standard*, January 5, 1946, and in *Smothered Under Journalism*, p. 18.

240 **"the jackdaw inside"**: "Just Junk—But Who Could Resist It?," *Evening Standard*, January 5, 1946, and in *Smothered Under Journalism*, p. 19.

240 **"plans to throw up his journalism"**: Fredric Warburg to Roger Senhouse in *Smothered Under Journalism*, p. 38.

240 **"give expression to the Sancho Panza"**: "The Art of Donald McGill," in *Orwell: My Country Right or Left*, pp. 162–63.

241 **"It is foully cold here"**: Letter to Geoffrey Gorer, January 22, 1946, in *George Orwell: A Life in Letters*, p. 287.

241 **"There is a time to sit"**: This and subsequent quotes are from "Bad Climates Are Best," *Evening Standard*, February 2, 1946, and in *Smothered Under Journalism*, pp. 90–92.

242 **"The grained woodwork"**: "The Moon Under Water," *Evening Standard*, February 9, 1946, and in *Smothered Under Journalism*, p. 99.

242 **"But meanwhile man's power"**: As I Please, *Tribune*, January 11, 1946, and in *Smothered Under Journalism*, p. 32.

243 **"but I have been putting it off"**: Letter to Dorothy Plowman, February 19, 1946, in *Smothered Under Journalism*, pp. 115–16.

243 **"There isn't really anything left"**: Letter to Anne Popham, March 15, 1946, in *Smothered Under Journalism*, pp. 153–54.

243 **"At this period, after his long fast"**: This and subsequent quotes are from "Some Thoughts on the Common Toad," *Tribune*, April 12, 1946, and in *Smothered Under Journalism*, pp. 238–40.

244 **"I'm going down to Wallington"**: Letter to Inez Holden, April 9, 1946, in *Smothered Under Journalism*, p. 230.

245 **"Recently, I spent a day at the cottage"**: "A Good Word for the Vicar of Bray," in *Smothered Under Journalism*, p. 260.

245 **"the little disused reservoir in the village"**: Letter to Anne Popham, April 18, 1946, in *Smothered Under Journalism*, p. 249. He apparently left the letters behind, and Esther Brookes, the next inhabitant, burned them.

245 **"Polyantha roses on E's grave"**: *George Orwell Diaries*, p. 418.

246 **The postwar city was also**: Betsy Mason, "Bomb-Damage Maps Reveal London's World War II Devastation," *National Geographic*, May 18, 2016, https://www.nationalgeographic.com/science/article/bomb-damage-maps-reveal-londons-world-war-ii-devastation.

246 **"Thinking always of my island"**: *George Orwell Diaries*, p. 288.

247 **"during the bombing he was looking after Richard"**: Susan Watson in Coppard and Crick, *Orwell Remembered*, p. 220.

247 **"there's no policeman"**: Letter to Michael Meyer, May 23, 1946, in *George Orwell: A Life in Letters*, p. 312.

248 **At one point, Richard Blair**: Richard Blair in a talk for the Orwell Society, February 21, 2021. "The Orwell Society George Talk Barnhill A Most Ungetatable Place," The Orwell Society, February 22, 2021, YouTube video, 1:20:44, https://www.youtube.com/watch?v=BBRe0KNoB7M.

248 **"I'll tell you about how"**: Letter to Richard Rees, July 5, 1946, in *George Orwell: A Life in Letters*, p. 317.

# NOTES

248 **"The 'garden' at Barnhill"**: Email from Damaris Fletcher to the author, September 25, 2020. Still, extensive flower gardens exist at the castle on the Isle of Skye a little to the north, and Bernard Crick writes in his biography of Orwell, "The climate was mild. Elaborate critical theories of Orwell's character and of his last writings have been built on isothermic fantasy. . . . Twenty miles down the Sound, for instance, lies the island of Gigha and Achamore House Gardens with one of the finest rhododendron, camelia and azalea collections and arboreta in the British isles." Bernard Crick, *George Orwell: A Life*, p. 354.

249 **"driven home, as it were"**: *Tribune*, February 15, 1946, and in *Smothered Under Journalism*, p. 108. It might be worth noting that he imagines a male reader whose wife is "already asleep in the armchair."

249 **"want day nurseries"**: "On Housing," *Tribune*, January 25, 1946, and in *Smothered Under Journalism*, p. 78.

249 **"One of the chief memories"**: Richard Rees, *George Orwell: Fugitive from the Camp of Victory* (London: Secker & Warburg, 1961), pp. 151–52.

## "AS THE ROSE-HIP TO THE ROSE"

251 **"It is astounding how little"**: Vladimir Nabokov, *Speak, Memory* (New York: Vintage, 1989), p. 115.

252 **"he was already dead"**: *Nineteen Eighty-Four*, p. 33.

253 **"Suddenly he was standing on short springy turf"**: *Nineteen Eighty-Four*, pp. 35–36.

253 **"with what seemed a single movement"**: This and the subsequent quote are from *Nineteen Eighty-Four*, p. 36.

254 **"with that same magnificent gesture"**: *Nineteen Eighty-Four*, p. 143.

255 **"dream was still vivid in"**: *Nineteen Eighty-Four*, p. 189.

255 **"It would not have occurred"**: *Nineteen Eighty-Four*, p. 190.

255 **"a little chunk of history"**: *Nineteen Eighty-Four*, p. 168.

255 **"The paperweight was the room"**: *Nineteen Eighty-Four*, p. 169.

255 **"a monstrous woman, solid"**: *Nineteen Eighty-Four*, p. 159.

256 **"belonged to the ancient time"**: *Nineteen Eighty-Four*, p. 35.

256 **"The Party told you to reject"**: *Nineteen Eighty-Four*, p. 92.

256 **"We make the laws of nature"**: *Nineteen Eighty-Four*, p. 304.

257 **"It struck him for the first time"**: *Nineteen Eighty-Four*, p. 250.

257 **"She had had her momentary flowering"**: *Nineteen Eighty-Four*, p. 251.

258 **"Orwell has been accused of bitterness and pessimism":** Margaret Atwood, "Orwell and Me," *Guardian*, June 16, 2003, https://www.theguardian.com/books/2003/jun/16/georgeorwell.artsfeatures.

258 **"the essay on Newspeak is written":** Atwood, "Orwell and Me," in *Guardian*.

259 **"In the old days, he thought":** *Nineteen Eighty-Four*, p. 145.

259 **"The very act of trying":** Octavia Butler, "A Few Rules for Predicting the Future."

261 **"After I was certain what was wrong":** *George Orwell: A Life in Letters*, p. 377.

261 **"roses, poppies, sweet williams, marigolds":** *George Orwell Diaries*, p. 541.

261 **"Snowdrops up all over the place":** *George Orwell Diaries*, p. 562.

262 **"Sometimes of the sea or the sea shore":** *Our Job Is to Make Life Worth Living*, p. 203.

262 **"My novel *Nineteen Eighty-four* is *not* intended":** *Life*, July 25, 1949, and in *Our Job Is to Make Life Worth Living*, p. 135.

263 **"The essence of being human":** "Reflections on Gandhi," *Partisan Review*, January 1949, and in *Our Job Is to Make Life Worth Living*, p. 8.

264 **"Our job," Orwell declared:** "Reflections on Gandhi," in *Our Job Is to Make Life Worth Living*, p. 7.

## THE RIVER ORWELL

266 **In the year 885:** All the historical information about the River Orwell comes from W. G. Arnott, *Orwell Estuary: The Story of Ipswich River (with Harwich and the Stour)* (Ipswich, UK: Norman Adlard & Co., 1954).

# IMAGE CREDITS

### The Prophet and The Hedgehog

D. Collings, *Muriel the Goat*, 1939. (Portrait of Orwell at Wallington.) Courtesy of the Orwell Archive, University College London Services, Special Collections.

### Going Underground

Sasha, untitled image showing coal miners and coal wagon, Tilmanstone Colliery, Kent, 1930. D and S Photography Archives / Alamy Stock Photo.

### Bread and Roses

Tina Modotti, *Roses, Mexico*, 1924. Courtesy Michael Mattis and Judy Hochberg Collection.

Verso of Tina Modotti, *Roses, Mexico*, 1924, showing Vittorio Vidali's stamp. Courtesy Michael Mattis and Judy Hochberg Collection.

### Stalin's Lemons

Yakov Guminer, *2 + 2, plus workers' enthusiasm = 5*, 1931. Via Wikimedia Commons.

### Retreats and Attacks

Sir Joshua Reynolds, *The Honorable Henry Fane (1739–1802) with Inigo Jones and Charles Blair*, 1761–66. Collection of the Metropolitan Museum.

# IMAGE CREDITS

## THE PRICE OF ROSES

Rose production near Bogotá, Colombia, 2019. Image by the author.

## THE RIVER ORWELL

Vernon Richards, *Orwell and Son*, 1945. Courtesy of the Orwell Archive, University College London Library Services, Special Collections.

# INDEX